MANAGEMENT, WORK AND ORGANISATIONS

Series editors: **Gibson Burrell**, School of Management, University of Leicester, UK
Mick Marchington, Manchester Business School, University of Manchester, UK,
and Strathclyde Business School, University of Strathclyde, UK
Paul Thompson, Strathclyde Business School, University of Strathclyde, UK

This series of new textbooks covers the areas of human resource management, employee relations, organisational behaviour and related business and management fields. Each text has been specially commissioned to be written by leading experts in a clear and accessible way. The books contain serious and challenging material, take an analytical rather than prescriptive approach and are particularly suitable for use by students with no prior specialist knowledge.

The series is relevant for many business and management courses, including MBA and post-experience courses, specialist masters and postgraduate diplomas, professional courses and final-year undergraduate courses. These texts have become essential reading at business and management schools worldwide.

Published titles include:

Stephen Bach and Ian Kessler
THE MODERNISATION OF THE PUBLIC SERVICES AND EMPLOYEE RELATIONS

Emma Bell
READING MANAGEMENT AND ORGANIZATION IN FILM

Paul Blyton and Peter Turnbull
THE DYNAMICS OF EMPLOYEE RELATIONS (3rd edn)

Paul Blyton, Edmund Heery and Peter Turnbull (*editors*)
REASSESSING THE EMPLOYMENT RELATIONSHIP

Sharon C. Bolton
EMOTION MANAGEMENT IN THE WORKPLACE

Sharon C. Bolton and Maeve Houlihan (*editors*)
SEARCHING FOR THE HUMAN IN HUMAN RESOURCE MANAGEMENT

Peter Boxall and John Purcell
STRATEGY AND HUMAN RESOURCE MANAGEMENT (3rd edn)

J. Martin Corbett
CRITICAL CASES IN ORGANISATIONAL BEHAVIOUR

Susan Corby, Steve Palmer and Esmond Lindop
RETHINKING REWARD

Ian Greener
PUBLIC MANAGEMENT (2nd edn)

Keith Grint
LEADERSHIP

Irena Grugulis
SKILLS, TRAINING AND HUMAN RESOURCE DEVELOPMENT

Geraldine Healy, Gill Kirton and Mike Noon (*editors*)
EQUALITY, INEQUALITIES AND DIVERSITY

Damian Hodgson and Svetlana Cicmil (*editors*)
MAKING PROJECTS CRITICAL

Marek Korczynski
HUMAN RESOURCE MANAGEMENT IN SERVICE WORK

Karen Legge
HUMAN RESOURCE MANAGEMENT: Anniversary Edition

Patricia Lewis and Ruth Simpson (*editors*)
GENDERING EMOTIONS IN ORGANIZATIONS

Patricia Lewis and Ruth Simpson
VOICE, VISIBILITY AND THE GENDERING OF ORGANIZATIONS

Alison Pullen, Nic Beech and David Sims (*editors*)
EXPLORING IDENTITY

Jill Rubery and Damian Grimshaw
THE ORGANISATION OF EMPLOYMENT

Hugh Scullion and Margaret Linehan (*editors*)
INTERNATIONAL HUMAN RESOURCE MANAGEMENT

Colin C. Williams
RETHINKING THE FUTURE OF WORK

Diana Winstanley and Jean Woodall (*editors*)
ETHICAL ISSUES IN CONTEMPORARY HUMAN RESOURCE MANAGEMENT

For more information on titles in the Series please go to www.palgrave.com/business/mwo

Series Standing Order

If you would like to receive future titles in this series as they are published, you can make use of our standing order facility. To place a standing order please contact your bookseller or, in case of difficulty, write to us at the address below with your name and address and the name of the series. Please state with which title you wish to begin your standing order.

Customer Services Department, Macmillan Distribution Ltd,
Houndmills, Basingstoke, Hampshire RG21 6XS, England, UK

Public Management

2nd edition

Professor Ian Greener
School of Applied Social Sciences, Durham University, UK

palgrave
macmillan

First edition 2009
Second edition 2013

Published by
PALGRAVE MACMILLAN

Palgrave Macmillan in the UK is an imprint of Macmillan Publishers Limited, registered in England, company number 785998, of Houndmills, Basingstoke, Hampshire RG21 6XS.

Palgrave Macmillan in the US is a division of St Martin's Press LLC, 175 Fifth Avenue, New York, NY 10010.

Palgrave Macmillan is the global academic imprint of the above companies and has companies and representatives throughout the world.

Palgrave® and Macmillan® are registered trademarks in the United States, the United Kingdom, Europe and other countries.

ISBN 978–0–230–35399–2

This book is printed on paper suitable for recycling and made from fully managed and sustained forest sources. Logging, pulping and manufacturing processes are expected to conform to the environmental regulations of the country of origin.

A catalogue record for this book is available from the British Library.

A catalog record for this book is available from the Library of Congress.

10   9   8   7   6   5   4   3   2   1
22 21 20 19 18 17 16 15 14 13

Printed and bound in Great Britain by
CPI Antony Rowe, Chippenham and Eastbourne

Contents

Tables

Preface

The second edition of this book has led to it being rewritten to take greater account of two ideas that were present in the first edition but that in the period after 2008 have needed much greater emphasis.

The first edition of the book was written in 2008 and published in 2009 when we were just beginning to get a sense of the size of the financial crisis, its causes and its implications for public management. Since that time good academic work has begun to appear that deals with all of these questions, and needed to be incorporated in the text to consider the question – what is public management like in the post-financial crisis period we now face? The major economies of the world face an extended period of austerity, and that has to have consequences for the practice and study of public management. This book is a still early attempt to get to grips with these problems.

Second, the book takes further a theme from the first edition, that of public management as paradox. To that end, it works through a number of paradoxes in public management and explores how they play out in both the realms of ideas and practice. In the time since I wrote the first book, the theme of paradox in public management has been taken on by a range of scholars to become a key area of the field, and Deborah Stone's classic text *Policy Paradox* has been republished in a new edition. I believe that exploring public management through the lens of paradox is not just an intellectual exercise, but can illustrate the real problems public managers face 'on the ground' in dealing with a range of problems that seem never to be fully resolved. This book aims to make contributions to both academia and practice through this theme.

It is a vital and exciting time to be studying public management – the boundaries between public and private organizations have never been more fluid, and the urgency of the kinds of dealing with the kinds of problems public managers deal with are increasing as the economies of the developed world struggle to deal with austerity. We need new ways of thinking about the discipline and new ways to make the case that public management is not only a distinctive field in its own right but also an important one. If I have made any progress towards that goal, the time spent writing will have been worthwhile.

Acknowledgements

Thanks to Ursula Gavin for giving me the opportunity to write this second edition, and to Palgrave Macmillan's reviewers for their helpful suggestions on how it might be further improved. Most of all, as ever, thank you to Linda who continues to put up with me despite everything, and to Anna, Bethany and Emily for not (quite) managing to spend all the money.

1

Introduction

As both an area of study and of practice, management is still very much in thrall to the ideas of its founding fathers such as Taylor and even Drucker, in attempting to come up with ways of achieving organizational goals through the application of planning and rationality. This seems like a sensible and worthwhile enterprise – we are unlikely to be successful unless we know what we are trying to achieve, and once we have an idea of that and the steps that are necessary to achieve our goals, we will surely progress more quickly. Many books on management, both academic and practitioner, for both public and non-public settings, are about organizations achieving greater success through plans that achieve their goals, and implementing these plans.

However, there are a number of problems with this goal-setting, planning and implementation model of management. First the environments within which organizations operate are becoming faster moving and more complex. The 'PEST' (political, economic, social and technological) frameworks taught on courses don't really deal with the way that public and private organizations can be held to account and pressurized to change through rapid campaigns in the media and social networks. Public organizations can find themselves at the receiving end of a campaign exposing poor practices within extraordinarily short periods of time, and have to be able to respond. Hospitals can find local and national newspapers and television channels outside their front doors and be expected to answer questions about poor care, with patient groups, organized through Twitter, trying to simultaneously and noisily hold them to account.

At the same time as this, the regulatory frameworks public organizations work within are growing ever-more complex, and the customers ever-more demanding. Much has been made by politicians of the need for public organizations to be more responsive to their publics as they increasingly face 'consumer societies' where the public expects choices and high standards of customer services as well, and in which the 'one-size-fits-all' model of provision is no longer acceptable. At the same time public organizations are required to be more efficient and, in an era of austerity, to do more and more without increases in budgets.

What all of this amounts to is public organizations facing increasingly fast-moving complex environments at a time when there are no extra resources to deal with the new demands. What should they do?

One answer to these problems is to plan more, to try through top-down means to speed up decision-making to make organizations more responsive and to introduce customer-service practices where they had not really existed before. And, of course, to do all of this in such a way that it does not increase costs. Politicians have encouraged (even demanded) that public organizations go down this road. To that end, they have tried to introduce market mechanisms into public services to enforce competition (often with existing or new-entry private or not-for-profit providers) on the grounds that increased competition will force these kinds of changes upon public organizations, and that managers will raise their games as a result. If there is a common sense in public reform in the 2010s, it is that.

The idea that the use of market mechanisms to solve problems is remarkable in that, in a period after the biggest financial crisis since the 1930s, during which there is at least a reasonable degree of consensus that it was the deregulation of market mechanisms in finance that was a significant cause of the problems, you might have thought that markets would have got a bad name. Indeed it seemed for a while that this was the case when a range of critiques of the inappropriate application of market ideas appeared (Cassidy, 2009, Elliott & Atkinson, 2008).

However in 2012 as I write this, market-based ideas are dominant again. Republican candidates for the US Presidency are claiming that the financial crisis was caused not by too much deregulation, but by not enough. Market reforms in public organizations are proceeding apace, and countries with financial problems exacerbated by the financial crisis face restructuring packages that involve huge public sector cuts and radical programmes that involve making much greater use of private provision (and often funding) to deliver public services. For good or for ill the default option for public reorganization has become the wider use of market mechanisms, apparently regardless of the lessons about their misuse academics and policywriters drew from the financial crisis.

Paradoxes in public management

The combination of the increased speed and complexity of public organizational life, the need to deliver more with no increase in resources and the preference for market mechanisms at a time when we might have stopped to doubt their efficacy in dealing with public problems all point to problems in the standard managerial model of organizational planning that is based on setting goals, making plans and implementing them.

Instead of assuming that public managers can proceed through careful planning and implementation cycles, what happens if we accept that plans are likely to be too slow, and the goals of organizations contradictory? These problems are by no means exclusive to public management but perhaps are brought to the fore there. Public organizations are required to be efficient and parsimonious in resource use, yet customer-focussed. They are required to detain prisoners under lock and key or teach students and grade their work, but also increasingly to regard them as customers of their service. They are meant not only to implement the policies of the government of the day, but also to be responsive to local needs. How do you mean to put together a plan when the goals of that plan actually conflict with one another?

This book argues that dealing with what often appear to be contradictory goals is not an exceptional part of public management, but is instead central to its endeavour. What we, therefore, need is not to try and resolve such contradictions (which is probably not even possible), but instead to accept contradictions and to learn to work within them. By being aware of the tensions and contradictions that are embedded in public management, managers can learn to understand the trade-offs that decisions entail, and students of the field can generate a richer understanding of how public organizations work. Before we can progress any further, however, we'd better be clear about what we mean by 'paradox' and what this concept means for public management.

Paradoxes

The philosophical literature on paradoxes is concerned with ideas or arguments that appear sound, but lead to unacceptable or contradictory conclusions. The claim 'I am lying in this sentence' is paradoxical in that it cannot be true (it cannot be true to say you are lying) and it cannot be false (if you were lying about lying, you'd be telling the truth, and yet you say you are lying). This kind of example gives an idea of what it is like to work within a paradox – where we are in a situation where competing demands (here between truth and lying) generate a result, which seems unsatisfactory as it does not have an obvious solution.

Paradoxes, therefore, tend to be equated with puzzles in philosophy, as examples almost of trickery where, if we can find the contradiction, we can resolve the puzzle. There is a great deal to be said for considering public management as a puzzle or perhaps as puzzling (Heclo, 1974), but this approach seems to imply that there is a right answer to the apparent contradictions public managers face, and it seems unlikely that such complex problems can be reduced to single correct solutions.

The term paradox has been used in a number of ways in academic management literature. Stone (2012) does not define her term in detail, but in practice seems to use it to highlight a range of tensions in policy and practice that public managers face. This is very much the way this book will use the concept, but it will try and work through examples in a way that deals more directly with public management than Stone's book does, and with each paradox explored in more depth, with the trade-off that less paradoxes can be explored as a result.

More recently 'paradox' has been used in a more general sense to include a wider range of situations in public management, where policies introduced have unintended consequences (Hood & Peters, 2004, Margretts *et al.*, 2012). This work is excellent, but this definition will not be used here as it perhaps stretches the concept a little too far for the purposes of this book, and its application in this way here would lose the distinctiveness of the idea as Stone uses it.

More relevant to this book is work from Wendy Smith (e.g. Smith & Lewis, 2011) which she has developed over ten years. Smith differentiates paradoxes from dilemmas. A dilemma situation is one in which an organization faces contradictions, but is able to choose between the two goals or challenges by assessing the costs and benefits of each. Where there is a paradox, however, there is a duality where contradictory elements co-exist over time, and the organization must simply live with them – there is no opportunity to choose as both the contradictory elements are inescapably part of the organization.

From a public management perspective, there are numerous examples of paradoxical goals. Public organizations are often organized in such a way as to try and achieve efficiency by treating professional time (such as that of a doctor or a teacher) as a scarce resource. So appointments are made to see doctors according to the hours they spend in the organizations, and timetables and school opening hours based on the availability of teachers. This is sensible and efficient. However, at the same time, public organizations have been criticized for being inflexible in terms of opening hours and customer responsiveness – it is not possible to get appointment times to see doctors outside of the standard working day, or to get schools to open for longer hours so that parents can drop children off before work and pick them up afterwards.

Public organizations therefore face an apparently contradictory situation – they must achieve productivity gains and be more efficient, especially in a period of austerity, but at the same time work longer hours and find ways of organizing that are not based on their scarce resource – professional time.

When faced with a contradiction public managers and academics interested in researching and writing about it, face a choice. They can either try and find a way of reconciling the contradiction by taking apart the problem or putting it back together in such a way that the contradiction disappears. This is how paradoxes are treated in the philosophical literature with which this chapter began, and there are certainly situations in which, by redefining the problem being considered, answers can be found that appear to remove the contradiction.

There are at least three problems with treating public management paradoxes as resolvable through this kind of strategy. First of all it almost inevitably leads to recommendations that end up simplifying the challenges managers are facing. By redefining contradictions we can find creative new ways to think about how we go about our work, but working at increasingly abstracted levels can hinder us in dealing with the very messy reality of having to manage a public organization. Abstractions can be helpful, but believing that they can create magic solutions does not seem like a good starting point for good management practice (Greener, 2005c).

Second even where we can resolve public management paradoxes and find appropriate solutions, those solutions will be based on our considering one paradox at a time. In the redefining of a problem there is the inherent danger that we will simply end up creating a new contradiction with another problem we will need to face. This is because, as the work of Christopher Hood has made so clear, management decisions often carry unintended consequences – we may think we have solved a problem only to create a new one somewhere else.

So, for example, as a part of trying to resolve the paradox between efficiency and customer service above, we might decide it is a good idea to define service users as customers to change staff attitudes towards them. But that may end up creating contradictions in our public engagement strategies, which typically position the public as citizens instead, and so not lead to dialogue and debate in those forums, but instead to customer-based demands, giving us a new paradox to deal with. In this situation, citizens can end up turning into customers or consumers, leading to apathy and no chance for informed discussion (Barber, 2007a). The end result is a new paradox – that to improve our public services, we need representative service users to engage in 'voice' through discussion and debate with those providing services to them, but they instead engage as customers, and so do not regard themselves as representing other members of the public or wish to discuss or debate with them but simply to choose public services. Because public management challenges are interrelated, a redefinition of roles in order to avoid one paradox can simply lead to the creation of a new one.

Finally – there is the possibility that treating public management problems as paradoxes is a creative answer. It avoids simplification, reduces the risk of shunting contradictions into other areas of practice, and it asks us to confront the competing challenges that managers actually face (Stone, 2012). Managing organizations involves making decisions about which goals are most important, but at least as frequently having to make trade-offs between what seem to be contradictory goals, behaviours and principles. Treating public management problems as paradoxes opens up the opportunity to work through and discuss the challenges or work in a complex and challenging environment in which there really may be no simple answers. That seems to me to be a much richer starting point than simply ignoring contradictions, or trying to make them go away.

Bearing in mind the centrality of paradoxes to what follows, the book is structured as follows.

Chapter 2 provides an overview of the financial crisis, giving both an explanation of what happened and then going on to explain its importance for public services. It asks how it is that, after the biggest financial crisis since the 1930s, we have not seen a radical new agenda in public service reform away from the market-driven models of the 1990s and 2000s?

Chapter 3 considers the role of the state in public management, exploring how ideas about government changed in the post-war period, and also the extent to which those changes inadvertently helped contribute to the financial crisis. It presents ways of understanding the broader context within which public managers must work, and considers what has happened to the economies since 2007–08 with which public managers must work.

Chapter 4 considers how ideas about the way we understand the role and functions of public management have changed in the post-war period, and asks what the impact of the financial crisis seems to have been on our understanding of public services. It asks why we have not seen a major movement against the use of markets, competition and privatization after the financial crisis.

Chapter 5 considers the way we pay for public services, before looking at the state of government finances after the financial crisis, asking where we go from here, but suggesting at the same time that it is often when the economy is in its worst state that the government can achieve the most benefit from investing in public services.

Chapter 6 looks at professionals in public management. Many public services are characterized by strong professional groupings, which have, in turn, strong views on how best to run public services. This chapter considers the consequences for public managers of having to work in an environment where professional groupings are so important.

Chapter 7 looks at the roles the users of public services have been positioned as playing, especially in terms of the balance between thinking of them as customers (and so having demands and wants) and citizens (and so being there to hold public services to collective account). Present public service changes tend to place a considerable premium on the former rather than on the latter. Why is this?

Chapter 8 considers the role of markets in public services. The extension of market-style relations to public services has been a defining characteristic of attempts at public reform for nearly 30 years, but seems to have considerable problems associated with it, especially after probably the biggest market failure in history – the financial crisis. Why do we persist with market mechanisms in public services, and can they work?

Chapter 9 looks at the increased use of performance management in public services, asking whether top-down attempts at change through the use of targets and plans can work, and suggesting that they come with a range of issues that public managers need to be aware of to have any chance of achieving success.

Finally, Chapter 10 tries to present a summary of the main tensions and problems that arise from considering public management as a paradoxical discipline and practice, along with the many roles that public managers must learn to occupy as a result. Examples are used both in the text and in case studies that are present at the end of some of the chapters (but not all, to keep the book at a manageable length).

So, having outlined the book, let's get on with it with perhaps the biggest question our governments are facing today – what caused the financial crisis, and what are its implications for our public services?

2

The financial crisis
and its public management
consequences

Introduction

It is not exaggerating to claim that the financial crisis that began in 2007 is the most significant series of economic events to face the global economy since the 1920s and 1930s. To understand its importance, we need to understand both the causes and implications of the crisis, as the former can outline the mistakes that were made that contributed to its being so severe, and the latter presents a series of constraints on public policy and public management that look to be with us for a generation.

The explanation of what happened requires engagement with the world of international finance – not an immediately obvious place for a book on public management to start. But to understand the financial mess we are now in, we need to understand how we got here. Therefore, the book begins with this topic.

So, to turn to the first question – what on earth happened?

The causes of the financial crisis

In the cold light of day, and with the benefit of hindsight, the events leading up to the financial crisis seem rather incredible. Where to start the story is a difficult choice – when we consider the wider context of public management in Chapter 3, we'll go back several decades to explain how the economic crisis of the 1970s set in train the events that led up to the crisis of 2007, but for the moment present a narrative that does not take account of this wider context.

In both the United States and the United Kingdom in the 1980s and 1990s, governments came to believe that central to their enterprise was the idea of a property-owning democracy. In the United States, legislation was passed to attempt to correct what was seen as home-lending practices that discriminated against particular ethnicities, and arguments were made that banks should become active agents in extending homeownership into new groups and income classes. In the United Kingdom, Prime Minister Thatcher sold social housing to tenants in the belief that property owners would have a greater take in their communities and the economy than they would as 'council house' tenants (as well as realizing how popular it would make the government selling off public housing at subsidized prices). In addition to this, the United Kingdom deregulated its financial services industry so that building societies were able to convert themselves into banks, completely changing their business models, which became far less risk averse and eventually leading to some of them offering mortgage deals up to 125 per cent of the market value of a house.

However, it was not intrinsically the extension of mortgage lending (in the United Kingdom) or the creation of 'subprime' lending in the United States that led to the crisis. If this were the case, the financial crisis of 2007/8 would have been contained to a few overstretched financial institutions that had lent homeowners too much money. The problem was more systemic than this. The financial institutions that made 125 per cent mortgages or originated subprime loans did not hold the debts themselves (old-fashioned 'originate and hold'), but instead packaged them together and sold them on ('originate and distribute') as a form of bond (a mortgage-backed security, or later, as a part of what became known as a collateralized debt obligation or CDO). In these bonds, the purchaser of the financial asset received a return linked to the modelled risk attached to the mortgages or other loans upon which the returns on their bonds were based. Loans measured as high risk (in terms of either them defaulting or being repaid early, so reducing potential profits) gave high returns, and loans that were low risk, lower returns. Risk was assessed on the basis of financial models that indicated it was almost impossible to have a nationwide housing price fall, or systemic default on housing loans, because the data series, which measured that risk did not go far enough back in time to include it as a possibility (Shiller, 2008).

Once financial assets had been packaged together they were sold into the deregulated international financial market on an 'over-the-counter' basis, which effectively meant they were tailor-made ('bespoke') assets (which gave banks large fees), and not traded transparently through an exchange where everyone could see what price they were trading at, or of what kinds of financial assets the bonds comprised.

The demand for these financial assets came from oil-rich nations in the Middle East or rapidly developing nations such as China, whose sovereign hedgefunds were looking for investment opportunities to reinvest the savings and surpluses appearing in their countries. Rising demand for financial assets led to even greater financial innovation and engineering taking place, and to the creation of new financial assets, which were effective bets on the likelihood of firms or assets such as CDOs defaulting (which were called credit default swaps), and which could themselves be combined to make new bonds, which could be modelled into synthetic CDOs. This created a huge upside-down pyramid of trillions of dollars of financial assets and was built on the basis of relatively few 'real' mortgages at its base, as subprime mortgages were converted into CDOs, which were effectively pools of mortgages, and synthetic CDOs, which were bets on the mortgage defaults (credit default swaps) combined into bonds that too were based on mortgages.

As the prices of housing continued to rise, and default rates on housing remained manageable, financial asset-based mortgages appeared safe and were widely purchased throughout the financial services industry across the world. Individuals, seeing housing prices rise and finding loans easier to get, took out more and more debt. Mortgage companies were happy to lend as they could sell on those mortgages, apparently without regard as to how risky they were, to other financial institutions packaged as CDOs. Financial institutions chased new financial products as they were literally awash with case from the Middle East and China.

The combination of reckless borrowing, careless lending, the upside-down pyramid of financial assets being built on the property market, and investors not really knowing much about the financial assets they were buying led to huge asset bubble being inflated. When the mortgages at the bottom of the pyramid began to default systematically, and the financial assets based upon them gradually become worthless, the whole edifice came crashing down, with governments bailing banks out with taxpayer money for fear of repeating the Great Depression of the 1930s. Governments then had to face the consequences of these bailouts as they struggled to repay the debts they incurred as a result, having to make cutbacks in public expenditure, which were further exacerbated as economic growth turned into recession as banks stopped lending to private businesses, business confidence generally collapsed, and job lay-offs in the public sector resulted in further unemployment and further falls in economic activity. By some measures, the world lost nearly 50 per cent of its wealth between 2007 and 2012. This leads directly to the problems experienced, especially in Europe in 2011 and 2012, of governments struggling to repay their debts or having to reach agreements for their organized write-down.

There is a great deal more to the financial crisis that those last couple of paragraphs – there is a whole literature on the topic (e.g. Davies, 2010, McLean & Nocera, 2010, Ormerod, 2010, Roubini, 2010, Stiglitz, 2010). But what concerns us here is the role of government and public management in allowing the crisis to occur, and what the implications of the crisis have been for public management since 2007.

The role of government and public management in the crisis

At an ideological level, it is relatively straightforward to divide accounts of the economic crisis into those that see it is a collective, societal failure that involves us all in some way, those that blame the government for it, those that blame a bunch of bankers that went out of control, and those that regard it as a failure of capitalism.

Blame everyone

A first response to the financial crisis therefore is to lay the blame at everyone's door – to say that we all contributed to the crisis, and so must face the challenges it offers today together. In the United Kingdom, the Prime Minister and the Deputy Prime Minister have been keen to stress that to solve its problems we must believe we are 'in it together'. The official US investigation into the financial crisis reads as perhaps the clearest articulation of this view, working systematically through all of the errors that went into constructing subprime and amplifying its effect so it spread around the world.

At a common-sense level, this discourse makes a great deal of sense – if mortgage brokers hadn't got greedy and offered their products to people who obviously couldn't pay them back, and the people themselves hadn't taken out loans they didn't appear to understand and certainly couldn't afford, there would have been no subprime problem. If banks hadn't passed on the risks of their loan book to others, obscured by financial mathematics so that no one could really assess the size of their underlying risks, and then used statistical modelling techniques that were probably inappropriate to price them, backed by credit rating agencies that made huge errors in assessing the risk of those assets to suggest they were as safe as US government bonds, then the crisis wouldn't have occurred. If other banks hadn't purchased those assets, despite not really understanding them, and then engineered them into even more financial products and sold them on (often back to the banks that sold them the original financial assets), then the crisis wouldn't have occurred. If financial traders hadn't taken out loans to purchase more of the assets and driven up their prices to an unsustainable point, then the crisis wouldn't have occurred. If governments hadn't sat by and watched all this going on, reassured by the taxation revenues it all seemed to be generating, then the crisis wouldn't have occurred. When written down this way, we were all to blame to some extent – even if we just ran up a little credit card debt or make a small profit on the sale of a house, we were all part of the same financial system.

Of course, this argument also has serious weaknesses. It seems odd to blame a poor family from California who were missold a mortgage for the financial crisis to the same extent as a governmental regulator who was meant to be overseeing the system. It is unbalanced to suggest that a banker who has ended up being paid millions of pounds in bonuses has come out of the financial crisis in the same state as someone who has had their home repossessed. Neither blame nor the effects of the financial crisis fall on us all equally – and attempting to construct an explanation that blames everyone is something of a negation of duty in pinpointing those whose actions played the largest roles.

Equally, the financial crisis was not caused by people borrowing beyond their means or even by unscrupulous mortgage brokers or bankers lending to them – it was caused by the massive financial investment system of CDOs, Credit Default Swaps (CDS) and other alphabet soup assets being built upon those mortgage loans. In the scheme of things, it was the regulators and bankers who were meant to be overseeing this system and so were more responsible, rather than the small-scale participants themselves.

Blame the government

In the process of elections during 2011 and 2012, leading to the selection of the Republican candidate to challenge Barrack Obama for the presidency, the blame for the financial crisis has been laid firmly at the foot of government. The argument is that, counter to most accounts of the causes of the financial crisis, it was not the deregulation of financial services that caused the crisis, but instead that they were not deregulated enough. If only government had allowed a free market in financial services to be established, the argument goes, the crisis would have been averted, or at least those who were responsible would have been accountable as there would have been no need for government bailouts as the market would have dealt with the problem of failing banks through their efficient liquidation and takeover.

Accounts, which suggest that markets should have been deregulated further or allowed to resolve the financial crisis tend to come from the political right or free-market economists such as Thomas Sowell who argues that the roots of the crisis lie in sincere but misplaced attempts to spread homeownership to those that could not really afford it, and which were bound to fail as they led to markets being distorted. By interfering with market decisions, governments set up markets to fail.

A second means by which governments are regarded in this viewpoint as having contributed to the crisis is in bailing out failed financial institutions after the crisis occurred. This led to what economists call 'moral hazard', in which banks do not have to face the consequences of poor lending or buying assets that prove to be worthless, as they know the government will bail them out if they make mistakes. In the eyes of free-market economists what should have happened is that more prudent or successful financial institutions should have been allowed to take over those that were failing, even if it meant acquiring them as bargain prices, or led to disruption and uncertainty for savers or mortgage holders. In this view, government regulation does not help – banks can be depended upon to control their own behaviours and the risks they take on because of the fear of bankruptcy if they do not (the idea of 'counterparty risk').

From the perspective of those arguing that government was the problem in the financial crisis, there is little room for public services or therefore public management. If you believe that markets are self-correcting and lead to efficient, optimal outcomes, it is hard to see much of a role for public services. If you don't believe that markets can fail under any circumstances, then there are really no such things as public goods and the only role for government is that of protecting the property rights upon which private markets are based.

The trouble is that it's hard to see how the often beautiful (mathematically) models created by free-market economists bear much resemblance to the reality of the world, especially post-2007. The financial crisis seems to involve a whole string of market failures – mortgages being missold, financial assets being mispriced, and banking failures requiring massive government interventions to prevent the collapse of the entire financial system.. The Bush administration can hardly be regarded as a bastion of anti-market collectivists. Its Treasury Secretary at the time of the crisis was Hank Paulson, clearly someone who believed in free markets in his long and successful career as a banker at Goldman Sachs, but who admits in his book how the events around the financial crisis shook his faith in deregulated financial markets (Paulson,

2010). Even former Chairman of the Federal Reserve, Alan Greenspan, a strong believer in the working of the free market to the point of belonging to US novelist and philosopher Ayn Rand's radical pro-capitalist 'objectivist' movement, admitted in his evidence to the financial crisis hearings that the idea of self-regulating financial markets had proven deeply flawed. Although free-market economic theory is theoretically elegant, it is harder to see how it is helpful in either explaining the financial crisis as experienced by those closest to it, or in dealing with its consequences.

The failure of free-market economic theory to explain the financial crisis in anything other than very abstract terms also means that its critique of public services might also be misplaced. If market failure exists, there is a need for public services.

Blame the bankers

If we turn to the claims of the camp that suggest that the financial crisis lies in bankers running out of control, then this argument rests on government regulators, especially in the United Kingdom and the United States, allowing financiers to operate in an increasingly deregulated environment in which they were able to take on greater and greater risks. The ratio between bank capital and debt increased, and the boundaries and barriers between retail and invest-ment banking eroded so that it was not just financially sophisticated investors that were putting their money at risk, but effectively everyone.

The argument in favour of financial deregulation in the 1980s, 1990s and 2000s was that, in a globalized economy, there was no alternative but to let financial flows roam the world in search of greater returns, and that it was actually more efficient to allow that to happen. If countries retained barriers to the kind of inward investment that these capital flows could lead to, they risked missing out on the opportunities that it might bring. If regulatory regimes in one country were stricter than another, those with the strongest rules risked losing out as the money flowed to more deregulated economies.

As the declared profits from financial services grew, governments became more dependent on them for tax revenues (UK Chancellor Alistair Darling reports in his book that 25 per cent of all UK taxation revenues came from the City of London in 2006 (Darling, 2011)), and financiers were brought in to advise government not only how to regulate financial services to achieve the best possible levels of profitability but also how to deal with issues in areas not obviously within their areas of expertise, such as public sector reform. In the United States, bankers entered government (we have already mentioned Hank Paulson, the former Chief Operating Officer of Goldman Sachs, becoming

Secretary to the Treasury in 2006), and politicians often seemed to retire to take on roles as directors of banks. It does certainly seem to be the case that governments and bankers got very close to one another. This was justified at the time in claims that banking was becoming so complex that only 'insiders' could understand it sufficiently to oversee it, but, with the benefit of hindsight (and indeed without it for many writers who were critical of the move), it does appear that the influence of the financial service sector on government led to it being given freedoms it was subsequently unable to cope with.

After the financial crisis, both the United States and the United Kingdom were left with both massive debts from the bailouts of the bank (and so hugely increased debt interest repayments) and a significant hole in taxation revenues. As the profitability of finance institutions specifically and private business more generally has fallen, so has the amount of taxation they return to the government. Unemployment has risen leading to both an increase in benefit payments and reductions in taxation receipts. The combination of all these events creates a situation where, at exactly the time that the government has less taxation revenue, its spending commitments have risen significantly, and resulted in substantial budget deficits.

The financial situation governments find themselves in, therefore, is parlous and has been made worse by the financial system that governments were required to bail out 2007 putting those same governments under considerable pressure to formalize budget austerity plans or face increased interest rates on their debts and runs on their currencies.

In 2012, governments are therefore left in an extraordinary situation. Having bailed the banks out, the deficits that have resulted from reduced tax takes, increased benefit payments, and increased debt commitments are now leading to governments struggling to meet their commitments. Speculative financial flows appear to be moving from country to country, driving up the interest rates on their debts and even leading to Prime Ministers having to resign (as happened in Greece in November 2011), and yet nation-states seem powerless to stop them.

As such, the 'blame the bankers' discourse about the financial crisis appears to have some credibility – both before and after the crisis – as an explanation for the problems we now face. The bigger problem now is what we should do about them.

Dealing with the financial crisis as a problem instigated by the bankers, however, points the finger pointedly back at the governments that allowed speculative activity to get so out of control, and a rethinking of the way that we govern our economies. One response, mooted by former UK Prime Minister Gordon Brown (Brown, 2010) (but with a long history before that) and picked up by the European Union in 2011/12 (ironically, with current UK Prime Minister David Cameron vetoing the suggestion), is that the introduction of a tax on financial transactions (a 'Tobin Tax'). A tax on financial transactions would reduce the speculation that led to the financial crisis, as well as helping reduce the speculative pressures that governments are now facing because of their increased debt commitments. There seems to be great deal to commend this idea, if it can be introduced in a coherent and systematic way across the world. However, such a tax will do little to deal with the debts that now hang over many nations and have resulted from the crisis, and this is the main legacy that public services now confront.

In the United Kingdom, the 2010 general election was dominated by discussions about the scale and size of the budget cuts that would be needed, with a figure of an average of 20 per cent across all government departments being settled upon. Cuts on this scale resulted in the Governor of the Bank of England suggesting that the political party that was unfortunate enough to win the election would put themselves in a position where they would be so unpopular that they would end up being out of power for a generation afterwards. The US President Obama has faced budget-related rebellions as Republicans voted against the raising of the 'cap' on the total US national debt, and so has been frustrated in his attempts to break free from recession in the United States through increased infrastructural investment.

The 'blame the bankers' argument then seems to have at least something to commend it, and suggests that government needs to take a much more proactive role in the financial services industry. In the context of public management, it would also ask questions whether the deregulatory reforms instigated by politicians during the 2000s in public services were, in retrospect, as ill-advised as those made in the financial services industry, and to suggest that we need to look at reforms in a more radical way. This leads on to our third argument that the financial crisis represented a failing not only of the financial services industry but also of capitalism itself.

Blame capitalism

Finally, there is the argument that the financial crisis represents a failure of capitalism itself, and that we must now rethink to come up with big reforms that change the way it operates, or even look for different modes of economic organization entirely. The failure of capitalism argument has a number of versions. In its weakest form, it suggests that the financial and asset markets, which were at the root of the crisis became skewed in such a way that some groups were able to disproportionately profit from them, with others being excluded and often now having to take their share of the pain in economies that are stagnating and which have accumulated vast debts. The solution for writers in this tradition is for economic reforms to reduce the dominance of large monopoly firms of all kinds to drive economies to become more competitive and distribute their rewards more equally so that the massive inequalities in income and wealth that have resulted from the financialization of the US and UK economies are now addressed (Hutton, 2010).

A stronger form of the failure of capitalism argument comes from the resurgence in Marxism, and requires a longer story about the development of capitalism in the twentieth century to be told, and so will be explored more fully in Chapter 3. However, in outline, it suggests that the US and UK economies, in placing such faith in a finance-driven model of economic growth from the 1980s onwards, took a catastrophically bad turn, weakening labour movements and creating gross inequalities in income and wealth that have resulted in the inflation of vast asset bubbles and left those economies holding debts they will now struggle to service. In contrast, countries with economies, which have balanced financial expansion with investment in their industrial base and infrastructure, such as Germany, have come out of the crisis comparatively well, and are now much better placed to be able to secure economic growth in the future.

Countries such as Germany have tended to invest in the skill base of their people, making their economies more competitive through a strategy of investment ('flexicurity') rather than the US or the UK model in which labour markets have been made more competitive by reducing the power of trade unions, reducing the barriers to labour markets, and so increasing the insecurity of the workforce (Harvey, 2010) or a strategy of 'flexploitation' instead. It will be extraordinarily difficult for countries that have based their competitiveness on labour market flexibility rather than labour market investment, to move away from the financialization model back to what the government in the United Kingdom has described as a more 'balanced economy' again.

The failure of capitalism argument is more systemic than the others covered above, and suggests that we must look more radically not only at the causes of the crisis but also at their implications for the way that we run our economies, including the role of public services within them.

I believe that this last argument is the richest and most persuasive of those covered here. In the United States and the United Kingdom, we have based our economic policies since the 1980s on the idea that there is no alternative to the rise of globalization than to embrace the growth of the financial services industry, deregulating it, and becoming dependent on taxation revenues from those services to pay for public services, but with the result at the end of the 2000s in the United Kingdom was net state loss of more than £50bn – the financial services sector cost the government more than it brought in revenues during the decade (Engelend *et al.*, 2011, p. 31). It is surely time to question the advice of the bankers brought in to advise government during that decade which led to the extension of market mechanisms into public provision, and the default assumption that competitive forces are the best way of driving public reform. We have recast the roles of public managers from being administrators and custodians to being managers and entrepreneurs.

We now need to consider the consequences of the financial crisis for public services specifically to begin to get a sense of the scale of the challenges we face in the 2000s.

The consequences of the crisis for public services

Having explored how we can understand the events leading up to the crisis, it is also important to understand their subsequent consequences. There are two main interpretations of the implications of the crisis for public services today.

The mainstream interpretation of the crisis is that economies that were heavily based on financialization, such as the United States and the United Kingdom, and those that have been on the receiving end of the collapse of world trade and were already indebted, such as Greece, Italy, Portugal, Ireland and Spain, now face substantial budget deficits and must introduce deficit reduction programmes or face speculative flows acting against their countries to either bid up interest rates on the debts they face, and so face potential debt default, or, if they are outside a large currency such as the zero, driving down the value of their currencies.

This interpretation carries with it a range of paradoxes – it is saying that the bailouts of financial institutions have now resulted in a situation where the United States and the United Kingdom face censure from speculative flows *from the financial institutions that they bailed out in the first place.* It also suggests that the international capital markets are the appropriate judge of a country's economic success, *when the same markets appear to have fundamentally mispriced the risk associated with financial assets for much of the 2000s.*

These paradoxes are perhaps most clear in the case of the credit rating agencies, such as Standard and Poor's and Moody's, who routinely graded financial assets based on subprime mortgage assets as being as safe as US government bonds in terms of risk, but who made headlines in 2011 by downgrading their grading of US debt from the highest possible rating, and who are threatening (as I write this) to put the United Kingdom under review for a similar downgrade. The credit rating agencies continue to play a significant role in the financial markets despite being massively discredited by the financial crisis when their previous ratings were shown to be so incorrect. The central problem here is that we still seem to be judging economic success on the same criteria as we did before the crisis – but surely the crisis should have led to us questioning those criteria given the colossal failure of the economic model that it appeared to imply?

The solution to the problems we now face (most immediately, the governmental budget deficits) is dependent upon the private sector filling the gap left by the state as it is forced to introduce a range of cuts to public spending. However, this is effectively asking private investment to take place at a time when economic growth is stagnant, and when banks are unlikely to lend to them, not least because they continue to have substantial capital problems of their own. Assuming private enterprise will fill the gap left by a reduction in public services therefore seems unlikely – would you want to expand or start a new business when people are losing their public sector jobs and it seems more likely that firms are going to close than be successful? And would you, as a banker, want to lend to private business when the economy is not growing? Governments have attempted to address the latter point by effectively printing money and exchanging it for non-liquid financial assets by the banks, to attempt to encourage them to lend (so-called 'quantitative easing') but to only limited success in terms of getting banks to restart lending.

Politicians also appear to be reluctant to re-regulate the financial institutions whose actions played such a significant role in the financial crisis. This seems odd – don't we want to stop it from happening again? However, financial institutions are now extremely powerful in the United States and the United Kingdom, having strong lobbying groups, which threaten to move operations abroad if regulation does not suit them, and, in any case, given the lack of economic growth from the rest of the economy, we may find ourselves being dependent on exactly the banks that got us into this mess, now getting us out again. This is, of course, madness, especially given the calculations above that the banking sector actually cost more in state revenues (including the bailouts) than the taxation revenues they paid out in the 2000s. However, banks appear to have such a grip on our imaginations as creators of wealth that government policy towards them has a strong sense of 'business as usual' about it, based on the hope that they can restore profitability in order for government-held assets to be sold off, and for corporation tax revenues to rise again and meet the increased interest and debt repayments government have been left with.

The danger, however, is that by depending on the banks to get us out of the crisis, we neglect thinking about whether we want to continue to run the economy as if the crisis had never happened for those whose actions led to it, whereas the rest of the economy (including the public sector) is asked to either make sacrifices or exist in an environment of reduced opportunity (and reduced credit) in the meantime. By not taking the opportunity to reconsider the balance of financial and industrial and commercial economic activity in the United States and the United Kingdom, we risk not only repeating the crisis but also being so dependent on our financial institutions for growth and tax revenues that we are never able to reform them.

Equally, by not learning the wider lessons from the financial crisis about market failure and inappropriate deregulation, we do not transfer that learning to our understanding of public reform. If we treat the financial crisis as something that has no implications (other than budget cutbacks) for public services, then we seem to be missing the bigger lessons that we might draw from them, and risk going down public reform roads that are based on discredited ideas.

It is this kind of logic that leads to a second interpretation of the situation governments and public services now face. Rather than reducing public expenditure, perhaps we now need to be investing in the infrastructure and skills and training our economies are going to need in the future, and putting people to work to those ends. In order to do this, we will first have to tame the financial speculators that would drive up interest payments on the debts that would be necessary to achieve these goals through the use of tools such as the Tobin Tax, which imposes a small charge on short-term financial transactions.

A significant, state-led investment would benefit those economies in its receipt both now and in the future in the development of new technologies such as the 'green' solutions we will need to build sustainable futures, as well as rebalancing them away from the excessive financialization, which the United States and the United Kingdom have embraced to a situation where banking becomes once again an instrument of making investment and achieving growth for the wider economy rather than just itself. This argument suggests that only by investing now can we hope to pay off the debts we have to face both now and in the future.

In this viewpoint, public spending, so long as it is an investment, is entirely justified. This thinking is disputed, with Keynesian economists such as Paul Krugman arguing that it has a 'multiplier' effect in the wider economy so that every pound spent has a magnified effect as it works its way through as pay, which is spent and allows further employment and investment. Free-market economists dispute this, but frankly after the disasters their policy prescriptions seem to have led to in terms of the financial crisis, it seems to me as if we should give another set of ideas a turn to see if they can deal with the crisis more effectively than simply allowing those who got us into this mess to try and dig us out again.

In both the United States and Europe (and gradually in the United Kingdom) we have seen stimulus packages put in place, but there is a danger of them being too small to make a difference, and so leading to accusations that money is being wasted on building infrastructure when it could be used to pay down the deficits. This investment expenditure may have prevented things from being even worse than they are now, but it has yet to lead to strong economic growth. Without international financial reform it is hard to see how governments can go much further, however, as they are likely to face the censure of debt speculators who force their interest repayments up beyond the 7 per cent, which is regarded as being the limit for sustainable state financing.

Equally, asking difficult questions about the causes of the financial crisis inevitably leads to us questioning whether the public reforms of the 1990s and 2000s were the right thing to do, as they were based on the same kinds of ideas, such as deregulation and increased private competition, as those that led to the financial crisis. The financial crisis, in these terms, is too big and important an event for us to waste the learning from it for both private and public reform.

Conclusion

There are two paradoxes associated with this chapter. The first is that the financial crisis, a colossal market failure (possibly the biggest we've ever seen), did not lead to us reforming financial services and rethinking our approach to the use of markets in the public sector, but instead to accelerating their usage in the belief that there is no alternative to governing in a period of austerity than to make a greater use of market mechanisms and privatization. A large part of the justification for the use of markets and competition involving private providers of services is based on a second paradox – that the financial markets, whose failure led to the crisis of 2007 and 2008, are now attacking nation-states for the level of debts that they have to repay, when those debts were largely incurred bailing out financial services firms in 2007 and 2008.

The world, at the beginning of 2012, is in something of a mess. The financial crisis has not led to significant financial reform, even though there appears to be a general acknowledgement (not least from the Managing Director of the IMF, Christine Lagarde) that re-regulation is necessary, and the introduction of a measure like the Tobin Tax is entirely appropriate. Unless that reform takes place, it is hard to see how governments can avoid the austerity measures that they are presently imposing on their people, but by imposing those austerity measures, countries such as the United States and the United Kingdom, which now face huge deficits and have become dependent upon financial institutions to generate growth and taxation, risk a decade (or more) of economic stagnation, whilst at the same time always risking a recurrence of the economic crisis should asset prices be allowed to inflate to unsustainable levels again. Countries such as Germany have shown us that there is an alternative model of achieving economic competitiveness, but we seem remarkably reluctant to learn from them, still being largely in thrall to economic doctrines that were surely discredited by the events of 2007 and 2008, and yet seem to dominate our thinking.

This lack of imagination in thinking of an alternative to austerity means that public services face not only cuts but also a challenge to their very existence. Governments are increasingly making use of private and not-for-profit provision in what used to be public service areas in the name of increasing competition and driving up efficiency and service responsiveness. No one is denying that public services are in need of improvement, but whether these measures will improve things is questionable at best. If private healthcare is the answer, why does the United States have the world's most expensive healthcare system, but only mediocre health outcomes? If transport services are better run by the private sector, how come public sector French trains are so much better (by almost any criteria) than the United Kingdom's, which have been in private hands since the mid-1990s?

The financial crisis then has led to the governments of countries, which had been dependent on the profits of financial services to now deal with the deficits that resulted from bank bailouts, from the economic stagnation that has occurred post-2007, and the financial debt speculation that now jeopardizes their ability to pay for those deficits. Even countries that had little involvement in the crisis itself face an uncertain future because of the collapse in world trade.

In such an environment, public management faces an uncertain future across a range of issues. Does the financial crisis show that we need public services as a bulwark against the excesses of the market, or that we can no longer afford them? If public services aren't able to provide the level of service we expect from private companies, does this mean that we have no alternative but to privatize them and to organize them on a competitive basis? If we are to retain public services, how should they be accountable to those they are meant to serve? If we must retain some public provision as a provider of last resort (in the event of private provider failures), then does this undermine the idea of a competitive marketplace? This book attempts to address these issues, along with a number of others. The financial crisis did not cause all of these problems, but did raise their importance and urgency, as well as, I believe, giving us the opportunity to revisit them and to ask whether we have taken the wrong road in reforming our public services. How we respond will shape our economies and societies for decades to come.

3

The context of public management and the changing role of the state

Introduction

Chapter 2 explored the financial crisis and its implications for public services, suggesting that it is crucial now to look fundamentally at public reform to make sure that same errors in understanding that led to the financial crisis are not being used as a basis for public reform. Central to this message is that public management does not exist in a vacuum, as the state sets the rules and political context within which public managers have to work (Hood, 1998). Managers in both the public and private sectors are clearly influenced by the activities of the state – laws passed by the government apply equally to public, private and not-for-profit sectors. However, in the public sector the state will also set the budget, the goals of public services, the dominant mode of governance (market, state or hierarchy), which conditions the relationships they have with other public organizations and the public, as well as the means by which public services are held accountable or judged to be a success or failure.

This is the longest chapter in the book as it has to fill in a great deal of history that is relevant to our present predicaments, as well as explaining how we got here. It, therefore, sets a wider context for the problems we face today, as well as exploring how we responded to the last economic crisis in the 1970s.

The relationship between public managers and the state is fertile ground for a number of academic disciplines: political scientists are often interested in how power is deployed and legitimacy established; sociologists in how relationships are constituted, especially those involving professionals and the public; and organizational theorists in how to organize public services to improve efficiency or to empower staff.

This chapter makes use of these disciplines (and more), asking the question 'how does the state work, and how changing ideas about the role of the state affect public management?'

The working of the state in contemporary capitalism is worthy of a book in its own right, and indeed, several are already available. This chapter attempts to set public management debates in a broader context by exploring how ideas about the state and its relationship to public services and public managers has changed, especially over the long-term, and how different interpretations of the position today can be drawn to illuminate different approaches to public management.

The chapter begins by exploring how the state developed in the twentieth century, and it is to this topic that it now turns.

The development of the state in the post-war period

The post-war economic settlement

After the Second World War, there was a general trend amongst developed nations towards the expansion of public services. This expansion did not occur in the same way in each country – the United Kingdom put in place a comprehensive welfare state quickly, as did countries like Sweden. The United States, in these terms, was a laggard, only catching up with the reforms of the Johnson government of the 1960s, and still struggling with the idea of comprehensive healthcare provision or high-quality public schooling. Developing nations, equally, often find it difficult to find the appropriate time to put in place greater public provision – a significant challenge that China will face in the twenty-first century is the extent to which it chooses to provide more government-sponsored services for its people, or expects families to save in order to access healthcare or to make their own provision in the case of long-term unemployment.

In the context of the developed nations in the post-war period, however, there were several drivers leading to the extension of public services, with two of the most important being based, first, on the experience of the industrial economies before the Second World War during the Great Depression (and so being extremely relevant to our thinking about public services today); and second, the implications of the war itself for the way that government was conceptualized in terms of its proper role and the range of activities it should occupy.

During the 1930s, the world went through a significant recession (Aldcroft, 2001). The stock market crash in the United States in the late 1920s had a profound effect on the world economy as countries resorted to protectionism in order to try and look after their own economies in a global economic slump, but with the end result being a rise in unemployment across the world, and a rise in instability that eventually led in Europe to the Second World War.

At this time, most states offered only minimal unemployment insurance, and so when people lost their jobs, it was largely up to them to find a way of coping. Governments, driven by a philosophy of balanced budgets, often reduced public expenditure and support as taxation revenues fell and made things worse as a result by increasing uncertainty and by reducing demand in the economy at a time when things were already in a poor state. So entrenched was the view that public budgets needed to be in balance that even President Roosevelt, originator of the US 'New Deal', argued in favour of them in his campaign to be President, before doing something entirely different when elected to office in a range of attempts to boost the flagging economy.

According to tenets of classical economics, when there is a fall in demand for goods and services their price should fall to compensate, and balance between supply and demand be re-established. The problem is that prices often do not fall as quickly as they rise – especially labour costs – and so there is a collective action problem in which it would be best if everyone would take a pay cut so that people do not lose their jobs, but no one, individually, wants to receive a pay cut. Equally, classical economics assumes that people are able to move freely to find new work, and that workers can quickly retrain in new skills should their own no longer be valued in the marketplace.

Free-market economists, especially those of an Austrian persuasion such as Hayek and Von Mises, believe that recessions are the price that needs to be paid for poor capital investment decisions in the past, and during which corrections take place in which prices need to be allowed to reach more sustainable levels. In time, new investments will be made that lead to profitability in the next rise in economic activity. This view of the world, if also held by those in power, leads to a belief that government should be involved in the economy as little as possible, as doing so will distort market signals, interfere with the free movement of supply and demand and actually prolong the recession as the market adjustment will take far longer to occur, making the pain greater for everyone involved.

Keynes

The great economist John Maynard Keynes, rather than starting with the assumption that markets were automatically self-clearing, believed both that there was the potential for prices to be 'sticky', in that they do not move freely up and down, and that there could be substantial problems with the 'animal spirits' of investors, who, instead of making careful and rational decisions about which projects and stocks they should be purchasing, were engaged in a rather odder game. In Keynes' view, the stock market was not about working out the trying to price assets accurately, but instead the prices were set by traders attempting to guess what other traders would do next and outsmart them.

Combining this view of prices and investment, Keynes suggested that in a recession there is a danger of a vicious circle setting in which a fall in confidence leads to falling investment and job lay-offs, which leads back to a further fall in confidence and a potentially destructive spiral downwards.

In these circumstances, waiting for the economy to correct itself or reducing interest rates will have little effect. It may take years for prices to fall and for business confidence to rise again. Hoping interest rates will stimulate the economy is like trying to move an object by pushing (rather than pulling) on a string – as even at low rates people (especially investors) will not want to borrow for fear of what the future holds, especially in relation to their own employment. Instead of trying to reduce interest rates and waiting for prices to fall to the point where markets return to equilibrium, Keynes suggested that unemployment and falling output might require the government to intervene and 'pump-prime' demand by increasing public spending, especially on 'works' programmes (or investment).

Keynes' view ran directly counter to the free-market-driven view of the economy; in a period of recession, tax receipts fall as there are less profits, and so the government, according to that view, should also reduce its expenditures in order to balance its overall budget. Keynes suggested the opposite; that government should deliberately generate deficits in order to boost the economy as a whole and remove the deficiencies in demand. This was revolutionary stuff (Aitkenson & Olseon Jr, 1998).

Keynes acknowledged that in the long run, markets would probably re-establish some kind of balance, but he did not believe that the pain and suffering that would take place as a result was necessary. Instead of waiting for the correction to come, why shouldn't government get involved and drive up demand so that the pain could be avoided? The implications of Keynes' ideas were profound. He was suggesting that the government should increase its involvement in the economy on almost moral grounds because it did not adjust quickly enough (because of sticky prices and the 'animal spirits' of investors) to come back into balance itself, and so economic recession would mean that the population suffered the waste and indignity of unemployment when it was not necessary, and could be avoided.

Keynes suggested that 'public works' programmes be instigated in periods of economic recession where the state invested in the country's infrastructure. When the state could not find any worthwhile projects to invest in, he even went as far as saying that the unemployed should be employed to dig up disused mine shafts on the grounds that this would give the unemployed work, and which would lead in turn to demand being boosted in order to push the economy out of recession.

The flipside of Keynes' logic was that, when the economy was expanding, the government should reduce its expenditure commitments, winding down public works programmes, as the lack of demand in the economy had been remedied and government intervention was no longer necessary. Public expenditure was therefore viewed as a kind of automatic economic stabilizer, to be increased in periods of recession and decreased in periods of economic growth. The government had a legitimate reason to get involved in the running of the economy where there were economic problems (as there were in the 1930s, when Keynes' book was being written) but should withdraw again in better economic times. In practice, the former (spending more in recessions) was relatively straightforward to achieve, but the latter rather more difficult, as the account below will make clear. However, the importance of Keynes' ideas in the extension of the role of the state in the post-war period cannot be understated – his work gave governments the intellectual basis for expanding the role of the public sector.

The experience of war

The second factor affecting the role of the state in the economy was the experience of war itself. During wartime, economic production is transformed from having large numbers of private enterprises self-organizing around markets, to production being concentrated into government-funded or government-provided industries designed to wage war. The wartime economic transformation, especially in the United Kingdom, had a profound effect on many of the politicians who experienced it, and who regarded the success of planning during the war as a justification for extending the role of the state into nearly every area of life. States set rations on what food could be eaten, introduced production schedules on what needed to be made and organized the workforce to try and make sure that essential tasks were carried out from fighting through to factor production through to scientific research. Countries in Europe (and even the United States and Australia) developed wartime economies that were dramatically different from those they had in peacetime. After peace had been re-established, the countries where battles raged often had their private productive capacity effectively destroyed, and looked to their governments to re-establish them through massive investment programmes. Loan and grants from the US government through Marshall Aid provided to be the means through which war-torn Europe was able to get back on its feet again.

The huge expansion in the state's involvement into every aspect of their country's governance meant that there was a cohort of politicians who came to see how large-scale organization could be accomplished in the wartime situation, and believed that this could be carried forward into peacetime. In countries where production had been substantially destroyed by the war, particularly Germany, it was a matter of life and death that governments intervened to rebuild infrastructure and production capacity. In the victorious nations, the huge debts incurred during wartime held the potential to bankrupt economies, but despite this, in the United Kingdom, the nationalization of strategically important industries such as steel and coal and the establishment of a welfare state were regarded as being the road to re-establishing economic efficiency (Hennessy, 1994). Politicians believed that wartime had not only shown how it was possible for the state to run the economy but also that Keynesian economics suggested the state had an intellectual basis and an ethical reason to be involved more fully in the economy. The alternative to Keynesian management of the economy was a return to the private market, and market forces were blamed for having caused the Wall Street Crash and Great Depression. Governments also believed it as crucial that an international fixed exchange rate system be put in place to facilitate trade, with Keynes again being central at the 'Bretton Woods' discussion in the United States that led to the establishment of such a system.

The post-war public settlement was therefore based on an expansion of public services that were justified through the ideas of Keynes and the experience of greater state involvement in wartime. Depending on how you view subsequent events, the greater international co-operation in trade coming from the post-war international economic settlement, combined with Keynesian economic planning and greater government involvement, led either to a sustained period of economic growth until the mid-to-late 1960s or to a period of lost opportunity where government over-expanded but was fortunate not to ruin the world economy because of the relatively calm economic waters of that time. What is apparent is that the 25 years after the Second World War was a time of growing prosperity and year-on-year economic growth of a kind that has been seldom seen before or since.

The crisis of Keynesianism – Fiscal crisis, crowding out, and other crises

A number of problems led to the 'golden years' (as they were subsequently known) of Keynesian economic management and fixed exchange rates being undermined. In the 1960s, the fixed exchange rate system came under increasing pressure as the United States funded overseas wars and so gradually lost its ability to control the value of its own currency because of the sheer volume of dollars that were traded outside of its own geographic borders. Countries such as the United Kingdom appeared to struggle to trade at the fixed rate set for the pound, as its comparatively poor economic performance meant that downward revaluations of the pound were necessary, whereas countries that experienced strong economic growth, such as (West) Germany, had to revalue their currency upwards or their exports would have been underpriced outside of their home country.

The fixed exchange rate system underlying the post-war economy came apart in the early 1970s as currency problems grew further as a result of oil price shocks, in which the oil-producing nations (OPEC) reached agreements that resulted in them limiting production to drive up the oil prices. The world's dependence on oil by the 1970s meant that this led to huge oil price rises, with fourfold increases occurring. Countries importing oil also directly imported inflation, with general prices rising dramatically and inflation taking hold. Public workers demanded pay rises to match the general price rise in the economy, leading to huge increases on the demands of the government purse at exactly the time that economies were stagnating because of the huge prices.

Governments appeared to face a perfect storm of exchange rate uncertainty, inflation, rising unemployment, and union militancy. A new word, 'stagflation', or economic stagnation plus inflation, was invented for a situation in which governments appeared powerless with no idea of what to do – the Keynesian solution to falling demand was for government to engage in public works programmes, but governments faced dire fiscal situations in which they would have to run up massive debts to engage in expansionary programmes, which might also result in even greater inflation as prices were pushed up even further. Again, there are strong parallels with the position in the 1970s and the situation today.

A range of ideas appeared in the 1970s to try and explain what was happening, which have a considerable resonance with today's debates.

Fiscal crisis

By the 1970s, the state had expanded considerably from its position at the end of the Second World War, as more services were provided and expectations about the role of the state were raised. However, this led to questions as to whether this expansion could continue indefinitely, with the government taking a greater and greater proportion of gross domestic product (and so higher and higher taxation), or whether there would come a point where the public sector was no longer affordable. Similar to today, the claim was made that the government had simply become too big, and now had to be scaled back.

The fiscal crisis argument, originally based in the Marxist literature (O'Connor, 1973), suggested that state expenditure was dividable into two categories: social capital and social expenses. Social capital was state investment in the productive economy. An example of this is government spending on education to make the workforce more productive, or improving infrastructure so that trade could better flourish. Social expenses, however, were provided by the state to prevent the workforce from becoming so disaffected by capitalism that protest and rebellion undermined it. Examples of social expenses might be benefit payments to workers who don't contribute to economic growth, or healthcare expenditure on non-urgent or non-life-threatening conditions. Social expenses were often provided after a great national sacrifice, such as that of war as a means of rewarding that sacrifice, as well as means of achieving popularity for the politicians who introduced them.

The problem is that social expenses tend to have what is called a 'ratchet' effect – once they have been introduced it is very difficult politically to subsequently withdraw them. As we noted above, this is one of the problems of Keynesian thinking – in periods of economic prosperity, the government should be reducing its expenditures to help stabilize the economy, but this is extremely difficult to accomplish for politicians who work on four- or five-year electoral cycles – do you want to be the one that cancelled a works programme or withdrew a benefit? It is a brave government that antagonizes its electorate. Today's attempts by governments to scale back on benefits and the protests they inevitably lead to show what happens when you try and take away government benefits that people have come to regard either as a right or as a mark of their country's fairness.

Social expenses therefore have a tendency to rise and rise, and O'Conner suggested that this creates a dynamic where the state is required to pay for a wider and wider range of public services until a point is reached where 'fiscal crisis' is reached – where the government is unable to afford its planned expenditure, and is unwilling or unable to raise taxes any further to pay for them. The government is therefore unable to meet its commitments – a situation that Greece particularly has found in 2011–12 as the result of a combination of decades of the tolerance of tax avoidance and the crippling interest payments it now must meet.

O'Conner hoped that fiscal crisis would eventually lead to the overthrow of capitalism, but this of course didn't happen. The fiscal crises in the 1970s led to dramatic cutbacks in welfare expenditures in many developed nations, but more importantly created the space for the introduction of non-Keynesian ideas on how to run the economy, and for very different ideas about how best to run public services.

Crowding out

A related idea to that of fiscal crisis is that, if the public sector gets too big, it will result in investors using their resources to buy public debt rather than being investing in private organizations. According to this view, as more and more public debt is generated and sold to investors, its purchase 'crowds out' (Bacon & Eltis, 1978) private investment, and the productive, wealth-generating part of the economy allowed to stagnate as the state grows instead. 'Crowding out', if it exists, results in a different form of crisis to O'Connor's, in which the private economy is unable to support the large public sector as its taxation demands have grown too great, and the private economy stagnates because it is unable to generate sufficient investment to renew itself. The result is economic stagnation, with private firms, even if they have excellent ideas for new products or services, unable to attract the investment they need.

The idea of crowding out has less resonance in the 2007–08 crisis because the debts of the United States and United Kingdom are not entirely held by investors from their own country, with large proportions held overseas instead. Having large overseas debt in a globalized financial economy has led to other pressures; however, as Chapter 2 made clear, with speculative capital investors driving up the price of debt in countries they believe are vulnerable, and making debt repayments unaffordable for those nations.

Bacon and Eltis wanted a roll-back in the state to allow the vibrant private sector to grow without interference from it – a message that has strong resonances with governments today.

Other types of crisis

Along with fiscal crisis and 'crowding out', there was an associated form of crisis coming from the state losing faith in its ability to deal with the full range of problems for which it has taken responsibility (Pierson, 2006). One variation on this is the theory of government 'overload', where the government reaches a size where it can simply no longer discharge its responsibilities. This might be due to what economists call diseconomies of scale, where the size of an institution becomes so large that it is unable to co-ordinate its activities or control what it does, or it might be due to the state entering areas of activity it has no expertise to be able to manage. As with Bacon and Eltis, the solution is to reduce the size of the state in response, and to re-privatize services.

In addition to ideas about crisis that explain it in material terms (especially in terms of money and debt) there is also 'ideational crisis', which occurs when governments find that they can no longer depend upon the ideas or principles upon which they have been previously governing. This occurs most visibly where government policies seem no longer to work – as in the case of Keynesian economic policy in the 1970s.

As we noted above, in the 1970s major industrial economies suffered from simultaneous rise in unemployment and inflation (or 'stagflation'), which was not meant to happen according to Keynesian economic ideas (Greener, 2001). As such, governments found themselves effectively caught in a situation where their policies appeared to be failing, and they needed to look for alternatives (Hall, 1993, Oliver, 1997), especially as the fixed exchange rate system failed, governments experienced rising inflation and rising unemployment, an emerging worldwide recession, and yet appeared powerless in the face of these challenges. These factors undermined the legitimacy of Keynesian economic thought and created the opportunity for advocates of different views of economic and political governance to gain a hearing from the governments of the world.

The state response to the crisis of Keynesianism

In response to the crises of the 1970s, governments have increasingly cast themselves not as a paternalistic planners of the economy, as they became under Keynesianism, instead occupying more managerial roles (Clarke & Newman, 1997) in which they favour entrepreneurship and enterprise, and with the main aim of government policy not being to achieve full employment, as it often was under Keynesianism, but instead to make the economy more competitive in a globalized world. In this view, the state attempts to intervene not in the demand side of the economy, to boost demand through investment and employment, but instead in the supply side, to try and make its industries, both private and public, more competitive and productive.

The most recent manifestation of this idea is the 'social investment state' associated with the ideas of Anthony Giddens and the language of the 'Third Way' (Giddens, 1998), where the state becomes a kind of super loss-adjuster on behalf of its citizens. In these circumstances, the state does not 'spend' its taxation revenues, but instead 'invests' them to the end of achieving greater economic competitiveness, with only those that are demonstrably unable to work, or are actively retraining or seeking work, receiving state support. These ideas also fit remarkably well with the notion of the 'Big Society' central to David Cameron's thinking in the United Kingdom election of 2010, where the state must withdraw from public service provision in order for local groups to fill the gaps instead (Norman, 2010).

In the social investment state or big society, the public no longer receive state support unconditionally – they also have responsibilities, which the state demands in return. There is a move towards means testing and limiting access to benefits to promote independence and autonomy. The state should invest taxpayer money where the best returns for the economy as a whole can be generated, with none of the sentimentality of the past where failing industries were supported on the grounds of social cohesion, or people being allowed to receive benefits where they could be in paid work instead.

Explaining changes in the state – The work of Bob Jessop

The work of Bob Jessop (Jessop, 1993, 1994, 1999, 2002) is of considerable help in explaining how and why the state has changed over the last 50 years or so, and of reconsidering the role of public management within it. Jessop utilizes four analytical spectrums through which it is possible to explain and explore change. These crystallize around two 'ideal types', or forms of the state that capture its form before and after the crisis of Keynesianism. They are meant to hold explanatory potential rather than provide a detailed empirical study of any particular case. They are summarized in Table 3.1 and described in greater depth below.

From Keynesianism to Schumpeterianism

First, Jessop suggests that the role of the state has moved from one predominantly concerned with Keynesianism to one oriented instead around what he calls 'Schumpeterianism'. Keynesianism has been covered above and is based

Table 3.1 The changing formation in the state

Change in welfare state	Description
Keynesianism to Schumpeterianism	Move from paternalistic planning and focus on demand side of economy to enterprising, entrepreneurial supply-side focus.
Welfare to workfare	Move from social benefits being a right to having duties associated with them – the duty to earn benefits, for example.
National to post-national	Move from national basis of economy and policy to use of both international and local bodies.
State to regime	Move from centralized state provision to a plurality of providers often organized in a network form.

on Keynes' view that economies, left to their own devices, may not always come into balance (equilibrium) at a point of full employment. Keynesianism (the approach of economists building on the work of Keynes, but not necessarily entirely representative of it) advocated greater state investment in public services in times when the economy may be below full employment, but can also be read as a means of attempting to stabilize economic cycles (periods of growth and recession) by justifying states paying benefit to those out of work, for example, in order to stabilize the economy in periods of recession. Keynesianism held the achievement of full employment as its central economic goal, within a relatively closed economy in which large international capital flows did not exist, or could not affect the value of the currency in a fixed exchange rate. It is a paternalistic approach to running a relatively closed economy, based on expert advice and opinion, and aiming to benefit the public through full employment.

Schumpeterianism in contrast emphasizes competition and enterprise in an economy, suggesting, in line with the changes discussed in the previous section, that the state should be concerned not with the demand side of the economy (expenditure), but instead with the supply side (product and service provision), because the globalized economy is no longer relatively close to international trade and currency speculation. Schumpeterianism aims to create a more competitive economy through the reduction of state control and deregulation, the simplification or outright removal of rules believed to be hindering business.

The Schumpeterian view of the state, being based on the need to try and achieve competitiveness within a global economy, is seen by its advocates as inevitable – a globalized world requires firms to be internationally competitive, and if the state is to have a role, it is to support private business in doing so.

Schumpeterianism is based on a globalized economy rather than the relatively closed economy of Keynesianism and suggests that there is a need for a halt in growth or reduction of the public sector. Public services, in this view, cannot satisfy the consumers of the twenty-first century, being too inflexible and bureaucratic. Equally benefit payments need to be scaled back as people are regarded as having become too dependent upon state handouts rather than taking responsibility for themselves. This view is very much associated with neoliberal agendas about personal freedom and responsibility (Harvey, 2010), and the political right (Murray, 1984), but has more recently been acknowledged by other writers concerned about the disempowering effects of becoming entirely reliant upon the state for their income, and the lack of life chances this might generate as a result (Le Grand, 2007).

Under Keynesian thought, public administration is an expert-led, paternalistic affair, dominated by highly educated technocrats who are relied upon to demonstrate fairness through the creation of public systems for administering budgets and services for the benefit of the people. Services tend to be professional dominated and supply centred rather than being focused particularly on the needs of the individual receiving them (Stewart & Walsh, 1992).

Schumpeterian public management, however, is about providing public services in a competitive marketplace, with public provision giving way to private and not-for-profit (even if the state continues to fund services). Services become business-focused, dominated by professional managers aiming for innovation and enterprise to successfully compete to provide the best service with the greatest efficiency. Schumpeterian public management aims to create lean systems of control for the delivery of user-responsive services and is suspicious of strong professional groups that may not be perceived to be acting in the interests of public service recipients, seeking to bring them under the control of public managers through techniques such as performance management and performance-related pay.

From welfare state to workfare state

Jessop's second analytical spectrum is concerned with social policy. The idea of a welfare state is associated with the view that services should be universal and given as a right to citizens. This means that the state effectively guarantees the provision of a range of public services, which are granted not on the ability to pay, but instead on the basis of need. This clearly has strong overtones of attempting to achieve fairness, and a fit with Keynesianism, which has a complementary fit being based on the idea of an interventionist state.

Workfarism, on the other hand, emphasizes both rights and duties. In return for receiving state support, citizens are required to do something to support the competitiveness of the economy. An example might help illustrate this.

Under welfarism, unemployment benefit might be given as a right to those out of work in the name of fairness, but also on efficiency grounds (see Keynesianism above). As such unemployment benefit payments can be expected to rise during an economic downturn, and help to stabilize the economy from falling into a severe recession. A workfare approach, in contrast, would grant unemployment only if individuals could show they were actively seeking work, and require those receiving benefits work in the community in return, perhaps cleaning up graffiti or mending public facilities. It is even possible that they might be required to work in public or private organizations in return for their benefits on the grounds they are achieving work experience, and then the benefit might only be payable for a fixed period of time after which the state withdraw its support. Workfarism is based on the principle that individuals must earn state support, but also to show they are not in danger of becoming dependent upon it.

Jessop suggests that there was a move from welfarism to workfarism as the twentieth century moved on, as discourses appeared, which positioned benefit claimants a 'scroungers' or an 'underclass' that were not contributing to the economic well-being of the nation. Workfare policies were pioneered in the United States in the 1980s, but perhaps summarized best by the UK politician Norman Tebbit who suggested that the unemployed should get 'on their bike' and seek work if they were unable to find it.

The move from welfarism to workfarism leads to employment-related services such as what used to be called 'job centres' being privatized and performance managed so that targets are given for the number of unemployed that need to be found work. Benefits agencies, instead of being organizations, which pay out universal benefits, carefully assess claimants to determine whether they are eligible or not, and may too be privatized on the grounds that competition will drive down the cost of such systems to the state, as well as making them more efficient and better-run.

The claim that private employment agencies are superior to public ones at getting people back to work, and that the private sector is more efficient at administering benefits systems, both need careful consideration. Private organizations may have strong incentives to return the unemployed to work, but whether the jobs they are able to fill offer any kind of permanent solution to unemployment is more questionable. Incentivizing reductions in unemployment registers for fixed periods of time risks them being 'gamed' and people forced to take jobs that they are unsuited for simply so agencies appear to be succeeding. In the United Kingdom as I write this, one such private agency A4E is being investigated for fraud in relation to concerns they have been engaging in 'gaming' activity.

Equally, as eligibility criteria becomes more complex under a more workfare-based systems, more information has to be gathered and processed about claimants in order to assess their cases, and to make sure that they have earned the right to receive any available benefits. This risks creating a complex bureaucracy, which will need to be managed to make sure that decisions are made in both a fair and timely way, and if organizations are being incentivized to reduce benefit payments through the unthinking use of eligibility criteria, there are real risks that real financial hardship can be caused to the most vulnerable. Benefit systems need to be made to work both fairly and efficiently, but the more complex the system, the harder this is to achieve. In an era where the state routinely gathers more and more information about its citizens, data management and data security become increasingly more important, and those managing benefit systems must develop an increased awareness not only of the potential of IT to assist in their decision making but also of how they can make information systems containing public information secure. Well-publicized cases concerning hackers breaking into government computer systems, or even government officials losing laptops or data DVDs illustrate the problems here.

From the national state to the post-national state

Jessop's third analytical spectrum runs from the state being organized primarily nationally to instead a moving both upwards to global levels and downward to regional ones. Keynesian economics was based on the premise that economies were relatively closed, with the state using economic policy to secure full employment on a national level. This was a situation, in other words, where countries could regard themselves as largely masters of their own economic destinies. However, as competition became more globalized, and international finance became deregulated and moved freely of individual countries and their borders, the nation-state became regarded as less important as a unit of analysis, and the global economy came to the fore. At the same time as this, a reaction to national government failing and globalization mean that regional government assumed a greater prominence, being potentially more manageable and responsive than the national state was able to achieve.

Globalization has meant that economies are increasingly unable to act independently of one another – with the financial crisis being the exemplar of this as a US and UK housing problem spread rapidly to the rest of the world. The mobility and sheer scale of financial capital means that an economy not seen as performing well will experience an outflow of investment and potentially an increase in the interest it has to pay on its debts (as Ireland, Greece and Italy discovered in 2011). This economic form of globalization means that countries have become more interlinked through capital flows, which have come to dwarf the economic transfers made for direct trade.

The second sense in which post-nationalism is relevant is that the state, where it has reached the point of 'overload' (see above), typically needs to get organizations and political bodies at more local levels to take greater responsibility and for central government itself to occupy more a 'regulation' role in overseeing their activities rather than participating in them directly. The state becomes a regulator and overseer rather than necessarily a provider of services, and the organization of the public sector becomes more fragmented and locally organized in the name of increased efficiency and local responsiveness.

Stronger regional government is one answer to this, with Germany and Australia as competing exemplars – one based around an activist model (Germany) and the other a more liberalized one, but with both having strongly regional orientations in which national government has a much smaller role than in centralized states such as the United Kingdom.

In the United Kingdom, the discourse of the 'Big Society' is a suggestion that not-for-profit and charitable organizations, as well as self-organized community groups, need to take a greater role in social organization, taking over formerly state-run activities. This is desirable not only because the United Kingdom faces such considerable financial deficits (see Chapter 5), meaning that the coalition government is attempting to reduce its spending commitments (although this is certainly a strong motivator), but also because the state has been regarded as becoming too intrusive into people's lives, taking away their sense of responsibility to both themselves and their local communities.

Third, post-nationalism, as well as suggesting the state needs to delegate more, also means it must take into account decisions by supra-national bodies such as the European Union (EU), NATO, or the World Trade Organization (WTO), into its decision making. In the case of the EU, law can be passed that is legally binding upon member states. In the case of the WTO, agreements can be signed that determines the extent to which public services can be insulated (or not) from competitive forces (something the EU has also become increasingly involved in).

For public managers, post-nationalism means a range of complex tensions have appeared. On the one hand, it has often led to a decentralization of the provision of services as the central state passes provision to more local levels in an attempt to reduce the overload it is experiencing, as well as potentially to reduce central government's responsibilities for delivering public services more generally. This is often associated with a further devolution of control through the greater use of private and not-for-profit local service providers so that public policy is implemented by a wide range of different types of organizations. On the other hand, it often also means that the state is able to claim that it is passing the responsibility for delivering services away from itself, who may find that government-imposed rules and regulations mean they have little discretion in how services are run, but have to take the blame where things don't work out well. Equally, because the state sets the rules by which services are run, it may change them at any point, or decide to reorganize frequently, making it extremely difficult for service managers to plan or organize effectively. These tensions will be returned to in later chapters as they represent significant concerns for today's public managers.

From state-based organization to regime-based organization

Jessop's final analytical spectrum runs from state-based organization to regime-based organization. State-based organization is centralized, run from a definable centre, and with a bureaucracy and top-down implementation in place. The state is organized in a hierarchy with central decisions passing down through organizational chains to the local level where they are implemented. This clearly has overlaps with the characterization of the state as being nationally based, but adds analytical depth because it shows the possibility of national organizations having an unbroken line of command and a unified system of rules – the classic public bureaucracy.

A regime-based organization is one where networks of providers from the public, private, and not-for-profit sectors combine to perform services for users at the local level. Instead of national organization, organization attempts to achieve a more responsive local provision through provision that works across all types of providers. Service users cross organizational boundaries between public, private, and not-for-profit provision with the aim that the service appears seamless to them. If the state-based organization emphasizes universality, standardization, and control, regime-based governance attempts to achieve instead responsiveness, flexibility, and diversity in provision. Jessop suggests that as states have experienced overload and attempted to pass their responsibilities to more local levels, regime-based governance has become more prevalent. This shift has been fostered by new approaches to managerial thought emphasizing 'N'-form (network form) governance (Kickert *et al.*, 1997).

When regime-based governance becomes dominant, public managers have a new role in trying to link together the disparate range of service providers to form a coherent service. Public 'network' management is about managing networks of different providers, many of whom may not be public providers, into coherent services that meet the needs of the local population. This is an entrepreneurial role for public managers in the sense that they are required to join back-up provision for service users so that it appears seamless and involves them working across organizational boundaries to that end (Burt, 1993) in order to configure and reconfigure provision to closely match individual service user's needs. Public managers become responsible for overseeing the operations of these complex networks to make sure that they offer a high standard of service and responsiveness, and to stop users from being passed around the system without their needs being met.

Two ideal types – The Keynesian, Welfare, National State and the Schumpeterian Workfare Postnational Regime

The Keynesian, Welfare, National State (KWNS) was the first ideal-type 'fix' (in Jessop's terms) to the problem of managing economy and society in the post-war period. It aimed to create a stable environment for economic growth and to give guaranteed welfare rights for its citizens. It was organized on the basis of the national economy, with public services provided by the state, rather than by the private or not-for-profit providers. The KWNS formation had particular problematic (or 'crisis') tendencies built into it: there was a tendency for the government to take on new spending responsibilities in economic downturns that it did not relinquish when the economy improved; public resentment grew of the amount of taxation the public had to pay to support government in its increased range of activities; and as the economy grew richer, and the people more individualistic and consumerist the public came to regard public organizations as inflexible and unresponsive to their needs. Globalization meant that the national economy became difficult to administer as financial interdependence increased, with some decisions having to be made across whole economic areas (such as the EU) and some at a far more local level (at state or regional level) instead. As the economies of the developed world faced stagflation in the 1970s, they found themselves powerless in dealing with the challenge, and began to seek new approaches to governing their economies and societies.

The Schumpeterian Workfare Postnational Regime (SWPR) is, according to Jessop, the emergent response to the crisis of the KWNS that emerged from the 1970s onwards. It combines an emphasis on economic dynamism and enterprise with a requirement for citizens to take greater responsibility for themselves. It acknowledges the economic interdependence of states, and the need to pass the delivery of services to more local levels, making use of private and not-for-profit organizations, possibly to the exclusion of public provision entirely. However, there are tensions here too.

The assumption that the global marketplace is the ultimate arbiter of a country's worth assumes that financial flows always go to the most productive opportunities, and do not resemble the 'animal spirits' Keynes suggested existed and make errors of judgement. In the wake of the financial crisis, the idea of the global marketplace being the ultimate arbiter of value seems a hard position to sustain, not least because short-term financial instrument investment now dwarfs direct investment in plant and machinery creating the real possibility that much financial activity is not driven by the underlying performance of economies, but is rather driven, as Keynes suggested, by investors second-guessing what other investors might do. If global capital flows do not allocate capital efficiently or effectively, then the logic of the need for a Schumpeterian competitive state is undermined.

The globalized financial flows get things wrong on a national level is perhaps most apparent in the contrast between the German economy since 1990, which spent more than a decade struggling because of the pressures of reunification and the massive state-led investment required, but is now regarded as the strongest and most dynamic and Europe, compared to the UK economy, which was regarded as dynamic and efficient in the 1990s and in the first half of 2000s, but subsequently appears to have invested heavily in financial services that appeared successful, but created the need for massive banks bailouts and resulted in economic stagnation since 2007. Both Germany and the United Kingdom, it can be argued, adopted SWPR formations, with the former investing in the infrastructure and productive capacity of the economy in order to become competitive (but which was met with hostility in financial markets), and the latter in financial services (which financial markets regarded, perhaps unsurprisingly, as the right strategy). But the fortunes of each state, in the climate post-economic crisis appear almost the mirror images of one another, with Germany becoming the dominant economy in Europe, and supporting the weaker Euro-based nations, while the United Kingdom struggles to find any growth at all and debating whether to rebalance its economy away from financial services.

The SWPR formation also perhaps downplays the importance of state-based power by underestimating the importance of national governments. One of the lessons of the financial crisis was that, when it looked as if the financial system was in danger of collapse, the state was the only institution that had the resources to act and prevent the disaster. Without the state's massive interventions from 2008 onwards, the entire financial system would surely have collapsed, and along with it, the entire banking system.

As the comparison between the United Kingdom and Germany shown above, although the SWPR is the formation most redolent of recent state reform, there will be different emphases on each of the characteristics in any particular country. Stillman (1997), for example, asks why there might be differences between the contemporary forms of public administration present in the United States and Europe, and suggests, in essence, that Europeans 'deduce Public Administration from reason of state, whereas America's missing sense of state forces us to induct state from Public Administration' (p. 337). The absence of a sense of what the state is for in the United States, and the way that freedom is often defined in terms of freedom from the state, leads to the need for American policymakers and academics to try and work it out from the way that public administration is conducted. There are definable elements of the SWPR present in both countries, but substantial differences between the specific way the state operates in each as a result.

The SWPR and public management

If the SWPR is the ideal type closest to the contemporary state form, it is worth exploring what form of public management it encourages. Some of its aspects are shown in Table 3.2 and discussed below.

Table 3.2 The SWPR and public management

Aspect of SWPR	Description
Schumpeterian	Use of markets mean public managers must become more entrepreneurial, competitive, and concerned with contracts.
Workfare	'Active' approach to welfare with targets for benefit reduction and privatization. Close concern with assessing welfare claimant eligibility.
Post-national	Potential for more local delegation in management, but also for more influence from international organizations.
Regime	Need to 'boundary span' in a market-based environment to provide a seamless service.

Managers in public organizations under the SWPR are placed in a range of paradoxical situations. They are required to manage their organizations for the collective good (the definition of 'public'), but at the same time focus on meeting individual consumer needs in a competitive marketplace. Where they come from the background of the professional group that dominates their service (i.e. teachers in education and doctors in medicine), they may find that they have to change the established practices of their own peer groups as they call for greater user responsiveness and competitiveness, and so have to challenge their own identities – are they to consider themselves professionals or managers, and when faced with dilemmas, whose side should they take? Should headteachers demand their colleagues take greater account of student views, or side with the professional integrity of teachers where demands for greater responsiveness and exam focus are made, even if it places less emphasis on learning as a result, and more on the passing of exams?

Where managers come from non-professional identities, the situation is no easier. Managers may find themselves 'going native', becoming sympathetic to the view of the public professionals they come into contact with as they come to respect their expertise (Schofield, 2001). In such a situation, they may become defenders of the existing values of public organizations rather than implementing the reforms demanded by the state or the public. If public managers try and challenge public professionals, they may find their work frustrating and depressing, with public professionals apparently trying to block their progress at every turn, and providing numerous reasons why every change they propose cannot occur. Managers from outside of public organizations often regard the bureaucracies they encounter as suffocating, but the rules and regulations were often put in place to ensure fairness and transparency, creating further paradoxes as managers attempt to achieve those goals, whilst at the same time as treating users and individual consumers of their services. Bureaucracy is not automatically bad – in particular circumstances it may be a good thing or even necessary. Most of us would like to think that the drugs prescribed to us have been checked and rechecked rather than delivered to us at lowest possible cost. If user responsiveness and efficiency have their place, so do care, rules, and bureaucracy.

In addition to working within an increasingly competitive marketplace, public managers must also, paradoxically, find ways of creating increasing collaboration. As we noted above, this is because as regime-form governance becomes more commonplace, they must find ways of creating services that span several providers. Managers in local government might have to find ways of contracting for services for refuse collection that require the collaboration of private and public firms who are themselves positioned in competitive relationships with one another. Public managers must find ways of becoming 'boundary spanners' or, in social science terms, occupy 'structural holes' (Burt, 1993) that link together different providers and create added value for those separate services as a result, finding new configurations of existing and new services in a seamless web of provision.

Conclusion

The state has changed considerably in the post-war period, having profound implications for the way public management is conducted. Even though Jessop's ideal types do not reflect any particular state's experience, they are a useful guide in considering the tensions and difficulties that governments have experienced, and the implications of changing ideas about the state for public management. The ideal-type formations reflect the movement from the KWNS formation to that of the SWPR, but in any specific state there will be a greater emphasis on some of the particular elements rather than others. The United States, for example, was a relative latecomer to large-scale state involvement in welfare, not putting in place its medicare and medicaid programmes until the late 1960s, whereas the United Kingdom established its National Health Service with a larger-scale state involvement more than 20 years ago. The United States, even at its peak of public welfare commitment, was arguably closer to the SWPR than the KWNS, whereas the United Kingdom was the opposite. The United States has therefore found it more straightforward to embrace SWPR ideas than the United Kingdom, and become the world leader in the production of public management ideas (Moore, 1997, Osborne & Gaebler, 1993). This does not necessarily mean that it has better public services than everyone else, but its particular state formation has put it at the forefront of thinking about public service reform as it was already closer to the ideal type other states appear, to varying extents, to be moving towards.

Central to Jessop's analysis of the role of the state is the contradictions or 'crisis tendencies' that must be managed if reform is to be successful and a new 'spatio-temporal fix' found in which politicians, managers, and other stakeholders can understand their respective roles. One such fix that has received widespread attention internationally, especially within Europe and the far East, is that of the Third Way. The Third Way, perhaps most clearly articulated by (Lord) Anthony Giddens (1998, 2002, 2007), is an attempt to create what he calls a pragmatic basis for the reform of the state and public services in order to 'renew' and 'modernize' them in line with the demands of the twenty-first century. Within this perspective, the state is positioned as a site of social investment where it comes to act as a kind of super loss-adjuster for society at large, supporting people when they are unable to work, skilling them to meet the challenges of employment, but looking after those that are unable to do so for themselves.

Newman and McKee (2005), however, argue that the social investment state exhibits an instrumental form of the New Public Management (see Chapter 4 for a full description of this) and so its claim to be aiming towards longer-term goals of 'social investment' is likely to be compromised by a more mechanical approach. They suggest that wider political struggles around the role of women, children, and social investment are co-opted and stripped of their legitimacy because the policies addressing these areas are pale shadows borne of the neoliberal project rather than attempting to confront these issues in a systematic way. Their hope is that the idea of the social investment state can yet be mobilized for a range of more progressive projects, even if it might still be constrained by the instrumentalism of what became known as the New Public Management (NPM).

The strength of Jessop's framework is that it does not assume stability, but instead that the state is permanently facing a central contradiction, which it struggles to contain. Jessop refers to this contradiction in terms of Offe's paradox, after the German political sociologist. This observation is important as it demonstrates the central paradox to this chapter.

Offe's paradox suggests that capitalism cannot exist either with or without the welfare state (where a very large number of public managers work). The state cannot exist with the welfare state because the welfare state imposes a taxation cost upon the private sector meaning that capitalists are destined to be forever complaining that the welfare state is getting in the way of profitable expansion, as well as denying opportunities to provide public services on a for-profit basis. However, at the same time as this, capitalism cannot exist *without* the welfare state, as it is dependent upon it to provide its workers with the services they need to access in order to meet their basic needs, to stabilize the economy in periods of recession (and so keep demand up beyond a basic level), and so underpin successful capitalism.

Offe's paradox comes through clearly in Jessop's framework – the two ideal types (the KWNS and SWPR) are in tension with one another and are based on contradictory understandings of what the state is for, as well as containing internal contradictions that hold the potential to undermine any settlement or equilibrium that can be established, moving the ideal type back in another direction.

The state after the financial crisis

As noted above, the SWPR form towards which the US and UK economies were moving in the 2000s was based not on the German/Swedish model of 'flexicurity' through high-skill training and welfare support to facilitate training and mobility, but instead on a 'flexploitation' model in which an emphasis is placed on labour market deregulation to reduce labour power and make it easier for employers to hire and fire. When public services were allowed to expand, that growth was funded on the basis of taxation revenues from financial services, which subsequently appeared illusory.

After the financial crisis, the public sector has found itself facing a range of challenges, but mostly based on the problem of delivering more services for less public money. In the United Kingdom, we have seen the government trying to find ways of reducing public employment, pay freezes for those who retain their jobs, and pensions reform to reduce expenditure commitments in the future. This approach assumed that the private sector would create jobs into which those leaving the public sector could move, but this has so far not proven to be the case, and unemployment rising to around 8.4 per cent or about 2.7 million at the end of 2011. The United States, in contrast, appeared to be recovering slightly at the same date, converging at about the same rate as the United Kingdom but down from 10 per cent around which it hovered for most of 2010, but with pockets of far greater deprivation. Michigan, for example, peaked at a rate of around 15 per cent before falling back to 10 per cent, Nevada still over 13 per cent at the end of the year, and California over 11 per cent.

There are strong links between ideas about the present and future role of the state, and the way public management is conducted. Having given a broad overview of how public management has changed in the post-war period, Chapter 4 explores more specifically how the field of public management has developed in the post-war period, exploring in more details the specific ideas that have been advanced on how best to organize public services.

Case study – Public management in Europe

An excellent study of public management in Europe comparing France, Germany, and Italy was published by one of Europe's leading academics in the field, Walter Kickert, in 2005 (Kickert, 2005).

Kickert presents what he terms a 'historical-institutional' study of the three countries that shows how 'the study of public management is . . . influenced by the particular institutional context of state and administration in the respective country' (p. 539). In other words, the context inherited by politicians and public managers will strongly influence what happens within public management in any particular country. The three countries in Kickert's paper are influenced as follows.

In **France** there is a 'highly qualified and esteemed . . . administration' (p. 542) that has existed since the time of Napoleon, and which is run by an elite group of officials. There is also little difference between politics and administration, with senior politicians and official moving freely between the two. When near to retirement they are also able to retire to top positions in private and nationalized companies. National plans became commonplace since the Fifth Republic (1958), with the extensive use of economic forecasting, and there was an extension of nationalization of industry during the 1980s, in contrast to the United Kingdom and United States, where at that time privatization was far more common.

Since the mid-1980s, however, reforms have taken place due to social and political pressures, and because of economic recessions and budgetary crises. Four periods of modernization are suggested: between 1984 and 1986 when economic crises brought the ambitions of the Socialist government to an end; 1986–88 when a neoliberal reform programme was brought in by a more political right government, but to which the civil service responded in a defensive way that blocked much of the planned reform; between 1988 and 1992, the Socialists returned to power and attempt at government modernization using tools such as total quality management and which was followed by a fourth period of reform, which focused more at the state level, and which commissioned substantial reports into the future of the state in France. This led, from 1997 on, to attempts at decentralizing state activity, followed by attempts to improve HR and to simplify regulations.

France is still dominated by the notion of 'service public', which is strongly associated with the legitimacy of the state carrying out its activities in terms of the interest of the general public, through an administrative function that has legal guarantees of security and equality – giving public management a basis in administrative law not found in the United Kingdom or United States. Reform is made particularly difficult because the 'grand corps' of civil servants, especially given their close links to politicians, have been able to effectively block change (see also Flynn & Strehl, 1996). Cole and Jones (2005) suggest that the NPM in France has been 'domesticated' (p. 584) and that 'The ideological underpinnings of the NPM debate do not find a receptive terrain in

French public administration' (p. 584). In Minvielle's (2006) words 'reforms are established incrementally, much more slowly than in the English-speaking industrialized countries, because of the historical weight of the centralized state and institutional and political conservatism' (pp. 761–762).

In **Germany**, there has also been a tradition of legalism, but this has been gradually departed from since the Second World War, with a movement towards a neocorporatist social market economy, and the German state got more involved in planning in the 1960s and 1970s, followed by a retrenchment due to economic problems in the 1980s.

The legalistic view dominated public administration in Germany up to the 1960s, when it became viewed as a barrier to state modernization. Instead, administrative science was meant to form the backbone of the renewed civil service, with a core curriculum being established at university level, but much recruitment to the German civil service continued to be from graduates with a law background.

From 1989, debates have been dominated by reunification, leading to the establishment of new administrative curricula, and widespread municipal reform also led to a resurgence in interest in public management as a discipline. Reichard (2003) suggests that, comparatively speaking, Germany has retained its strong legalistic focus for administrative reform, being less pragmatic in terms of how policy is implemented than in other countries, with its reforms of public finance being most wide ranging.

In **Italy**, there is a more generalized dislike of the state than in France and Germany, brought on by the experience of dictatorship, but also due to the strong family tradition in the country. There is popular dissatisfaction with the political system, not least due to actual and perceived government corruption, and frequent changes in government still appear common.

The civil service inherited by the government after the Second World War was perceived by the government as being 'old-fashioned, slow, legalistic, overstaffed' (p. 553), but instead of reform, the government sought to simply circumvent it. Political appointees became common, and a parallel administration created, and an increasing number of jobs could be given to political supporters of those elected to power (a more extreme form of the 'spoils' system in the United States).

The Italian civil service is large, and consists largely of those from the south of the country, where the public sector is a hugely important employer because of high unemployment rates. Examinations are meant to determine civil service entry, but the system seems to have largely broken down, and public workers are portrayed as giving poor-quality and inefficient service and entering the service without the required qualifications. Politicians have little influence over the civil service, and exercise control through political appointments and creating their own cabinets, leading to a deadlock where distrust and sabotage between the two groups are common.

Since the 1990s, and huge state problems with corruption, administrative reforms have become more common in Italy. Local and regional government have become strengthened through decentralizing reforms, and top civil servants became far more dependent upon their jobs to politicians, who could now appoint to the 55 highest official posts. However, it is unclear whether much has really changed, with the legalistic paradigm of senior civil servants still dominating.

In summary, France has a strong legalistic tradition, with high status and prestige administrators dominating, educated at national schools of public administration. Administrative reform has struggled to make inroads into this elite, but with some decentralizing reforms occurring that attempt to achieve greater efficiency and effectiveness. Germany also has a strong legal tradition, and this has largely continued despite the best attempts of state officials to change it. No substantial reforms have taken place in the national bureaucracy, but public management reforms have been both more common and more successful at the levels of municipal and regional government, reforms that aimed at greater efficiency and effectiveness. Italy, in contrast, does not have a strong state tradition, with the civil service forming a separate bureaucracy bypassed by politicians, and leading to a parallel system of 'spoils' government. Corruption since the 1990s has resulted in some reforms to the system, but there remains a significant amount of resistance to them.

The legalism present in the three countries seems to have made reform difficult to achieve. In many respects, the goal of efficiency, especially economic efficiency, runs directly against the idea of legal accountability that dominates these systems, and so achieving greater flexibility and managerial reform remains a significant difficulty.

Further reading

Bob Jessop's work on state changes has developed over a number of years, and is most completely developed in his book *The Future of the Capitalist State* (2002), but many articles present shorter versions of his ideas (Jessop, 1992, 1994, 1999). Jessop's ideas have been applied to case studies in Scandinavia by Jacob Torfing, and make for fascinating reading (Torfing, 1999a, 1999b, 2001). Kickert's work on comparing European approaches to public reform compared to those of the United States help provide a contrast between the two approaches (Kickert, 1997, 2005), and Christensen and Laegreid's work on how New Public Management has 'transformed' different states is also extremely valuable (Christensen *et al.*, 2002). Two strong collections of essays considering the role of the state after the economic crisis are Engelen *et al.* (2011) and Casey (2011).

4

Changing ideas about public management

Introduction

This chapter considers the history of public management ideas in the post-war period, and therefore deals with the way that public management (both in terms of ideas and practice) has responded to the changing role of the state, and to the financial crisis. It begins by providing a basic definition of public management, before moving on to understand how ideas and practice in public management have changed, and concludes by considering both the practice and discipline after the financial crisis.

What is public management?

In recent years, there has been a blurring of what exactly counts as being a public manager. It used to be the case that public managers were those working in public organizations, paid for by the government and providing public services. However, as private organizations have been brought in to provide public services, private organizations paid for what we would have called public provision through community outreach activities, and the boundaries of what counts as public or private services brought under challenge, it has been harder to say exactly what counts as a public service.

What counts as a public service varies from country to country, but typically refers to those services, which we believe either should be available to everyone as a right, and so are paid for by the state and provided either free or on a subsidized or means-tested basis. Public services are often difficult to exclude people from, making charging difficult (as with streetlighting) or are services we recognize the provision of is a basic human right (as we might regard access to healthcare). We might also consider that there are a range of services, which is our collective interest as a society to provide for everyone (as in education, in order to improve economic prospects for everyone, and to allow more informed debate and voting).

Here, I am happy to recognize the wide range of claims of managers who can claim to be engaged in public service, and the diversity of funding means and organizational structures that now comes with that. However, we do need a starting point, and that will be to go for the most straightforward definition – a public manager is one who provides a public good or service on a non-profit basis, with that service paid for by the state.

Public managers work not for private companies, but for the government (at least indirectly), and can expect a far greater degree of public scrutiny as a result. This is right and fitting – they are being paid with taxpayer money, and taxpayers have the right to ask how that money is being spent. If private organizations provide services to the public sector, they will often be expected to comply with a range of additional rules and requirements as a result of receiving taxpayer funds.

The public administration model

A good place to begin in considering the changes to both public management (the practice) and public management (the discipline) is a review article published in 1999 (Dunsire, 1999). Dunsire attempts to link the 'world of thought and the world of action' (p. 360) by moving between what public management academics (or to give the subject is more traditional name, public administration) have written about their subject, and what changes he detects as having occurred 'in the field'. Dunsire suggested that the situation immediately after the Second World War was one dominated by the principles of 'traditional public administration', and which Stewart and Walsh (1992) suggest were

1. Public provision of a function is more equitable, reliable and democratic than provision by a commercial or voluntary body;

2. Where a ministry or other public authority is responsible for a function, it normally carries out that function itself with its own staff;

3. Where a public body provides a service, it is provided uniformly to everyone within its jurisdiction;

4. Operations are controlled from the headquarters of the public body through a hierarchy of unbroken supervision;

5. Employment practices (including recruitment, promotions, grading, salary scales, retirement and pensions) are standardized throughout each of the public services (e.g. the civil service, the local government service and the armed services);

6. Accountability of public servants to the public is via elected representative bodies.

(Dunsire, 1999, p. 361)

Traditional public administration, as an ideal type (perhaps most closely adhered to in the United Kingdom as well as in some other European countries such as Sweden) was, therefore, primarily concerned about the achievement of equity and fairness as goals, through public provision as well as public financing, attempting to provide a uniform provision of service through centralized control, utilizing standardized employment practices and legitimated through democratic accountability. This is a useful starting point because it is comprehensive in considering most of the relevant elements of public management and allows us to construct contrasts with other approaches to the practice and understanding of the subject.

The first principle of public administration is that public provision leads to services being more equitable and reliable than commercial or voluntary bodies. Public ownership should guarantee the provision of a particular service, whereas relying upon private and not-for-profit providers could both carry greater risk should those firms decide to leave public provision and simply become bankrupt. In both these situations, the state may have to underwrite service provision by acting as a funder of last resort to avoid private or not-for-profit services, leading to the obvious question, that, if it is going to have to be funder of last resort, why the state simply doesn't provide the services itself.

The idea that the state be responsible for public services leads directly to the second principle of public administration that it should not only plan for and finance the service but also deliver it. Again, there are sensible reasons for this. The easiest way to ensure that a service is accountable to the government is for it to also run it, that way it should be able to fully scrutinize its activities. However, whether the state (especially a central state) is capable of this level of scrutiny in practice is something of an open question.

The third principle of public administration, uniformity, is again based on the idea of fairness. If the state allows services to be privately provided, or if state provision varies from one place or one service user to another, then there is the danger that this might also be unfair, as it might mean that some people receive a better service than others. As such, public service fairness is more of a goal than an expectation – still presents a contrast with private provision, which is based on the principle of satisfying different user needs with different products and services.

The fourth principal of public administration is that there should be a hierarchical chain of command from the public service headquarters through to the delivery end of the service. The most obvious organizational form this approximates to is a bureaucracy. Bureaucracies put in place rules and define employee roles clearly with standardized employment practices (the fifth public administration principle) having a clear chain of command, and creating the opportunity for a link between policymakers, the heads of the public service, and those responsible for delivering the service itself. A unified chain of command should, therefore, aim to minimize what has been called the 'implementation gap', the problem of getting the policy made by the state implemented 'on the ground' in public services that might be hundreds of miles away from where the original decisions were made.

Finally, the public services are held accountable through democratic means. How this works in practice varies from state to state and depends upon the balance of power between local government and central or federal government. Where a strong local democratic tradition exists, local officials may be held accountable for local services with which they are in frequent contact, and with the possibility of a considerable variation in services from one locality to the next, to some extent contradicting to the principle of service uniformity. Equally, it is possible that senior public managers be elected, with the mayors of major cities being held accountable via the ballot box for their ability to run local services. Alternatively, in a more centralized democracy, politicians who have little or no contact with the day-to-day activities of many public services may be held democratically accountable for them, prompting the need for considerable information-gathering bureaucracies to be put in place so the politicians can try and find out what is going on within them.

Democratic accountability requires that public officials are held to account through the democratic process, and if this is not in place, there are dangers of 'democratic gaps appearing and services not being accountable to the public'. Fox and Miller (1995) write of the 'incredulity of representative democracy' (p. 25) and claim that the idea that public administration is accountable to 'the people' through the democratic process is a myth, as the public simply do not work within a 'loop' model of democracy in which the public vote for credible candidates to run public services, and reward those candidates if they do well. Fox and Miller demonstrate from data on congress elections that incumbents have a significant advantage in the election process, and that typically Americans have no idea of who their local politicians are, or what they stand for. This is clearly a significant problem for the traditional model of public administration; if it is not legitimated through democracy, then how should it be accountable? This problem will be returned to again below, as well as in Chapter 7.

Further problems with the public administration model

In addition to the problems already raised, Dunsire suggests that the six principles of public administration listed above are not underpinned by a coherent set of ideas, but are instead based more upon 'muddling through' (Hennessy, 1997) or an 'incremental' political process (Lindblom & Woodhouse, 1993) than being based on anything more rational. This problem seems to be particularly present in the United Kingdom in the 1950s and 1960s, where, in contrast to the United States, public administrators regarded the learning of management techniques as being largely irrelevant to their activities (Thomas, 1978). The lack of business schools and the lack of a national school of administration, as was present in France, meant that public administration often fell within the remit of generalist civil servants with little interest in achieving systematic public service improvement.

Dunsire also suggests that the traditional public administration model was unable to deal with demands, especially from the 1970s onwards, for a greater focus on the three 'Es' of economy, efficiency and effectiveness, as public officials saw the three 'Es' as contradicting the principles of fairness and equity with which they worked. Now the argument in this book is that contradictions are a central part of the world in which public managers have to work, so imagining that the three 'Es' could be ignored seems a poor decision.

The hesitancy of officials grounded in public administration thinking to deal with the 'three Es' led to policymakers becoming increasingly frustrated with what they perceived to be an 'implementation gap' in public services, where they found institutions that, from the perspective of reformist politicians, appeared resistant to change. The chain of command that was meant to be a central part of a public bureaucracy did not mean that central policymakers or managers actually held a great deal of control over how public services were delivered on the ground. Civil servants appeared to be overriding politician's wishes (as in the classic TV drama, 'Yes, Minister'), and entrenched professional groupings often held considerable autonomy with the ability to ignore the demands of central administrations to reform services. This ability to 'veto' policy often carried with it the ability to opt out of accountability mechanisms as well, leading to public services having the kinds of legitimacy problems Fox and Miller suggested in the previous section. If public services were accountable neither to politicians representing the public, nor directly to its citizens, in whose name did they operate? What were local people to do if public services were found to be lacking, and how could improvements be made?

The lack of responsiveness of public bureaucracies to either citizen or consumer demands led to two particular criticisms. The first was the democratic problem suggested above. If the democratic loop that was meant to lead to public service improvement was flawed, then public services might also be less accountable than their designers suggested, but this meant that there was little scope for the public improving them.

The second related criticism came from the users of services who, having received an extension of their welfare rights in the post-war period, now appeared to begin to take the right to use public services increasingly for granted and to demand that the level of service they were receiving be improved. Public service users began to become increasingly aware that they were not receiving services for free but were in fact paying for them through increased taxation, and as economies got richer and citizens paid more tax, they began to ask more question about how 'their' money was being spent (Haug & Sussman, 1969). In liberal economies, such as the United States, this discourse was especially widespread, with popular movements against the increasing role of the state being supported by lobby groups seeking to preserve the pre-eminence of private enterprise, and even for private firms to take over the running of public services. Even in countries such as the United Kingdom, complaints appeared about very high marginal tax rates and were encapsulated by the Beatles' song 'Taxman' in the 1960s, which suggested rather bitterly that the British people were in fact working only to raise funds for the Inland Revenue (the tax collection body) rather than for themselves. In the United States, this tapped into a stronger sentiment of anti-government feeling perhaps best presented in PJ O'Rourke's book *Parliament of Whores*.

This service user-based critique of public services was extended by the US theorists who criticized the self-serving nature of bureaucracies by claiming that they were often not run primarily for the benefit of those working within public institutions rather than those they were meant to serve. This 'public choice' approach suggested that the incentives public officials worked within (lack of competitive structures, prestige based on department size, and budget) meant that they were more likely to try and maximize their share of their organizations' resources than try and improve the quality of the services they were meant to be delivering to the public. Public managers were portrayed as being more likely to pursue their own interests rather than serve the public.

These two elements – the 'democratic gap' suggesting that public services were not democratically accountable, and the criticisms from service users demanding improved services, combined to present a damning critique of the traditional public administration view, suggesting that public organizations were neither accountable nor controllable. As societies became more individualized, the collective goals of public organizations and the administrators that attempted to achieve them began to look increasingly anachronistic and dated. New modes of organization for public services seemed to be needed.

Towards a public management

From the end of the 1970s, both the UK and the US governments went about turning the principles of traditional public administration on their heads. The Reagan and Thatcher governments shared a suspicion of large government and began to articulate new ideas (or at least the restatement of old ideas) for the way public services should be run. Thinkers of what became known as the 'New Right' (Flynn, 1989) advocated services being transferred into the private sector as liberal, minimal state ideas gained credence and politicians preached the virtues of individuals providing for themselves rather than depending upon the state. In such an environment, the market was presented as the ultimate arbiter of what was valuable and what was not, and the planners of the 1950s and 1960s were recast as meddlers and 'do-gooders' who interfered with the laws of supply and demand on behalf of the 'nanny state'.

During the 1980s, services that were formerly both financed and provided by the public sector were privatized where politically possible, and where full privatization was not possible, ways of subjecting public services to market disciplines were sought. Markets for public services (often referred to as 'quasi' markets in the academic literature) were created to get public providers of such services to compete with one another towards the goals of raising responsiveness to users and driving down costs – but to apparently little success. The model was then extended to try and get private and not-for-profit providers to complete with public providers, but again, strong evidence that this was leading to service improvements was hard to come by.

Instead of the state directing public organizations to deliver services through relationships based largely on trust (because of the difficulty of measuring the activity of public organizations and the presence of substantial professional groups), contracts were introduced that moved relationships instead onto a more legalistic footing and potentially put in place penalties for non-compliance (Walsh, 1996). These changes became associated with the idea of creating a 'hollow state' that no longer provides services but simply oversees contractual arrangements for them. Researchers exploring this topic (such as Brinton Milward & Provan, 2003) argue that the central task in the hollow state is the use of tools like 'contracting and collaboration to manage networks of organizations from all sectors – public, private and non-profit effectively' (p. 15) and that the aim should be to create a network with 'enough stability to maintain its ability to manage a set of jointly produced services' (p. 15).

The move towards a market-driven role with clearly defined contracts is a little ironic. At exactly the time that sociologists and management writers chose to emphasize the importance of businesses generating trust and exploring informal relationships (Burt, 1993, 2000, Granovetter, 1973, 1985), 'new' public organizations seemed to be going in the opposite direction, moving to contract-driven relationships instead. The view of public organization being based around market relationships often had the tendency, perversely given the goal of making them more business like and lean, to increase bureaucracy, as it was necessary to bill, pay-for and monitor large numbers of new contracts.

The introduction of market-based structures has not got rid of bureaucracies, but instead attempted to change them, with Boyne suggesting that the main challenge in relation to bureaucracy is 'not to replace it, but to make it work better' (Boyne, 1999, p. 4). Bradley and Parker (2006) share this view, suggesting that even though public managers might want their organizations to move away from resembling bureaucracies, they tend to persist despite their best efforts. Bearing this in mind, however, three tendencies can be seen: a movement towards increased service fragmentation and flexibility; towards treating service users as consumers and introducing charging; and towards the greater use of IT and performance management. The following section explores each in turn.

Fragmentation and flexibility

The entry of private and not-for-profit providers into public provision means that public services no longer have a monopoly over provision organized (at least theoretically in a hierarchical chain of command). Instead, services have become either market-based or 'N-form', networks of provision joining a range of providers from public, private and not-for-profit organizations.

In an ideal world, it would make little difference to service users whether their service providers were public monopolies, private markets or N-form, as public managers would ensure that they receive a seamless service. Even though public monopolies often struggled to achieve this goal, the difficulties involved in reaching it through markets or networks are almost certainly much greater as they involve not only working across organizational boundaries but also finding ways of linking together different types of firm (public, private and not-for-profit) into a single service. The inevitable result of using markets or N-form structures is increased complexity, but also increased fragmentation. Contracts being offered to a greater range of provider organizations mean that managers have to find ways to 'join-up' provision again to overcome fragmentation and to provide coherent services.

At the same time as public services have risked becoming more fragmented, demands for increased employment flexibility have come to the fore. Reformers regarded public service contracts with clearly defined duties and working hours as preventing them from managing in the markets or networks they now faced. Trade unions became regarded not as a partner in service production, but as a barrier to the functioning of free labour markets, and new legislation made it more difficult for them to engage in strike action. Public managers were expected to lead their organizations rather than acting as mediators between professionals and trade unions, driving forward reform in more dynamic, market-based settings.

Consumers and charging

Instead of delivering universal provision to the collective public, public managers were encouraged to treat public service users as individual consumers demanding improved levels of service. Viewing the public as individual consumers rather than citizens or being part of a general public meant that different conceptions of the management role appeared. Managers sought to increase their revenues by finding ways of charging for levels of service above those that were offered as standard. Hospitals offered superior facilities such as private rooms and access to telephone and televisions in return for additional payments, and school managers tried to find ways of offering before and after school clubs for the children of working parents where they might allow additional funds to be raised in the name of achieving greater 'public value'. Public organizations were encouraged to offer their services to those in the private market that might be willing to pay for them; children's libraries might offer busy parents crèche facilities and child activities where they could safely leave their children.

Information Technology and performance management

At the same time as all the changes above, advances in IT meant that public organizations could be placed under far greater central scrutiny than ever before. Computers and improved information systems made possible the routine recording and measurement of public organizations, and to the publication of comparative league tables provided the opportunities for citizens to see how good their local services were (or at least how good they were at meeting the centrally imposed measures) compared to those in other areas (Bloomfield & Coombs, 1992). In the United Kingdom, the faith in IT systems to be a central part of public reform led, however, to catastrophic failures such as the aborted National Health Service (NHS) information system in which at least £6bn was spent to little end.

Information technology found an obvious ally in demands by the government for stronger service accountability, but also from the increased emphasis on performance management. The combination of IT and the new emphasis on performance measurement meant that public organizations could be scrutinized for their resource usage more acutely both internally and externally, placing a stronger managerial emphasis on parsimony in the name of demonstrating that services were becoming more efficient (Hood, 1991).

The public 'naming and shaming' of poorly graded public organizations attempted to address the problems of democratic legitimacy discussed above in new ways. Instead of public services being theoretically accountable to elected public officials or to the electing population at large, but without clear mechanisms for exactly how this was to occur, they became increasingly performance-managed by central government, which acted as an evaluator on behalf of the public (Hoque *et al.*, 2004). This change in accountability was made in the name of increasing user responsiveness by increasing public service accountability upwards (but despite the claims that bureaucracies were being abolished), in which the central state acted on behalf of citizens, and citizens, in turn, decided who should run the state. As such, the state, in systems where top-down accountability where stressed, claimed to be speaking 'for the people', supplanting the professionals who had made the same claim in the past.

Leagues tables and the publication of performance data also led, if used alongside the introduction of market mechanisms, to the possibility that service users could choose which services they wanted to receive, with resources being allocated in line with service user choices to reward good performers, and penalize those not chosen by the public.

Table 4.1 Public administration and its opposites

Traditional public administration	Opposite
Equity and fairness	Differentiated service.
Public provision	Mixed provision (public, private and not-for-profit).
Uniformity	Differentiation and diversity.
Hierarchical, rule-bound and slow organizations	Flat, responsive and fast organizations.
Standardized terms of employment based on service	Differential, local terms of employment based on performance.
Democratic accountability	User accountability (through markets). Central state accountability (through performance management).

It is relatively straightforward to create a second ideal type of public management by simply taking the list of 'traditional' public administration principles and working out their logical opposites. Table 4.1 therefore summarizes the two ideal types of public administration and new public management (NPM). However, in the same way as public administration models appeared to have built-in problems, most countries have struggled to find coherent ways of dealing with the difficulties that the NPM has introduced. They have particularly struggled to reduce bureaucracy, with attempts at introducing public markets often leading to an increase in rules, regulations, and administrators collecting data. There also seems to be a difficulties in putting fragmented provision back together into coherent services, and of finding ways of improving services in response to users because of the pressures of top-down performance management systems the state has introduced.

A new form of public management

The movement from public administration (the traditional public administration approach outlined above) to public management (the second ideal type) has been widely written about, with authors creating competing typologies of the types of the 'NPM' that they have found in the institutions they research (Newman, 2000).

Whether the NPM represents a new paradigm, an entirely new approach to the management of public organizations, remains a moot point. Gray and Jenkins (1995), for example, suggest that the NPM is based on public choice economics, as well as on 'strands of corporate management thinking' (p. 93), but does not form a new paradigm because there is no new unified theory of public management within it. They suggest instead that it is necessary to adequately theorize what a non-public choice models of public management might look like, to add a constitutional dimension to public management that addresses the lack of democracy present in the NPM and to test new frameworks empirically to bring together public administration and public management approaches, exploring both the practical and political implications of policies.

Public management as an academic discipline

As the public administration model broke up, academic understandings of public management also appear to have become more diverse than before. Some writers have focused on the problem of achieving better implementation, showing how coalitions might be built to that end (Sabatier, 1988). Others have constructed detailed case studies examining both the successes and failures of particular public programmes in line with the approach often found in the private sector of examining businesses that exemplified particular practices to see how they achieved success or failure.

In the United States and the United Kingdom as well as across New Zealand and Australia, however, the most significant stand of new thinking came through the shift to examining what has become known as the NPM movement. Hood's inaugural lecture at the London School of Economics (Hood, 1991) focused thinking and defined the public management shift that had taken place as one moved the discipline away from studies of policy to studies of management. The new approach emphasized quantitative methods of appraisal and performance management above qualitative, judgement, and experience-based approaches. Organizations were characterized as breaking up hierarchies into semi-autonomous units of provision, contracting and moving provision 'out of house' rather than attempting to achieve a unified production of services. This came along with a focusing on outputs rather than processes or inputs for public services, creating the potential for incentivizing public managers through performance-related pay rather than paying them fixed salaries. Hood suggested that the NPM emphasized the freedom to manage rather than the need to follow rules, that it moved organizations towards a marketing approach rather than a producer-dominated one, and stressed public organizations becoming more self-regulating than central regulating (although, as we have already seen, performance management systems developed in the 1990s appear to have swung the balance back to more central regulation again). In Hood's view, these changes were a mix of responses to the criticisms of public choice writers in the 1960s and 1970s and an updated 'scientific management' where control could be exerted through the rational application of measurable management programmes.

The biggest problem with the NPM movement is that its advocates often define the term in many different ways. As such, just about any organizational form that doesn't represent the public administration archetype can be argued to be a part of it. Hood's work, however, provided a benchmark against which many kinds of organization can be compared.

Another problem comes with NPM-type forms apparently embracing both market and N-form arrangements. The difficulty is that term 'network' is in itself rather meaningless, and a host of contradictory definitions exist that attempt to capture what might be meant in its use. In some cases, networks are defined in terms of what they are not – they are neither markets nor hierarchies, but a third form of organization (Exworthy et al., 1999). Elsewhere networks are used as an all-embracing structural concept with hierarchies and markets representing simply particular configurations of networks. Networks are also characterized in influential literature as being a form of organization having no individual single, dominant central organizing agent and where organization is achieved through a 'differentiated polity' of links between government and the increasingly diverse range of providers it depends upon for the delivery of public services (Rhodes, 1997). Finally, networks are sometimes characterized as representing a form of governance where the state is no longer able to manage and organize by itself (having something in common with the government overload thesis of Chapter 3) and where managers must find strategies for managing within this new environment through consensus-building approaches (Kickert et al., 1997). The absence of a coherent understanding of exactly what networks are is a significant problem if they are a central feature of the NPM.

Post-modernism

A further development in the public management literature has come through its increasing interest in post-modernism. This approach often has a different understanding of the crisis in public administration of the 1970s, suggesting that its problems were not because of any particular events, but instead because of the inherent contradictory tensions present in attempting to organize complex social systems. Fox and Miller (1995) present a wide-ranging critique of the attempt at organizing public organizations through bureaucracies and particularly the attempt by public administration to legitimize its activities on democratic grounds. Fox and Miller share much of this analysis, and show how taken-for-granted approaches to policy and management depend inextricably upon the organizing concepts and ideas dominant in a particular time, inevitably favouring the already strong through the reproduction of power relations, and leaving out the disempowered and dispossessed time and time again.

Fox and Miller suggest that it is necessary to make public management part of a process of deliberative democracy, with far greater efforts being necessary to achieve public involvement in policy formulation and implementation. Fox and Miller therefore want public administration to reconnect to the people in order to regain its legitimacy. They therefore seek to replace assumptions about rational decision making with greater public deliberation and involvement in public services. This has parallels in more recent work by Bevir (2010), who presents a thorough critique of recent public reforms, and comes to similar conclusions as Fox and Miller.

In the post-modern view, traditional public administration failed because of its dependence on the meta-narratives of rationalistic decision making and democratic accountability, both of which might be interesting theoretically, but cannot be supported in reality. Public administration is portrayed as a modernistic project that is no longer sustainable.

There are two considerable problems with prescriptions to improve public management through greater use of democratic means; first, with political participation rates declining it is a lot to ask for people to get involved in the time-consuming and energy-taking process of scrutinizing and deliberating public organizations. As Stoker (2006) advocates, what may be required to resurrect public involvement in public services is a 'politics for amateurs' in which the public are able to engage with service change and direction on more straightforward terms than the very high level of involvement that Fox and Miller suggests. Second, it is not entirely clear how Fox and Miller imagine public administration delivering the goods once policy has been formulated. Does their rejection of bureaucracy extend to the implementation of policy as well as its formulation, and if it does, how do they envisage public services being organized? How should the public interact with public managers, and what would their roles be in doing so? These are both crucial questions to which this book will return to later.

Criticality

The turn of the public management discipline to post-modernism is part of its general tendency to become more critical in orientation. This move to becoming more critical does not mean that academics have criticized public managers or public policymakers (although a lot of this does go on), but instead suggests that public management needs to take a more critical stance (Learmonth, 1999, Marston, 2000). Advocates of this view suggest that it needs to become more questioning, and find ways of challenging taken-for-granted assumptions about the way public management works. This has led to the increased use of the analysis of public management practices through sociological approaches including deconstruction (where taken-for-granted assumptions about practice are exposed and those practices reconstructed to be more inclusive), discourse analysis (unpackaging the ideas and practices underpinning reforms typically through an exploration of their language), and, as a result, the analysis of power and power relationships has become far more significant in the public management discipline than was previously the case. It has become as common to ask 'who gains' from reform programmes as 'what happened' as a result of their introduction. The central problem here is that, if we accept there is no 'God's eye' or objective view from which to examine the field of public management, we also risk losing the ability to achieve change, no matter how emancipatory or improving it might be, as all claims to truth we can make are inherently from our own perspective.

Critical views of public management make us far more aware of the use of power, but can end up being debilitating if they offer us no way to do anything about the problems they identify. Writers such as Czarniawska (1997) suggest that it is necessary to regard policymaking and public management in a narrative-based exploring the stories told by managers and others working in public organizations to understand how both continuity and change are achieved.

Is the New Public Management now the dominant paradigm?

In terms of the public management academic discipline, the NPM continues as the dominant discussion, if only in accounts that are critical of it. It is, however, difficult to claim that there is one specific form of public management emerging, even if there is a general trend towards the sort of tendencies identified by Hood, not least because, after the financial crisis, there is a new urgency to focus on parsimony as a goal. Public management continues to be inclined to attempt to import private management techniques, to be more output-oriented and target focused, and it has been increasingly organized on a marketized basis.

This emergent form of public management has a particular direction, but is far from being a homogeneous form. The institutional and cultural inheritances of the state where they are being introduced will strongly influence the version of public management that appears there. Countries with strong localist tendencies will tend to try and to find ways of continuing in that tradition (Kickert, 1997), those with strong central governments and electoral systems that allow for majority governments to rule strongly will tend to produce the most radical reforms (Wilsford, 1995), and countries with separations between local and federal government will have to form compromises that other states may not find necessary (Johnston, 2000). Christensen *et al.* (2002) find that in Norway (where there was no perceived economic crisis and little incentive for change), a soft version of the NPM was put in place, whereas in New Zealand, which faced strong external pressures, weak countervailing cultural forces and a parliamentary form they call 'electoral dictatorship', a far more radical version of the NPM was implemented.

Changes are also apparent in particular geographic spaces. Lynn (1999) shows that, across North America, the nature of change in public management reflects the national politics and administrative histories of Canada, Mexico, and the United States. Canada has been searching for fiscal retrenchment at both national and provincial levels; Mexico has been influenced by the transition from oligarchy to democracy at federal, state, and local levels; and the United States has been preoccupied at the federal level by the initiatives from the 'Reinventing Government' movement.

If different versions of the NPM appear to have been implemented in different countries, then does it even make sense to talk about a single NPM? Pollitt (2000) suggests that the emperor is not quite naked, but rather in his underwear. He suggests that the NPM is not just 'windy rhetoric' (p. 195) as downsizing has occurred in many countries, measured efficiency has increased, and some services have become more user centric and flexible. However, unmeasurable aspects may have taken a turn for the worse, and many staff and citizens may have suffered 'degenerating conditions as a consequence' (p. 195). He does, however, suggest that the NPM has never really extended beyond Australasia, North America and the United Kingdom, with methods being applied more selectively in other countries.

There is therefore a need to take a pragmatic approach to understanding public management on a world-wide basis, accepting that reforms will work out very differently from state to state (Pollitt & Bouchaert, 2000). This is exciting as it generates a range of different findings and attempts at dealing with the problems experienced by the public administration approach, but it can also be frustrating as there really is no single best answer as to how public services might be best managerially reformed.

It is also possible that the NPM has already had its day. Denhardt and Denhardt (2000) have long suggested that the opposition between the NPM and old public administration is less relevant to the twenty-first century than they were to the twentieth century. Instead, they suggest that 'new public service' should be based on democratic citizenship, community, and civil society, and present seven principles by which the new public service should be run; they should serve, not steer, establishing shared interests between groups rather than attempting to control the public; they should put the public interest as their aim, not as a by-product of their reforms; that public managers should think strategically and act democratically, suggesting the need for collective efforts and collaboration; that public managers should serve citizens not customers, placing an emphasis on dialogue rather than the aggregation of individual self-interests; make clear that accountability isn't simple and must meet multiple aims and stakeholders; that public managers should value people, not productivity, leading to collaboration and shared leadership and based on respect; and that public managers should value citizenship and public service above entrepreneurship, leading to the goal of making a contribution to society becoming important than achieving an environment favouring entrepreneurship. Denhardt and Denhardt offer a view of public services that, in common with Fox and Miller, stresses the importance of public accountability rather than either the consumer-driven model of some versions of the NPM or the flawed democratic notions of the old public administration. Whether states are prepared to implement their ideas, however, remains to be seen.

Newman (2000, 2002) has also argued that a movement beyond the NPM is now discernible. In relation to her analysis of the situation in the United Kingdom, she suggests that modernization goes beyond the NPM in three respects. First, in that the negative consequences of market fragmentation were acknowledged in an attempt, especially apparent in the early years of the Labour administration, to move towards 'joined-up' governance. This leads to the second change, as collaboration replaced competition in line with contemporary business thought, moving to less adversarial and longer-term models of contracting. Third, Newman argues, there was the introduction of new discourses of citizen and user participation. User participation was extended to include not only choice (in addition to market research and complaints mechanisms) but also user voice through more active participation in service design and planning. These changes, however, have led to some significant tensions; managerial flexibility works against central performance management; 'joined-up' government requires new styles of leadership and management that don't fit well with the NPM as presently in place; managers have to find ways of delivering success for their own organization while working in collaborations and dealing with 'cross-cutting' issues; and there is the problem of trading long-term goals against short-term efficiencies. Newman suggests that these contradictions must be managed, but whether this can occur within the dominant discourse of NPM managerialism is questionable.

Public management dynamics

Following Newman, and other writers who have explored public management as representing a series of paradoxes or contradictions, it makes sense, based on the analysis above explore each in turn to consider its explanatory power. Table 4.2 and the next section work through a series of such paradoxes that form the basis of the discussion in the rest of the book.

Table 4.2 Contradictions in public management

Contradictions	Description
Both managers and professionals believe that they should be in charge of public services.	Public management implies that it is managers in charge of public services, when those managers often depend upon highly trained professionals who do not wish to be managed.
Public services must be both democratically accountable to their citizenry, but also achieve good results for their individual users.	Public services face the contradiction of having to manage resources for the benefit of their population as a whole, as well as for their individual service users who may want very different things.
Public services must be run according to public values, but also according to market values.	Public services are often associated with distinctively public values including collectivity and solidarity, but at the same time must work within individualistic market environments, requiring them to adopt market values.
Public services must be efficient, yet also deliver strong customer service.	Public services often achieve efficiency through organizing around professional schedules, but have to demonstrate customer service by organizing around user schedules.
Public managers are appointed by contradictory means (election or selection).	Public managers may have very different duties if elected or if selected, creating very different lines of accountability.

Both managers and professionals believe that they should be running public services

One aspect of public organizations that is discussed a great deal in more policy-oriented research (Haug & Sussman, 1969, Wilding, 1982), but which appears less frequently in public management discussions, is of the impact of professionalism on management (for an exception, see Exworthy & Halford, 1998). Public organizations often (but by no means always) have strong, established professionals working within them. The two archetypal professional groups are those of law and medicine, with both groups working for the public sector to varying extents depending upon the particular country in question. In the United Sates, public defenders and prosecutors often work for salaries far lower than those they could achieve working for the private sector, whereas in the United Kingdom the medical profession have had considerable autonomy in how they run health services for much of the NHS's history (Klein, 1990).

Professionals represent a significant problem for management in that the key characteristics of professionalism, autonomy, self-regulation, and practice based on expert knowledge tend to lead to those in professional groups expecting to be able to manage themselves to a considerable extent. Management, in itself, has been a recognized professional class in the United States since the early twentieth century, whereas in the United Kingdom the founding of Business Schools came rather later, and managers still hold less prestige and status (and qualifications) than their US colleagues (Wilson & Thompson, 2006).

Public management has, in addition, also developed within a particular context in which until recently, relatively poor rewards (compared to private management) were available. There are exceptions to this – in France, prestigious schools of public administration existed during the post-war period, and public management afforded a far greater cache than in most other countries. In South Korea, this is also the case, with public managers reporting that they have far higher job prestige and recognition from wider society than their private sector counterparts (Cho & Lee, 2001). In a situation where public managers are holding esteemed and respected positions, as in France and Korea, they also tend to have a greater capacity to challenge to professional groups.

Regardless of context, however, professionals have expert knowledge that makes it difficult for managers not trained in their specialist area to measure or question their performance (Freidson, 2001, Gillespie, 1997, Wilding, 1982) (see also Chapter 6). Professionals often believe that public managers simply don't understand the complexities of their jobs, and that they have no legitimacy or business challenging their professionalism. In addition, those in professional groupings often come from elite social backgrounds, and attended the best Universities to acquire their professional credentials. Where managers come from less socially elite backgrounds, they may find themselves undermined not based on their management competence, but instead because they are regarded by professionals as not being their social or intellectual equals.

The extent to which managers experience these problems depends upon the status of management in the societal context being examined, as well as the status, educational attainment, and prestige of the managers professionals are facing.

Public services must be accountable to the government, but also achieve results for their service users

A second organizational tension that particularly affects public services is the tension between the need for probity on the one hand, and for dynamism and responsiveness on the other (Sukel, 1978). Public organizations tend to highlight these differences because public money must be accounted for not only in terms of its effect but also in terms of normative expectations about conduct in public life. These constraints are apparent in both public and private organizations, but the need to achieve strong accountability is especially apparent in public services. It is not enough just to be a successful public official; public managers must also show that they have high standards of public conduct. In the private sector, the behaviour of President Bill Clinton in relation to his interns may have been regarded as unethical, but the prospect of impeachment would never have occurred – he would have been judged on his results rather than upon how they were reached.

Equally, former London Mayor Ken Livingstone was shown, in an edition of the TV journalism programme 'Dispatches' in January 2008, drinking what seemed to be an alcoholic drink at an evening meeting with the public, and held up to criticism as a result. Livingstone was not being judged on the basis of his efficacy as Mayor (in that particular example at least), his character was being questioned and his fitness to hold public office. It is far less likely that the Chief Executive of a private company would be held up to such scrutiny for drinking alcohol in an evening meeting with shareholders.

Private managers have also found themselves having to account for their behaviour as well as their results, especially since the founding of the corporate governance and social responsibility movements. The difference is that public managers have moved from a focus and concern with the processes of their jobs, particularly in relation to their conduct and their ability to follow rules and normative standards of behaviour, towards one concerned with results, whereas private managers have moved from a focus upon results towards one increasingly concerned with conduct. There is movement towards a meeting in the middle, but from different directions. However, it remains the case that private organizations will always, in the final analysis, be more concerned with outputs than with the means by which they were achieved than their public counterparts.

Managers may hold public values, but must also show they have market values

A dynamic related to the one between accountability and results (see above) is the one between public values and market values. Market values are associated with those of the private sector, where the standard approach to management is often portrayed as one which combines having the best product or service with good marketing and good customer service (Christy & Brown, 1996). There is a strong sense of the market being the ultimate arbiter of what constitutes a good product or service, of deciding in an objective way who has the best marketing, and of what good customer service comprises. Managers, in the end, are judged by the ability to meet the needs of the market, as judged by the individual consumers that comprise it. If managers are able to satisfy the market, and turn a good profit, then shareholder satisfaction tends to follow.

Organizations that exist outside of the market environment, however, have to find alternative sources of legitimacy. The success of public services means that they are measured in terms of their ability to not only provide a service to individual members of the public but also to meet the needs of the public collectively. Private organizations have to meet the needs of many customers, but usually one at a time. Public organizations, in an age where they are expected to provide good customer services as well as meeting the collective need, face the tension between serving the public as a whole, and looking after the particular individual requiring service today (Quirk, 1997). Whereas market-based organizations tend to underplay (although not completely remove) the problem of who receives the good or service – the ones both willing and able to pay – deciding who should receive services and how is a central part of public management. Public managers must be able to show not only that they are balancing the needs of the public as a whole with the needs of the particular user but also that they are making their decisions in a transparent and fair way.

The need for fairness in public organizations is likely to lead to the generation of rules and standard procedures, which will be used to make decisions

Table 4.3 Market values versus public values

Market values	Public values
Individual customers	Individual requiring service Public as a whole
Customer experience	Fairness
Market success as criteria for success	Accountability, probity and fairness as criteria for success

about who gets served and in what order – the creation of a bureaucracy. In today's world, 'bureaucracy' has become a term of abuse, taken to suggest a sclerotic, slow-moving organization that is rule bound and lacking in market or customer focus. However, if bureaucracies lead to greater fairness, probity, and accountability, then they may have much to commend them in non-market settings (or even in some market-based organizations where these values are important) (Du Gay, 2000). Indeed, Kirkpatrick and Ackroyd (2003) question whether new managerial archetypes, particularly those that are driven by market mechanisms, are any more effective than pre-existing forms of professional bureaucracies.

Table 4.3 summarizes the differences between market and public values.

Public services must be efficient, and so organized around professional schedules, but provide customer service, and so be organized around user schedules

The tension between market and public values leads, in turn, to another related problem. Because public services often require significant professional involvement, and professionals are a scarce resource, public services have tended to be organized around the amount of professional time available than for the convenience of the individual service user (Tallis, 2005). This may seem intrinsically wrong – it seems an axiom of good customer service to place the needs of customers ahead of employees, and one of the claims of the 'NPM' is that it has helped move public services towards a customer rather than producer orientation. But a little thought shows that organizing public services around professionals may actually be more efficient than a customer orientation.

Because professionals are the scarce resource in the production of many public services, their time is the limiting factor in the production of the good or delivery of the service. It makes sense to organize services to get as much from the limiting factor as possible – and this implies public service users working around the professional rather than the user.

An example of a public service often organized around professionals is hospital medicine. Here patients will usually be required to wait to see a doctor, and although they may have an appointment time, if previous patients have overrun, or if emergencies have come in, the doctor may be running very late, leaving patients with substantial waiting times. Doctors are the scarce resource – it would make no sense for hospitals to employ too many doctors (even if they were available), only for them to have spare capacity when they were not needed. It does make sense, therefore, for appointments to be made in an efficient way, and so be organized primarily in terms of doctors' time rather than patients'.

This idea of efficiency, however, does not mean that patients should be deliberately kept waiting. Too often in the past the lack of availability of doctors has been used to allow excessively poor service where receptionists do not accurately report waiting times so that patients can at least see how long they are likely to have to wait, where doctors routinely book patients in for the same appointment, knowing some will be kept waiting or with ridiculously short intervals between appointments. Organizing appointments efficiently does not have to mean that no care has to be taken over service users.

Public managers may be appointed through contradictory means (election versus selection)

A final tension in public organizations is between the appointment of representatives and officials via the democratic process, or election, compared to appointment to post via a selection process. Different countries approach this tension in different ways. In the United States, after political elections, a significant number of public official posts are appointed by those publicly elected (Ross, 1988), so elected representatives are able to make political selections (or appointments). The dynamics of this can lead to difficult outcomes through. In August 2005, New Orleans was tragically struck by Hurricane Katrina, which resulted in one of the most significant disasters in American history, where more than 1,500 people died. After the events of 9/11, disaster management in the United States had undergone a refocusing under the Bush government in which the leaders of the Federal Emergency Management Agency (FEMA) suggested there was an 'oversize entitlement programme' and so disaster victims should rely upon 'faith-based organizations' rather than the government for help (Schneider, 2005, p. 516).

The Federal Response to Katrina was initially led by Michael D. Brown, appointed head of FEMA. Brown was heavily criticized for his lack of expertise in the area of flood defences (he had no experience of disaster management before his appointment to FEMA), with the suggestion that his appointment had been based on political rather than merit considerations. In the United States, upon a change of Governor or President, a whole range of public appointments change because they are in the gift to those who have been democratically elected rather than being appointed through a selection process. This 'spoils' system also manifests itself in countries such as Italy, where political appointments, often based on familial affiliations, are still very common (Kickert, 2005, Putnam, 1993).

The alternative to being elected to public positions is for managers to be appointed through a selection process. Here the availability of a job will usually be advertised, and so potentially available to everyone who wishes to apply for it, with the aim of the selection process to pick the right person on the grounds of their expertise, experience and ability to the job. Intuitively, this seems an appropriate way for public officials to be selected. However, there are also problems with it.

Where public officials have to work closely with politically elected figures, they do need to be able to get on, and if neither party is able to make the relationship work, then the delivery of public services is likely to be significantly affected. The appointment of the Chief Executive of what was eventually known as the NHS Management Executive in England is a good example of these problems. Victor Paige, the first holder of the role, resigned from his job in June 1986 frustrated by political interference and the lack of profile for management in the NHS (Edwards & Fall, 2005). This, in turn, led to disruption and the need for the Management Executive to have to search for a new manager at a time when it was only just becoming established. Had government ministers appointed someone to the role, rather than it going through a national selection process, the problem might have been avoided.

Appointment via selection addresses the potential problem of political appointments being unfair, but, if those elected to public positions are unable to get on with managers selected to run public organizations, a problem of a different kind can emerge. Where the civil service of a government holds full-time permanent jobs irrespective of who is elected to government, politicians may feel frustrated or patronized by public officials who regard them as transitory and uninformed, and may attempt to change the way government works by appointing their own advisors or consultants and attempting to circumvent civil service procedures. These tensions were very apparent in both the UK

Thatcher and Blair governments (Barber, 2007b, Blair, 2010, Hyman, 2005, Jenkins, 2006).

The contradictions as ideal types

Table 4.4 summarizes the discussion above, showing the contradictions representing ideal-type public and private organizations.

The contradictions shown above are best thought of as spectrums rather than binary opposites. As organizations become more manager dominated, or where professional groups are weaker, we would expect managerial goals, language, and targets to dominate. This means that organizations become more archetypally private, even if they are publicly funded and provided. However, most organizations, be they public or private, can never get away from the logic of their opposite form entirely, and will have to engage with it. However, as I argued in the Section 'Introduction', this is a creative process that can help managers to be more aware of the challenges they are likely to experience. Exploring the mechanisms that underpin the differences between organizations more generally, even if they tend to be clustered in particular ways in public and private organizations predominantly, seems far more worthwhile. The rest of this book, in many respects, is about exploring these tensions in public organizations in greater depth (the role of professionals and users in public organizations, the use of markets and performance management), before exploring what they mean for public management in the Section 'Conclusion'. In doing so, it constructs an argument that public management is necessary because markets don't work in all circumstances, that we need professionals to run public services even if they need to be made more accountable, that public services need to be made democratically accountable even though this is difficult to achieve and in doing so we

Table 4.4 Archetypal 'public' and 'private' organizations

Archetypal public organization	Archetypal private organization
Professional-dominated	Manager-dominated
Accountability-focused	Results-focused
Public values	Market values
Efficiency-focused	Customer-focused
Public goods	Private goods
Elected managers	Selected managers

need the public to play their roles as citizens as well as customers of public organizations.

Conclusion

The main paradox explored in this chapter is that every generation of scholars and practitioners believe that they are doing public management the right way, but that what is regarded as the 'right way' changes considerably over time, ranging from the bureaucratic forms of the public administration model, to the business-like principles of the NPM. There are very good arguments for both the public administration and public management models – but what is striking is that these approaches often lead to very different ways of organizing, delivering, and making public services accountable. This is a crucial insight as it illustrates the basis of range of paradoxes about public management delivery that the book can go on to explore.

In the period leading up to the financial crisis of 2007/8, public management (in terms of government policy) increasingly became about adopting ideas more or less uncritically from the private sector. In the terms explored above, it moved more and more towards the private pole. Academics concerned about this shift launched detailed critiques of this change (Clarke *et al.*, 2007) and of its implications.

However, after the crisis, we find ourselves apparently having learned very little from it. Public professions are finding their voices ignored in government reforms based on introducing greater privatization and market-based reforms, and managers apparently powerless to prevent them even if they believe them to be wrong. There seems to be little discussion about the distinctive nature of public services, and instead only concern for their productivity or cost-effectiveness, so that we measure what services are for rather than asking what they are for. Public services increasingly position service users as customers only, creating few opportunities for democratic engagement in a meaningful way, even if experiments with those types of structures appear to hold promise, and service users request more active engagement (Callaghan & Wistow, 2006).

Despite the massive market failures of the financial crisis, we seem to be continuing down the road of public reform towards greater privatization without having considered whether this is appropriate or even effective. Later chapters in this book will explore in greater depth why this might be – but for the moment note that this chapter shows that there are other ways of thinking about public management than as an attempt to introduce private ideas into public organizations. There are alternatives to the present common sense.

Case study – Reinventing government

Michael Spicer is a US Professor of Public Administration who writes a great deal about the role of ideas in public management. His wonderful book on the relationship between the state and public administration (Spicer, 2001) illustrates how US and European public administration grew out of different ideas that shaped the way public organizations and public management developed.

Spicer's work also explores the reinventing government movement that became important in public management, especially in the United States, during the 1990s (Spicer, 2004). The central doctrines of reinventing government (expressed most clearly in Osborne & Gaebler, 1993) are the 'elimination of red tape; holding administrators to account for measurable results; emphasising customer satisfaction in agency dealings with the public; empowering front-line managers to make their own decisions; contracting out whenever possible with the private sector for public-service delivery' (Spicer, 2004). Osborne and Gaebler attempted to present their work as an objective restatement of the separation between politics and administration, and therefore as an ideologically neutral series of ideas for the better running of government that could be applied universally. In the words of one of the inventors of the approach, 'reinvention applies to all types of organizations' (Osborne & Plastrick, 1997).

Vice President Al Gore echoed the sentiments of the reinventing government movement in arguing in the US National Performance Review that entrepreneurial government was about casting aside red tape, and giving public managers a sense of mission. President Kennedy was held up as an example of what could be achieved using precursors to reinventing government in giving NASA a very public mission of landing a man on the moon by the end of the 1960s. This clarity of purpose was contrasted with the situation in many public organizations that had to meet multiple, and even competing goals, and with government itself seen as creating much of this confusion by giving public managers unclear objectives. Rationalizing government was about depoliticizing the process of governing public organizations to make it 'more rational and teleocratic' (p. 358).

Spicer makes the argument that, far from being an ideologically neutral series of tools, reinventing government is an example of reform based, following Oakeshott, on the principles of purposive association, which run counter to the constitutional form of governance found in the United States, those of the civil association. Purposive associations are formed when individuals recognize themselves as bound together for the 'joint pursuit of some coherent set of substantive purposes or ends. Individuals within such a state acknowledge themselves and their actions as instrumental to the attainment of the purposes of the state' (p. 355). Human activities are seen as being directed towards the cooperative achievement of something substantive, with individuals conforming in both their own actions and their own ends to the achievement of a common, shared set of ends. Civil associations, in comparison, are based upon the protection of diverse interests and ends, and of celebrating diversity instead through mutual support and protection. This can be linked back to constitutional idea of individuals being made free from the state wherever possible, and to the founding principles, in many respects, of the United States.

Spicer suggests that the US principles of civil association are in opposition to the purposive governance reforms of the 1990s encapsulated in reinventing government, and that it is necessary to find administrative reforms that go with the grain of this form of governance rather than against it, to work with traditions rather than against them. He suggests that there may be dangers of imposing a teleocratic approach to governance in a political culture that is fragmented and divided. Spicer suggests that the reinventing government reforms have not worked out as their formulators suggested, or as politicians imagined, because of the lack of fit between their proposals and the civil traditions of the United States.

Further reading

Stewart and Dopson's work provides an excellent account of the public administration approach (Stewart & Walsh, 1992), and Dunsire's paper a neat summary of how the discipline has changed (Dunsire, 1999). Readers interested in debates around the Public Administration should have a look at a wonderful collection published as the approach began to come under fire in 1971 (Chapman & Dunsire, 1971). The reinventing government movement is expressed most clearly in its original manifesto (Osborne & Gaebler, 1993) and the later guidebook (Osborne & Plastrick, 1997), both of which were authored by David Osborne. In the 1990s and 2000s, the Public Value approach has been important, and follows on from many of the themes of reinventing government. The original book is well worth reading (Moore, 1997). Christopher Hood's classic papers on the transition to the 'NPM' are hugely important

(Dunleavy & Hood, 1994, Hood, 1991), as is Christopher Pollitt's book on the growth of managerialism in public services (Pollitt, 1993).

The most recent comprehensive review of public and private management differences appearing in an academic journal remains George Boyne's (Boyne, 2002), who has also examined the differences between HR practice between the two sectors (Boyne, 1999). Boyne's work is heavily based on US studies carried out by, amongst others, Barry Bozeman (Bozeman, 1988, Bozeman & Bretschneider, 1994, Bozeman & Kingsley, 1998) and Hal Rainey (Rainey, 1989, Rainey & Bozeman, 2000, Rainey *et al.* 1976, 1995). The first chapter in Christopher Pollitt's *Essential Public Manager* is also a very good summary of the discussion around differences between public and private management and whether they matter (Pollitt, 2003), and a personal favourite study was published in the prestigious *Academy of Management Review* in 1985, so is a bit dated, but well worth a look (Smith Ring & Perry, 1985).

5

Paying for public services

Introduction

Public finances in many developed countries have been left in a dreadful state by the financial crisis, with massive deficits resulting from bank bailouts and economic stagnation threatening the ability of governments to pay their debts. Critics of government and public services have suggested that the state has grown too big, and that now it is the time for a radical reduction in its size and scope. Private finance is playing a more significant role in the financing of public services as public organizations are increasingly trying to attract funds from the private sector through a number of means, including user charging. Public financing is a hugely complex and political area, and it is crucial to begin to get to grips with it to understand the present public service context.

Before we come to the debate concerning public finance after the crisis, we first need to explain why governments pay for services at all, and to work through the debates around the public financing of services. We can then move on to explore the state of government finances after the financial crisis, but first, begin by presenting the case for the public funding of public services.

The case for the public funding of public services

The classic form of public financing is where the state collects money through taxation, and uses the available funds, along with payments for items such as benefits and repayments of government debt, to pay for public services.

Services might be financed through the state because they are regarded as being located in natural monopolies, or those goods are non-excludable, or because they are too strategically important for the state to depend on market mechanisms.

The argument for financing services based on the existence of a 'natural' monopoly assumes that, in some circumstances, it is actually more efficient to have only one provider of a service. Having two train lines running alongside one another makes little sense, and so the state might provide a monopoly on train lines. In areas where competition is impractical allowing a private monopoly carries the danger that the market might be exploited through higher than necessary prices. If the public sector runs the monopoly instead, however, and it can be held accountable for the running of the service (although this might be a big 'if', as Chapter 4 makes clear), it may make economic sense for the public sector to provide a particular facility or service as a monopoly, funded through general taxation.

Non-excludability is perhaps an even stronger argument for public funding. Non-excludable goods are those that are needed by many people, but which are difficult to charge for per item of use. Streetlighting is the example used earlier – the people in a local area are taxed with that money then being put into a fund to pay for it on the grounds that everyone will benefit, whereas attempting to charge for lighting as it is used would be expensive and complex. Equally, asking people for voluntary contributions towards the cost of streetlighting is unlikely to work because some people, even though they may be extensive nighttime travellers and so substantial beneficiaries of streetlighting, might attempt to 'free-ride' by assuming someone else will pay. If everyone takes the 'free rider' view, no funds will be available for lighting, and so a collective outcome is reached, which is in few people's individual interest. The use of taxation provides a means for overcoming this problem.

The strategic importance argument for funding public services comes from the idea that some services are so important to the country and economy that they should be made available to everyone, free at the point of their delivery. Education and healthcare are strong cases of this, but for different reasons. Education is strategically important because achieving equality of opportunity for young people in an economy is the best way of ensuring the future vibrancy of the economy – we want the most able people to prevail, not to prevent those from poorer backgrounds from receiving their full potential, as might occur if parents have to pay for education. Equally, we want our citizenry to choose good politicians to govern them, and to participate in our democracies more widely, and this is more likely if they have a good education and can make informed decisions. Healthcare is important because we might regard it as an important principle that people can access it without concern of their ability to pay, and so justify public funding for it on those grounds.

There are other arguments in favour of the public financing of public services as well. First, there is the case where charging for a service, which is generally used by the population will discriminate against those on lower incomes as they will have to pay proportionately (in terms of their income) more for that service than those on higher incomes. The use of taxation, which is collected at least partially proportionally to income through income tax, suggests that it might create a fairer way of paying for services used by large numbers of people. In publicly funded healthcare systems, to continue with the example above, everyone has the same access to the same services, but people pay different contributions to the cost of the service based upon their individual tax contributions, which in turn are related to their incomes.

Finally, there is also an argument that paying for some services via taxation might be the most efficient way of paying for them. Where a service is provided to a large number of people, and collecting charges on an individual basis might be expensive and time consuming, it might be more efficient instead to collect extra taxation to pay for it and to fund the services through the state instead. This view often provides an argument for the preservation of public services than for new services becoming public. In situations where there is a political consensus that the charging of services should be attempted, but the costs of collecting the proposed charges would exceed the revenues of imposing them, they represent a poor policy decision. Another healthcare example works here – publicly funded systems occasionally see debates about the introduction of charges for visiting general practitioners or for staying in hospitals, but the costs of collecting those charges, especially where many patients would probably gain exemptions from them on low-income grounds, would probably exceed the revenues they would generate. The efficiency of public financing, therefore, seems to represent an argument for not changing existing public funding arrangements.

The problems of public funding

Paying for public services with public funds has several arguments in favour of it. However, there are also a number of problems. One of these is directly related to the taxation collection system as a whole.

General taxation funding

General taxation represents the taxation revenues available to the government for spending across the full range of its activities. Funding services from general taxation means not having specific programmes attached to specific taxes, but instead the government decides what to do with the sum total available from taxation. Provided those taxes are general (not linked to specific public services or programmes) they are made up of direct taxation (typically income tax and corporation tax) and indirect taxation (typically sales tax or value-added tax).

Paying for public services from general taxation requires the government to tax its population. An increase in funding for a particular public service will require an increase in taxation unless savings can be found from cutting government services in another service (which may be unpopular – see below), or the economy is growing and so giving the government an increased taxation take, or the government funding the service by running up additional debt (which will certainly, in the modern world economy, make it a less attractive place to invest on international financial markets).

Increasing taxation is unlikely to make a government popular unless it is able to demonstrate that the increase is necessary and the area where it is being spent is regarded sympathetically by the public. An increased spending on child welfare may be popular, but the public may not be quite as sympathetic on giving increased benefits to single mothers, even though the two may come to much the same thing. Keeping taxation constant may even prove to be unpopular in a situation where the public believe they are already paying too much tax, and it is a standard electoral strategy for right-of-centre political parties to campaign at election times to decrease the tax burden on the population.

Politicians therefore face a paradox – they can become more popular by offering more public services, but doing so is likely to make them less popular because that will require a rise in taxation. In a growing economy, there is scope for public services to grow as the economy does, but a period of recession, such as the one we now face, leads to difficult choices about whether to cut back on public services or increase government debts.

Funding public services through general taxation does not guarantee any public service a set budget; rather it makes available a general fund, which is used to pay for them. Each individual service must then usually make its case to the government department in charge of finance, or to the body responsible for running the government, for the amount of funding it requires. If a particular service has done well in public financing in the past compared to others, however, this does not mean that the less well-funded services will be better funded in the future, even where there is a strong case for funds being reallocated.

Future budgetary allocations will tend to bear a strong resemblance to the present and the past ones with typically only marginal changes in funding either up or down, so that budget allocations tend to be incremental (Wildavsky, 1997). If a particular service receives a considerable reduction in funding, it will certainly lead to a reduction in its provision. However, once the state has started to provide services, it can be politically and organizationally very difficult to reduce from public provision. Once the public become used to receiving a service funded publicly, they may resent having to pay for it again themselves, or even be unable to afford it.

Equally the public might resent a reduction in the level of public service provided compared to that previously received – there might be less schools to choose from or rubbish collection occur less frequently. This phenomenon, where the public experience a reduction in the services provided to them adversely, tends to lead to a 'ratchet' effect – once services have been paid for by the state, it can be politically difficult for it to stop (this is an argument strongly related to the 'social expenses' argument by O'Connor – see Chapter 3). Where services are no longer publicly funded, or where public managers have to ask the public for contributions towards their running, this can lead to both the government and managers becoming unpopular, and both groups are often reluctant to make such a move.

The ratchet or social expenses problem means that the pattern of public funding for a particular service can become disconnected to its value or to its need. If a particular state has always spent a considerable amount of funds on, for example, healthcare, it can be very difficult for it to reduce these sums, even if it believes that the money would be better spent elsewhere. Cutting back on health service spending might be badly received by the public, and the government in question have to pay the electoral price for their decision, even if it was the right one to make.

A second problem is that because public services tend to have a significant proportion of wages and salaries in their total cost (as services tend to generally), an increase in funding for public services may reward better those working in them, but not necessarily increase the measurable output of the service. The problem is generally known, after another economist, as Baumol's cost disease, and suggests that the pay rates of public services will tend to rise faster than productivity improvements available within them – professionals expect to be well-paid, but increasing school class sizes or asking doctors to see more patients through shorter appointment times will not improve the service on offer.

The problem of measuring whether increasing funding for public services actually improves their performance is exacerbated by the intrinsic difficulties in assessing the quality, and even quantity, of their output more generally. It is difficult to measure improvements in the performance of a school or a hospital because of the nature of the service it provides. If a school's exam results improve, does this mean that it is educating its children better, or simply that it has become better at coaching them for exams? If one hospital has a lower death rate for a particular treatment than another, does this mean that it is curing more people, or that it is treating more healthy people?

Increasing the funding of public services may not necessarily lead to an increase in the outputs, which politicians are using to measure standards, even if they have improved. If politicians cannot demonstrate a definable improvement in performance, they may be reluctant to increase funding, even if it is justifiable on the grounds of staff simply deserving pay awards or historic underfunding. The issue of performance management in the public sector is picked up again more fully in Chapter 9.

Hypothecated funding

An alternative to the general taxation method of funding services is to 'hypothecate' funding for particular services. In this method, the public will be told that a particular percentage of their taxation contribution is being used to pay for a specific service, with the idea being that this increases the accountability of the funding system. Services that are popular, such as healthcare, might be suitable for this kind of funding. Hypothecating funding in this situation might allow politicians to argue for increases in taxation to fund a particular service, so launch a campaign for extra sums for the education of young children, or to pay for improved healthcare.

The danger with hypothecated funding is that it is fine for the public to have their taxation linked to services they are happy to pay for, but what if finance is hypothecated for areas they do not agree with? Defence expenditure might be necessary for the security of the state, but is unlikely to be popular amongst all sections of the community, who may wish, if expenditure is hypothecated, to want to withhold that part of their taxation payment. Hypothecation makes clear the links between taxation and expenditure, but where public expenditure is in areas that particular sections of the public do not agree with, marking it out so visibly may incur resentment from them.

The problems of financing public services from public funds – Summary

The difficulties of funding public organizations from public finance are concerned primarily with the taxation burden that they create, and which is increasingly unpopular with the public in most nations. The public want better services, but don't want to pay for them through increased taxation, and will often resent politicians who ask them to pay for services they have previously received free from the state.

The alternatives to the public financing of public services

If using public finance to pay for public services comes with significant problems, what are the alternatives?

Using private financing to pay for public services

Private financing can entirely replace public funding, or be a supplement to it. Parents might send their children to a public school, but receive extra school trips, more tuition, and a wider range of learning materials if their parents are prepared to pay additionally for them. Public hospitals may offer a basic level of service to the entire public, but be able to provide private rooms, a choice of food, bedside telephones, televisions, and private rooms, to those who are prepared to pay extra.

Public organizations have increasingly had to find ways of providing higher standards of service, and one way of achieving this is to charge because of the reluctance of politicians to provide increased finance for them. This also allows politicians to demonstrate that public services are becoming more efficient because they are offering higher levels of service (admittedly for an extra payment) for the same level of public funding. However, providing extra services at an extra cost is a divisive answer to these problems, as not everyone will be able to afford the additional payments necessary to access extra levels of service.

Where private charging is introduced into public provision, then this also tends to mean that services are at least partially provided by the private sector as well. Although the financing and provision of services is at least theoretically a separate issue, with there being good reasons why privately financed services might be publicly provided (to guarantee provision and minimum standards of service, for example), private financing will often lead to private provision.

Table 5.1   The range of possibilities for public and private funding

Public funding with no private charging.
Public funding with charging for non-standard services.
Public funding with charging encouraged, and public provision offered to the private market.
Public funding given income targets for private income generation.
Public–private partnerships.
Private funding.

In schools, extra tuition might be provided by private tutors; in hospitals, extra services provided by private telephone and television companies.

It is important to be clear about what balance is expected between public and private financing for a service. A range of options are possible as summarized in Table 5.1.

At one end of a spectrum services are entirely funded by the public sector. Public schooling, where parents are not asked to make any financial contributions (such as for textbooks or tuition or school trips), might be an example.

Next we see a situation where private financing might be used to provide an additional service that most of the population do not regularly require, but for public funding to still pay for the majority of standard services. For example, in refuse collection, the state may not routinely take away particular kinds of rubbish, especially those that are particularly bulky or potentially dangerous. In these circumstances, it might be legitimate to expect the individuals who require such refuse services to pay additionally for them. Public managers will need to arrange for such 'additional' services to be managed as efficiently as possible and to try and make sure that the costs of providing such a service do not exceed the costs of running them, but this is a relatively straightforward role compared to the difficulties that come from a more widespread use of charging.

Next along the spectrum of public and private financing we might imagine public providers extending their range of offerings to those that lie a little outside of their usual services with the aim of extending their revenue base. Local authorities or local governments might have a range of in-house experts in a range of areas, despite the move to sub-contract services as much as possible from the 1980s onwards, and there may be opportunities to charge for the provision of these services on the open market. Estate services such as gardening and maintenance, for example, might be offered to the private sector through the market. Engineers are employed in civil maintenance departments, and occupational health employees can advertise their services to the private sector in addition to their public employers. Public employees in these areas still work the majority of the time for their own public service, but also look for opportunities to try and raise additional income from the private market as well, particularly in times where they may not be at full capacity workloads in their public work.

If public services can be offered to the private sector, it is a relatively short leap to giving public managers income targets for the sums they are expected to raise from their private activities. Where this occurs, there is a shift in attitude from private income being a supplement, to being an important part of public service funding. In the UK Universities, for example, it is becoming increasingly common for overseas students to be targeted through recruitment because of the extra fees they bring, and for academics to be given income generation targets. These income targets might be met by taking on additional teaching or consultancy, or by successfully applying for research grants. Income targets might be made up from raising private sources of finance (through consultancy or teaching private sector students on short courses) or from public funds (through additional public teaching, or raising public research grants). Perversely, however, Newman *et al.* (2001) suggest that targets can lead to a stifling of innovation, especially where they are accompanied by an attempt for a central or federal government to exert greater control. They found that inflexible targets created barriers to innovation, especially with regard to the proliferation of performance indicators, and sometimes even to local authority managers having to take the risk of not meeting a centrally imposed target in the short term in order to deliver long-term benefits locally.

Where public employees are expected to find additional sources of funds, public managers will be expected to find ways of incentivizing and policing reward systems so that income generation targets are fair, and that the targets are set over appropriate timescales. To continue with the example of higher education, bonuses or promotions might be awarded to academics whose work is judged to have been successful, but finding an appropriate timescale to make a judgement might be difficult. Annual timescales might be too short to consider successful research grant applications, and it may be several years before it is clear where a particular research programme was successful or not. If academic papers are cited by lots of other writers, this may be an indication that they have been influential, but it can also be an indication that they are widely recognized as having significant problems. Academic managers will also have to give serious thought to what they will do in circumstances where staff are either overly successful or appear to be struggling. Either case brings with it its own problems.

If academics are very successful in raising external funds, they might find themselves in a situation where they become overloaded, perhaps as a result of taking on too much consultancy, or being unexpectedly successful in grant applications In this situation, managers will have to find ways of supporting academics to make sure that they are able to honour all of their commitments, or perhaps encouraging them to involve colleagues more often in their activities to reduce their individual workload. At the other extreme, where academics are not able to attract external funding, perhaps by not succeeding in grant applications, or being unable to provide consultancy, this will result in them appearing, by these criteria, to be unsuccessful in meeting their goals. However, this may not always be the case; some academic disciplines will, at any point in time, tend to have more funding opportunities available to them than others, and it seems odd to demand staff apply for grants that may not be actually available. The careless imposition of income targets can act as a disincentive as well as potentially leading to high-quality staff leaving, and so must be handled with some care – another of the paradoxical situations that public managers must face.

Public–private partnerships

Where the system of public service financing goes beyond putting in place external income targets for public services, more regular collaboration with the private sector might be sought. The form of financing that might be encouraged in such a system is the use of public–private partnerships (PPP). The PPP is a relatively recent idea in implementation but has existed theoretically for several decades. In this situation, public organizations, as the name implies, work with the private sector in some form or another to combine expertise or funding through the formation of an organizational partnership of one form or another.

The term 'PPP' conceals a great deal as the exact structure of the arrangements between public and private organizations might vary considerably from country to country (Grimshaw *et al.*, 2002). One model, favoured in the United Kingdom, is to get the private sector to provide construction expertise to the public and to get it to invest in infrastructure, with the public sector then paying for the capital project involved over an extended period, perhaps as long as 30 years. In this circumstance, the public sector often gets much-needed capital infrastructure investment without having to pay for it upfront (as such, it is a lot like a hire-purchase arrangement), with the private sector partner benefiting from a guaranteed income source for several years, often at a considerable profit.

The private finance initiative (PFI) has been an example of a PPP that has gained momentum over the last ten years and resulted in a large number of hospitals and schools being built that would simply not have otherwise appeared, but the long-term costs of this building programme remain hugely contentious (Public Finance, 2007). Perhaps the best way of thinking about the PFI version of PPP is as a risk transfer. The public sector transfers to the private sector the risk involved in putting together a significant capital project, but the private sector transfers to the public sector the risk of making sure that the contract is drawn up on terms that are good value to the public purse. It seems, on balance, that the private sector has got the best out of this risk transfer so far, utilizing its expertise in contracting to make considerable profits against local public managers lacking expertise in negotiating and contracting (Asenova & Beck, 2003). In both the United Kingdom and Australia, significant concerns have been expressed over the value for money of the scheme in prominent capital building projects. In early 2012, the UK government was forced to find an extra £1.5bn to support public hospitals unable to meet their PFI commitments, suggesting that the problem is going to be a long-standing one that requires governments, rather than simply finding additional sums of money to support what seem to be bad agreements, but to take a second look at those agreements to see if they are providing reasonable expectations of the public purse.

In Europe, the idea of the PPP has been extended to try and include more social goals, and in Germany and Switzerland particularly, the notion of 'Public Social Private Partnerships' has become more prevalent. These attempt to combine long-term financing within an explicit social agenda that encourages co-operation between a larger number of partners (they must have at least three) and which attempt to combine both financing (the main area of focus of PFI) with a framework for dealing with the practical delivery of services. Unlike many PFI agreements, which have limited disclosure agreements for fear of breaching commercial confidentiality, openness, and transparency are amongst the key principles that partnership must sign up to, and, for the private partners involved can be a way of displaying greater corporate social responsibility. These European innovations are important because they demonstrate a different stress on PPP compared to those often found in the United Kingdom and Australia, moving away from simply raising of public finance towards more genuinely collaborative arrangements. However, only time will see if these new approaches create genuinely better value for money than has often been seen on previous projects.

Private provision

At the final end of the spectrum between public and private financing would be a model where private financing dominates in both public and private provision. Even advocates of a free-market approach would probably suggest that some public employees remain funded by the public sector – particularly the police – especially where their responsibility is to protect property rights. However, it is possible to imagine a model where the state is dramatically reduced in size and the private sector expected to finance most of the things we presently regard as public services. The logic behind this is an appealing one – if we all paid a lot less tax, then we would be richer, and so be able to afford to pay school fees for our children, healthcare insurance for our families, and we could subscribe to pay for access to roads we needed to travel on. The argument behind this view is that individuals, rather than the state, are best placed to decide how their money should be spent. Receiving a pay slip and seeing exactly how much money has been deducted in terms of taxation, or having to meet a very large annual payment to the state to discharge taxation responsibility, can be a demoralizing one, and even the most strongest supporter of public services can sometimes wonder what on earth it is we are getting back for all the money we pay to the government.

This individualistic view of society is appealing in that we would all have a lot more cash if we paid a lot less tax. However, we would all have to take a great deal more personal responsibility as well. Being unable to afford schooling for children would lead to a choice between not providing schooling at all (which would have significant implications for the future of the economy), of relying upon charitable schools for education (which were commonplace until not so long ago), or self-educating children at home (which families might struggle with where parents have to work full time), or of simply not having children until such a time that schooling can be afforded. The decision to bring children into the world would be based, even more explicitly than it presently is, on the ability of parents to afford them. The ability to drive a car would depend not only on the ability of individuals to afford to buy a car, petrol and insurance but also on being able to pay charges to drive on roads. If the public sector did not provide them, all roads would be toll roads.

In a television documentary broadcast on British Television in 2011, *The Street That Cut Everything*, one street received a refund of their local taxation payments ('council tax') in return for losing all locally provided public services such as streetlighting, rubbish collection, and street maintenance. Chaos quickly ensued. This by no means was a scientific study but was alarming viewing for those that think we are better off taking responsibility for the provision of public services ourselves.

In a private market, public managers would not really exist. If provision was private, then either banks or shareholders would have to be satisfied, and so profits made. There might be opportunities to work in charitable institutions with not-for-profit goals, but the constant concern in such enterprises would be ensuring continuity of funding to allow services to continue to be provided. Charitable funding means that services depend upon contributions, and sometimes substantial benefactions from the better-off, in order to be able to continue to operate. In times when giving declines, difficult choices might have to be made about the future of services. In these situations, the role of managers in the third sector (in charities and other not-for-profit organizations) becomes an outward-facing one, attempting to raise money from potential givers, as well as trying to make the best possible use of the money raised. To some extent, all organizations need to do this, but the pressure grows considerably where funding is solely from either market transactions or charitable giving, and there may be a tendency for time horizons of planning and work to become considerably shortened in an environment where money is continually being sought to allow services to be offered in the next period (Hutton, 1996).

Funding and the nature of public services

Making use of market mechanisms is a challenge to the nature of public services. When we started which services might be funded and provided publicly, a key element was that market mechanisms would not work. There would seem to be something of a contradiction here – public services are those which markets tend to underprovide, or where market failures mean that public funding and provision is required, but the present common sense of public reform is to try and use market mechanisms (and at least some private financing).

The use of market mechanisms, private provision, and private financing, then, asks some fundamental questions about public services. If public services can make use of private financing and private markets, how are they public anymore? If it was market failure that led to the introduction of public services, why are we reintroducing markets?

These issues can be usefully reviewed looking at the situation in the US hospitals based on private, and to some extent, not-for-profit provision. Hospitals that have to satisfy the needs of shareholders as well as those of their patients may have a need to deny access to medical care for those that are unable to pay for it through insurance, or where the hospital to able to offer it on the grounds of need (pro bono work). Assuming that in the United States, as elsewhere, doctors and nurses are motivated by doing public good; this may cause a considerable clash between their personal values and the ability of their organization to do good while at the same time making profit in a competitive market environment. Michael Moore's film 'Sicko' presents a damning indictment of such a system where he shows insurance companies attempting to find ways of not funding their clients for healthcare treatments they need by attempting to find even the smallest errors on their original application forms. This doesn't seem to be what public service ought to be about.

More recently in England (but not Scotland or Wales), the successive Labour and coalition governments have attempted to make greater use of market mechanisms in the National Health Service, encouraging private and not-for-profit organizations to compete with publicly owned providers of care, and offering patients more choices. The Health and Social Care Bill of 2011/12, which is still going through Parliament as I write this, has provoked a strong reaction from a range of medical representative groups, as well as raising a petition through the government website, signed by more than 160,000 people, asking for the Bill be dropped. A recurring theme in the criticisms of the direction of health reorganization is the concern that healthcare will be privatized in England so it becomes more like the United States.

Funding public services through private means does not change the nature of the service intrinsically; it does lead to managers having to deal with some difficult questions. An open-minded view of this dilemma is that it simply means that managers have to incorporate the wishes of shareholders or other financial partners into decision-making processes in the organization alongside the range of other stakeholders with whom they must deal on an everyday basis. The concern is not that managers have to make themselves more financially accountable – this is a fact of life for all employees in public organizations more generally. It is that the financial imperative of making sure that services break even or generate a surplus becomes the overriding emphasis of all decisions to the extent that they lose their public mission. Different funding mechanisms do not automatically change the nature of public organizations, but they do have a tendency to make more explicit the underlying logics of their operation.

Public funding after the financial crisis

To explore the consequences of the above ideas in relation to the challenges faced by governments after the financial crisis, we first need to consider how public finances vary from country to country, and to consider what effect the financial crisis has had upon them.

Some facts and figures

The size of the public sector varies considerably from country to country in terms of its size as well as whether it is growing, contracting, or staying about the same. Table 5.2 gives a sense of this.

What we can see in Table 5.2 is both the variation in government outlays as a proportion of GDP, ranging from the smallest (Australia, Japan, and the United States), to the biggest (Denmark, Sweden, and Italy). There is also a first understanding of the financial effects of the banking crisis of 2007/8. As a general benchmark (the OECD figure at the bottom of the table), but 2006 the average government spend as a proportion of GDP was 40 per cent. By 2010, it had risen to 44.6 per cent – a significant increase in a short period of time.

How was this rise in government expenditure as a proportion of GDP paid for? Table 5.3 shows the simple answer is debt:

Table 5.2 The size of public expenditure at a % of nominal GDP by selected country

	1994	1998	2002	2006	2008	2010	2013
Australia	35.9	33.6	33.6	32.6	33.5	36.4	33.2
Canada	49.7	44.8	41.2	39.4	40.0	44.1	41.2
Denmark	60.2	56.3	54.6	51.6	51.9	58.5	59.6
France	54.1	52.7	52.8	52.9	53.3	56.7	55.0
Germany	48.0	48.0	47.9	45.3	44.1	48.0	44.7
Italy	53.2	48.9	47.1	48.5	48.6	50.3	49.4
Japan	35.0	42.5	38.8	36.2	37.2	40.4	41.7
Sweden	68.3	58.8	55.6	52.7	51.7	52.9	52.1
UK	44.6	39.5	40.9	44.2	47.9	47.9	47.5
US	37.1	34.6	35.9	36.1	39.1	42.5	40.7
OECD	41.9	40.8	40.4	39.7	41.5	44.6	42.7

Source: Data from Annex table 25 – general government outlays (% of nominal GDP).

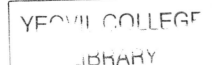

Table 5.3 Surpluses (+) and deficits (–) by government as a % of nominal GDP

	1994	1998	2002	2006	2008	2009	2010	2013
Australia	−3.2	1.8	1.7	2.1	0.5	−4.1	−4.8	−0.3
Canada	−6.7	0.1	−0.1	1.6	−0.4	−4.9	−5.6	−3.0
Denmark	−3.4	−0.1	0.3	5.0	3.3	−2.8	−2.8	−3.0
France	−5.5	−2.6	−3.3	−2.4	−3.3	−7.6	−7.1	−3.0
Germany	−2.5	−2.3	−3.8	−1.7	−0.1	−3.2	−4.3	−0.6
Italy	−9.0	−2.9	−3.2	−3.4	−2.7	−5.4	−4.5	−0.1
Japan	−3.8	−11.2	−8.0	−1.6	−2.2	−8.7	−7.8	−9.5
Sweden	−9.5	0.9	−1.5	2.2	2.2	−0.9	−0.1	0.7
UK	−6.8	−0.1	−2.0	−2.7	−5.0	−11.0	−10.4	−7.3
US	−3.7	0.3	−4.0	−2.2	−6.6	−11.6	−10.7	−8.3
OECD	−4.4	−2.1	−3.3	−1.2	−1.3	−8.3	−7.7	5.1

Source: Annex table 27 – general government financial balances (surplus or deficit % of nominal GDP).

Again, what is striking about Table 5.3 is the variation in government surpluses and deficits from the nations included – Japan had a very bad 1990s as it struggled to recover from its own economic crisis at the end of the 1980s, and running up considerable government deficits. However, Japan's situation was atypical, and even it was getting its finances back in balance by 2006, where the OECD average was had governments running a deficit, on average, of –1.3 per cent.

After the financial crisis, a huge shift occurred. In 2009, the average deficit rose to 8.3 per cent of GDP, but with considerable variation within that. Sweden appears to have barely been touched by the crisis in terms of its budgetary position, whereas the United Kingdom and the United States have run up huge deficits – even bigger than the OECD average. A large part of the reason for this was because of the huge importance of the banking sector and the dependence on profits (and so taxation revenues) on it in each of those countries. The United Kingdom also has an extremely open economy, and so is dependent upon world trading conditions in order to be successful – but with economic growth falling stagnant, the City of London no longer generating huge profits and rising benefits payments as unemployment increases, the deficit has risen and risen.

Before we can assess whether the government deficits being accumulated by many nations after the financial crisis are important, we must first understand how much debt the governments in question have. We can measure this by looking at government debt accumulation as a proportion of GDP, giving an indication of the extent to which countries have been financing public expenditures (including debt interest) from debt. This is given in Table 5.4.

Table 5.4 The government debt of selected countries as a proportion of GDP and ranking in indebtedness (all 2011 figures)

Country	Indebtedness as a proportion of GDP %	World ranking
Australia	30.3	97
Canada	83.5	19
Denmark	46.9	57
France	85.5	17
Germany	81.5	20
Italy	120.1	9
Japan	208.2	2
Sweden	36.8	83
UK	79.5	21
US	69.4	30

Source: CIA world factbook 2012.

What Table 5.4 again shows is a huge variety of indebtedness. As we noted above, Japan had been facing difficult economic times for most of the 1990s, and subsequently managed to decrease its government deficit in the 2000s, but still faces an extraordinary amount of indebtedness – twice its national income (only Zimbabwe has more debt as a proportion of GDP). From the countries above, Italy is ranked next, owing more than 120 per cent of its GDP. Next are countries such as France, Canada, Germany, and the United Kingdom with debts around 80 per cent of GDP, who as I write this are struggling to retain their 'AAA' gold standard debt status (with has a link with being able to borrow at lower rates of interest), and the United States, which has already lost its 'AAA' status because of the sheer scale of the debts it faces as the world's richest nation. There are some surprises in the list – Sweden and Denmark have reputations as high-public-spending economy, but their debts are far lower than its European neighbours. Australia is lowest ranked on the list of nations above, having a status as being a highly liberalized economy, which spends nearly 10 percentage points on public services than its European peers, and even less than the United States.

Interpreting government finance after the financial crisis

Interpreting all of the above takes care and effort. The obvious response when facing a deficit and accumulated debt is to cut back on expenditure, and this would certainly be the response we would have to face if considering these problems as a household. But countries are not like households.

If countries attempted to keep fully balanced budgets all the time they would cut expenditures in periods when the economy was slowing down, and increase them when the economic good times returned. This makes sense from the perspective of balancing the budget, but would only serve to make recessions deeper and expansions bigger. By cutting back on expenditures during recessions, the government would remove demand from the economy by reducing the scale of the public services it offered, effectively cutting back on elements such as infrastructural investment or cutting benefits. Equally, the government could raise taxes in order to find more money for public services, but this reduces the money individual have to spend themselves, reducing demand in the economy. Either reducing expenditure or increasing taxes would probably serve to make the recession deeper.

By increasing expenditure during a boom, when tax receipts increase, the government would invest in the building of new roads or other infrastructure, and perhaps pay more generous benefits mindful of having higher levels of taxation receipts to distribute. Alternatively, it could cut taxes, returning more money to people's pockets, so they would have more money to spend. In either case, the government increasing spending or reducing taxes during a boom is likely to add momentum to the economic expansion.

If governments work in this way, procyclically (as their spending decreases or increases in line with the rest of the economy) the budget may be balanced, but booms will be more bigger and recessions deeper. This doesn't seem like terribly responsible behaviour, adding risk to citizen's lives and leading to businesses facing extremes in their environment that are not helpful.

The alternative to this is for governments to work against the economic cycle, increasing expenditure in recessionary periods, and decreasing expenditures during booms. This is very much the Keynesian approach to macroeconomic management discussed in Chapter 2. However, this too has its difficulties – it requires governments being prepared to run up debts during recessionary periods, running deficits, but discipline in expansionary periods in order to pay those debts back. The evidence from Table 5.4 suggests that governments are rather better at running up debt than paying it back.

Public finance after the economic crisis

After the economic crisis, Governments with large amounts of inherited debt are facing huge debt repayments even as they struggle to balance their finances as they face increased benefits claimants and reduced tax takes. If governments fail to halt the rise in their indebtedness, they will reach a point where they are unable to afford to pay their debt interest as well as their public service commitments, and so face either defaulting on their debts (which is effectively the position Greece is facing in 2012) or cutting back on public service expenditure in order to accommodate the extra debt they are accumulating. Neither of these options is particular appealing.

Revisiting the data above presents us with a number of intriguing conclusions.

First, the size of the public sector is not necessarily related to the public indebtedness a nation faces. Denmark and Sweden, as well as frequently being rated as two of the best countries in the world in which to live, have extensive public services but also much lower inherited indebtedness than their European neighbours or the United States. These nations are considered as having a very different economic model to the rest of Europe or the United States and Australia, being based on a social democratic model paying comparatively high levels of benefits (Esping-Andersen, 1990) but having also dynamic private economies – Sweden's model has been described as 'bumblebee' in that it should not fly according to most economic models that advocate small states and big private economies, but is still remarkably successful anyway. Sweden and Denmark appear to show us that it is perfectly possible to have extensive public sectors alongside relatively low indebtedness – a very different model to the United States and, increasingly, the United Kingdom.

Another different approach to public services comes from Australia, which is often presumed to be like the United States, but which appears to have had a very different outcome after the financial crisis. Australia has comparatively low levels of public expenditure, but unlike the United States, comparatively low levels of indebtedness. Why have the two economies gone such divergent ways in terms of their fortunes after the economic crisis? A significant element is Australia's natural resource base, which has kept its economy stable as the world continues to need its exports, whereas the United States has become increasingly dependent on financial services (as has the United Kingdom) to generate profits and so, taxes. It is no accident that the United States and United Kingdom have run the biggest deficits of the countries considered in this chapter.

Looking at the very different outcomes economies have experienced after the financial crisis leads to the mundane idea that countries can come to very different decisions about the scale of public services that they offer, but also a more important one – that not all models appear to be equally successful.

It is possible to have extensive public services provided the population of that country are prepared to pay for them (Denmark and Sweden), and a dynamic economy can be allowed to work alongside them. The weakness of that model, however, is that should that economy fail, extensive welfare states impose significant costs very quickly as unemployment needs to be kept low, paradoxically, in order to be able to afford to pay generous unemployment benefits.

The case of Australia suggests that it is possible to have much smaller public sector provided the economy supporting it does not become over-dependent upon an area of activity, which leads it vulnerable to a crisis. A small public sector means lower levels of public services, which in turn need non-public providers to plug any gaps the lack of public services might lead to. This also requires a successful economy so that people can find work rather than having to depend upon charity or minimal public services. The UK and the US economies have experienced massive problems because of their over-dependence on their financial services industries, problems from which Australia has been relatively untouched. However, Australia's dependence on its natural resources poses questions of whether its model too is sustainable in the long-term.

Conclusion

The central paradox about paying for public services is, at the very time when public finances are at their most stretched, public spending can be most beneficial to an economy. In contrast, when it is most affordable – when the private economy is thriving and taxation revenues high – the government has least scope to achieve large benefit through its activities. Government spending on public services, as well as providing essential services for our lives, is also both an economic stabilizer through the provision of benefits and public services at times when the economy would otherwise have experienced a much larger fall in demand, and as a source of productive employment and investment in the economy.

The values of a particular society will play a strong role in terms of the choice made about how public services should be funded. Societal values produce institutional inheritances that strongly influence the choices made over service financing. In a country where individual freedoms are valued highly, and where a strong private market presence has been the case, as in the hospital sector in the United States, it will be extremely difficult to make an argument for greater public provision. Attempts to reform healthcare in the first Clinton administration failed so publicly that subsequent governments have been reluctant to try and face up to the problem of around 50 million Americans having to get by without health insurance. Strong interest groups from insurance companies and powerful hospitals will lobby fiercely to prevent change to the healthcare funding system, which is the most expensive in the world, but still fails to provide healthcare for the entire population. This is entirely understandable – if the free market is the preferred mode of governance, then inequalities will tend to exist as they provide the dynamism through which markets incentivize improvements. In working in a private sector-dominated environment, public managers face the dilemma of providing a service for their individual, fee-paying customers, and meeting their obligations to the public as whole, including those that may be unable to afford their services. If Obama is finally able to implement his plan to reform the US healthcare, it will be an astonishing achievement.

At the opposite end of the funding spectrum, a different dilemma is in place. Funding services entirely from the public purse may create a dynamic where there is little incentive for managers and public professionals to behave in a responsible way towards resources. In addition to this, there may be little incentive to provide a high-quality service as, with the profit motive lacking, public organizations may continue to operate whether they are making a substantial surplus or a substantial deficit. The challenge facing public managers in publicly funding settings is finding ways to incentivize high levels of performance whilst at the same time respecting professional autonomy. They must also find ways of getting those delivering services to treat budgets seriously where they lack the legitimacy and imperative that the marketplace confers on them. A publicly funded and provided service may mean that the collective good overrides the importance of the individual to whom a particular service is being provided, and that budgetary goals are seen as being unimportant.

After the financial crisis there has been a new focus on inherited levels of indebtedness and the ability of governments to afford the expanding interest repayments they now face. As I write this conclusion, Greece is engaged in a staged default of its debt, and other European countries are facing close scrutiny from financial markets because of concerns over their levels of indebtedness and faltering economic growth. However, it is important to make clear that the roots of the financial crisis were not in the public sector, even though it is through reductions in public spending that the crisis is being paid for as benefits are reduced, public employment reduced, and services scaled back.

What the financial crisis has done, perhaps, is highlight the fractures in flaws in different country's public funding models, showing some to be rather more robust than others, but making clear that all are potentially vulnerable in the face of recessions or faltering economic growth.

Case study – Public and private schooling

Schooling represents a case where public and private funding combines to create some extremely challenging results. In the United Kingdom, most children are educated in public schools, but in the United States, public schools are sometimes regarded as being where only the children of the poorest families are taught. Even this, however, is subject to considerable variation, as there are cities in the United Kingdom where many middle-class families choose to pay for their children to attend private secondary education providers because of concerns about the standard of public provision. This can contribute towards a self-fulfilling prophecy of poor public education as only those parents who cannot afford to give their children a private education send their children to public schools, and high-income parents who are also likely to be more highly educated and more likely to demand improvements from local schools, send their children to private schools instead. This has the danger of generating a failure of 'voice' (Hirschman, 1970) where the most articulate groups in society are no longer engaged with public services.

In private school education in the United Kingdom, other problems emerge. The United Kingdom has some of the most famous private schools in the world, such as Eton, and such schools have charitable status, implying that they do good not only for the pupils who enter them, often with their parents paying substantial annual fees, but also for the general community.

The charitable status of private schools has come under increased criticism in recent years, with some schools struggling to demonstrate that they are providing much good for the public at large. The present UK Labour government has suggested that private schools may need to do more to demonstrate this general good to the public than at present and to retain their charitable status. Private schools typically offer bursaries to students whose parents might struggle to afford their fees, but is this enough? Should managers in private schools be required to demonstrate that they are contributing in a far wider sense to local communities in order to be able to claim the tax advantages of being a charity? Private schools have to balance their commitments to their fee-paying parents by providing the best possible education to the children in their case, with a charitable duty to do good more generally. This is a significant challenge for managers within them.

In the United States, there is a strong concern with getting public schools to work better. The prestigious *Academy of Management Journal* published a forum discussing the work of Professor William Ouchi (Ouchi *et al.*, 2005). Ouchi's book *Making Schools Work* (Ouchi, 2003) suggested that the biggest obstacle to public schools improving was the large, centralized bureaucracies that often came with them. The solution, in Ouchi's view, is to 'decentralize decision making down to the operating subunits.... It applies to every industry in the country' (p. 930).

Ouchi compares New York City public schools with local Catholic schools, and found that 'the New York City public schools had 10 times as many students as the Catholic schools, about 1.2 million and 120,000, respectively. The Catholic schools had 22 central office staff; if the city had a proportionate number, it should have about 220. Actually it had 25,500' (p. 931). He argues that the creation of this bureaucracy takes the control of the individual schools away from their Principals. Ouchi compares the situation in Edmonton, where decentralization has occurred and nearly 92 per cent of the budget is controlled by Principals, with New York, where around 7 per cent of funds are under their control, and suggests that in Edmonton 'the public schools have become so popular that there are no private schools left' (p. 931).

Ouchi suggests that one of the main differences between public and private schools is that, in private schools everyone teaches through from the headmaster to the librarian, allowing them to have smaller assignment loads to mark and comment upon than public schools with large bureaucracies, and this motivates students to improve by offering them the chance for one-to-one tuition.

In all, Ouchi's prescription boils down to 'local solutions and autonomy' (p. 933) for the improvement of local schools – in many respects bearing a similar argument to the reinventing government movement (see Chapter 4). In terms of funding, however, his argument is arguably more radical in allowing individual school Principals the maximum amount of autonomy in how they spend their funds. Can devolving budgets and allowing autonomy really be the driver for improving public education? Ouchi seems to believe so.

Further reading

The OECD website is a little difficult to navigate and find particular series of data but is overall an excellent source of facts and figures concerned with public financing. A good place to start is at www.oecd.org/statsportal, but you may find that some of the data series require a subscription. If you are in Higher Education, your library may be able to provide access.

Ouchi's work on public schooling in the United States is frank about the need for a greater decentralization of funding and is worth reading as it tends to provoke extreme reactions from public managers (Ouchi, 2003). Charging is advocated by writers concerned with the public value movement (Moore, 1997) and an interesting discussion of the variation in public funding is provided by Jackson (2003).

6

Professionals in public management

Introduction

One of the key characteristics of public services is that they often make extensive use of professionals in the delivery of their services. Local government services have planners, hospitals have doctors (perhaps the most revered public service profession), schools have teachers and universities have academics. They are a distinctive part of public service organization, although of course not an exclusive one, as many of these professional groups work within the private sector as well.

Where public services have to be organized using professionals, it brings an additional level of complexity to their management. This chapter explores the challenges that professionalized services offer to public managers, raising questions of their relationship with both managers and users. It also examines the question of who should run public services – should it be managers brought in from the private sector or from other successful public services – suggesting that management is something of a generic skill? Should public services be run by the professionals themselves because of the specialist nature of their contribution to those services? Before it is possible to tackle these questions, however, it is important first to define what exactly professionals are, and to explore the implications of the dimensions of professionalism for those seeking to manage them.

The nature of professionalism

There is a well-established literature exploring professionalism going back to the 1950s and beyond in sociology, and which began by trying to explore the dimensions of professionalism to try and establish which groups could, and which could not, consider themselves to have professional status, noting the difficulties that public groupings such as nursing held in relation to their categories because of their lack of autonomy in the workplace. By the 1960s, work on professionalism became more critical, showing the potential the very autonomy and judgement that was held to be central to professionalism, had been sometimes been abused, especially in fields such as medicine, which has strong public service components (Coburn, 1992). In the 1970s, this theme was extended to explore how professionals fit in with the political economy of their countries and then to show how they compete with one another to create jurisdictional boundaries and areas they can put under their control (Abbott, 1988). In the 2000s, the focus has been on professional practices, exploring how professional judgements are made on the ground in interaction with those they are serving, with work becoming less overtly political (Sandberg & Pinnington, 2009).

In the public management literature, there is also an established literature base for considering the role of professionals in public services (Ackroyd, 1996, DiMaggio, 1991, Gillespie, 1997, Haug & Sussman, 1969, Kirkpatrick & Ackroyd, 2003, Klein, 1990, Wilding, 1982). This work has overlapping themes with the research on professionalism generally in that it is also concerned with the nature of professional work, the establishment of professional boundaries, and the difference that professional work makes for organizational life. A number of dimension of professionalism recur as being important to these questions. They are shown in Table 6.1 and discussed in greater depth below.

Professionals have expert knowledge

First, professionals have expert knowledge. This means that they have often been through long periods of training and have acquired high-level skills that are often not available to the general population. These skills might be based in the knowledge of complex laws, as with planners or those in the legal profession, or in the understanding of complex systems, such as the workings of the human body in medicine. Expert knowledge means that professionals have a special status in an organization and are able to argue that managers without their specialist knowledge cannot understand their work. How is a manager who lacks this expertise supposed to organize and direct a professional to do their work better when they do not necessarily understand the nature of the work? This is an age-old conundrum, but there are a few answers.

One way of dealing with the management of expert knowledge is for managers to measure not how work is done, but the outcomes or outputs of

Table 6.1 The dimensions of professionalism

Dimension	Problem to managers
Expert knowledge	They know things managers don't – so how can managers assess their work?
Socially powerful	They are often well connected and powerful – so how can managers challenge them if they face being overruled?
Autonomous	They are trained to work autonomously – so how can managers assess their performance?
Have confidential relationships with their clients	Their work often cannot be directly observed by managers, so how can they see if it is being done well or not?
Outputs difficult to measure	Their activities may be difficult to measure, so how can managers tell if it is being done well?
Have discretion over their work	Their actions are not programmable, so how can managers tell when professional decisions are poor ones?
Can do extraordinary things	If professionals have extraordinary powers, how do managers have legitimacy in challenging them?

the work, and to ask professionals to account for any significant differences between them and their peers. Where one surgeon has a very high success rate for a procedure, and another surgeon a low rate, this would seem to require an explanation. Where one planner appears to approve applications for development far more than another, there needs to be a reason for this difference.

The problem is that attempting to make professionals accountable this way may defer the problem of assessing expert knowledge from overseeing it as a process, to attempting to assess it as an outcome. Managers may not be able to assess whether the explanation given by the professionals for divergences in outcomes are sensible or not, as this too may depend upon expert knowledge.

Professionals can also be asked to assess the work of their peers; professionals might be given managerial roles and so be asked to oversee other professionals, or regular reviews put in place where teams brought in to assess the quality of work independently. In higher education, academics are regularly asked to peer review one another's work, and in medicine to participate in reviews of clinical cases to see what might be learnt from them.

Where professionals are asked to take on managerial roles, it can create conflicts for them where they believe the two are coming into tension, and in such circumstances they tend to revert back to their professional identity (Kitchener, 2000). This is hardly surprising – professionals will often be seeking to return to work with their peers when they have moved on from their managerial role, and so not wish to create problems for themselves later on by challenging their professional peers unnecessarily. Equally, having been inducted and trained as a professional, it is asking a lot to require that person to adopt a managerial identity and perhaps even to challenge the assumptions and basis of their own training.

When asked to review other professionals' work, there is a danger that the norms and standards used would not be those that managers or service users would wish. In that case, professionals might review one another's work and reach conclusions that appear bizarre to those outside of their grouping. Medical regulation procedures, for example, sometimes lead to doctors being allowed to continue to practice by their peers, while user groups campaign outside hearings for their licenses to be removed, often with the media making inflammatory contributions, professional hearings and reviews are accused of being 'old boys clubs', which are designed more to protect professionals than to prevent bad decision being made or harm to users occurring, and public misunderstandings abound (Tallis, 2005).

In the situation in which peer reviews are producing results that look odd outside of the professional grouping, managers are often caught between the demands of users for professionals to be removed and the demands of professionals that their colleagues be protected from media circuses or from unjustified complaints. This kind of dispute highlights the question of who should have the final say in how services are run – should it be service users, expert professionals, politicians, or managers attempting to get services to work as a whole? All these problems have their roots in the observation that professionals hold expert knowledge, and so it is extremely difficult for those not trained in that knowledge to hold them to account.

Professionals are socially powerful

The second key characteristic is that professionals often come from extremely well-connected backgrounds. In more recent times, professional groupings have become far more diverse than in the past, with increased educational mobility meaning that professionals are more likely than ever to come from both genders and from a range of ethnicities. However, they are still most likely to come from the middle classes of a society, from the ethnic group that is economically dominant within it, and to have the opportunity to form links with other powerful people through their training, which is often at prestigious universities. Professionals may then not only have their professional status to exert influence but also have attended the same schools (or at least the same universities) with others from their own and other professional groupings, and are likely to have been educated with other powerful figures (particularly politicians). Equally, professional groupings tend to have their own representative organizations having high-level access to politicians and other important decision-makers because of their social background and professional importance.

The leaders of professional organizations may regard themselves as having a right to contribute not only to the running of their own organizations but also towards national policy formulation and to government debates around their professional area. They may also expect to able to lead and participate in high profile media campaigns against the government of the day where they believe that their particular public service is not being well supported. Some professional groups, such as doctors, will be able to make these claims rather more strongly than others because of their public popularity and ability to generate stories that will be interesting to the media (with headlines of the type 'health services in crisis say leading doctors').

The social status of professionals hold means that public managers will find them to be powerful supporters but extremely difficult opponents. Professionals can often be strong allies where managers are seen to be supporting the profession's interest, but where they are challenging it, they can find themselves attacked in the media, by professional organizations, and even subject to legal challenge. Where legal action is threatened and management decisions are brought under the scrutiny of well-organized and influential professional bodies, managers who dare to challenge professional behaviour, or who threaten to remove professionals they perceive as under-performing, may find themselves under considerable pressure to reconsider their position.

Professionals are autonomous

The next characteristic of professional groupings is autonomy. Professional autonomy is based on a model of practice where professionals are regarded as having confidential relationships with their clients where they utilize their expert knowledge and make judgements about what is best for their clients, and means that they are often able to work remarkably autonomously from the organizations that employ them.

Professionals have often organized themselves into hierarchies separate from managerial lines of control on the basis of their professional ranking.

The most extreme version of this occurs in healthcare where a doctor's position in the medical hierarchy locates them in relation to other doctors in a way that is often entirely separate from any managerial considerations. Doctors who take management positions may even be regarded as failures by their peers, viewed as having opted out of the medical hierarchy because they are unable to be successful there, and so that they must be second-rate doctors as a result. In India, it is not unknown for doctor-managers not to tell their families they have taken on managerial roles, so strong is the prejudice against those choose to work outside of their professional area.

Professionals then expect considerable autonomy in their work. They may regard managers as being irrelevant or irritating bureaucrats who don't understand the nature of professional work, and even where the managers are practising professionals, they may be thought of as traitors or failures for 'crossing-over', with what matters their position in professional hierarchies. Many doctors have little or no respect for managers. Two solutions to this problem present themselves: for managers to show their ability to support doctors and build relationships of trust or to challenge doctors and confront their prejudices.

Where managers attempt to work with clinicians, they often frame their role in terms of attempting to help professionals overcome barriers to them achieving success. They might achieve this by perhaps showing them how their budgets might be managed better to reach higher professional standards, or by reorganizing work so that the professionals are given greater space to pursue their goals. If doctors engage with managers on these terms, it effectively reinforces professional autonomy, but at the same time may get professionals to regard managers as people to be worked with rather than enemies, and may foster trust and so eventually an ability to work together. This is very much a long-term project, however, and in public organizations where managers may change their jobs frequently, far more frequently than the professionals they must work with, it can be extremely difficult to achieve. Managers who have been in post for a number of years, however, often have reached mutual agreements with professional groupings where they have come to work closely together.

A second strategy is simply to try and exert managerial authority over professionals. This is likely to lead to a great deal of unpleasantness and requires the strong support of those in charge of the organization as an active human resources department to make sure that any challenges are legal and enforceable. This second approach is increasingly being used as professionals have their job descriptions standardized, and as their performance is increasingly tightly measured. However, one obvious downside is that it is trying to make relationships more straightforward in the future by causing conflict today. This requires a long-term commitment from both the managers challenging the professionals and the senior managers of the organization. If this commitment falters, or if professionals being to win appeals against managerial decisions, then managers may find that they are able to exert influence neither through trust nor through authority. Under these circumstances, a severely dysfunctional organization is likely to be the result. In hospitals and universities, professional groups have launched campaigns to have senior managers sacked, using all of their influence and power to disrupt board meetings and organize votes of no confidence.

Professionals often have confidential relationships with their clients

A fourth important aspect of professionalism, and related to their autonomy, is the confidential relationship professionals often have with their clients. Again law and medicine represent the archetypes of this, but it is also found in other settings. In this situation, managers may find themselves in a situation where it is extremely difficult to examine a professional's work, no matter how bad their performance is suspected to be, as the professional can argue that they are not able to discuss their confidential relationships with individual clients. If managers can neither measure nor control what occurs between a professional or a user, it is difficult to establish whether it is being done well (or badly).

There are various means for attempting to deal with the problem of confidentiality. One is for professionals, respecting both expert knowledge and confidentiality, to have their work overseen by other professionals who are able to view professional performance first hand in a way a manager cannot. This, however, can lead to accountability structures where professionals can engage in mutual favours (if you assess me, I'll assess you) rather than creating the opportunity for genuine performance feedback to be given. Equally, managers may still find themselves completely excluded from the process, and that the peer-review processes are extremely frustrating if not taken seriously by those involved in it.

Again similarly to the strategy suggested above for dealing with expert knowledge, an alternative means of addressing the confidential relationship is for managers to measure not individual cases, but the results of several cases and to ask for individuals to be held to account (by either themselves or their professional group) for cases that appear to be statistically or substantively unusual. If a particular doctor takes five days to discharge patients where others seem to take three, this might need some investigation to see if resources are being deployed appropriately. Managers might go further than this, calling multidisciplinary teams together to examine cases notes of users who have been anonymized (so not breaching confidentiality) to see if anything can be learned from those cases and improvements made in the future. This can be supportive if professionals believe that the process is about learning and improvement rather than allocating blame. However, where everyone on the panel knows, despite the anonymity in the case notes, exactly which case they are talking about and who the professional involved was, this process clearly fails and can degenerate into being perceived by professionals as a personal attack. High-profile medical cases tend to fall into this category, where despite case notes having all personal details removed, all the participants in the review know exactly which patients is really being talked about, and who the doctors involved were. As such, the pretence of removing confidentiality is removed, and a more difficult situation emerges. In cases such as this, and where high-profile problems have emerged, there is clearly a need for managers to approach reviews far more carefully, and to bring in reviewers with no personal ties to the case to make sure that the process is as independent and objective as possible.

Professional outputs are difficult to measure

The difficulty of measuring the 'output' of public professionals has been mentioned several times in this book already. If public managers find themselves in the unenviable position of being able to measure neither the process through which professionals engage with their service users (because of expert knowledge and confidentiality) or their output (because it is so difficult to measure), then the management role appears to be more about trying to motivate and support their professional peers than trying to control and measure their performance. This seems to have been largely the role associated with the old public administration approach that has been so under fire since the 1980s. Of course, this is something of a simplification – there are means of examining the processes involved in professional's interactions with clients and there are at least some measures of their outputs, even if they are imperfect. The problem comes, as Chapter 9 suggests, is in trying to choose indicators that capture the nature of the particular service rather than allowing what can be measured to dominate what the service comes to be about. It is relatively easy to measure waiting lists, but they may not be a good indicator of the performance of the agency for which people are waiting.

Professionals have discretion in their work

Perhaps the defining feature of professionalism, however, is that professionals have discretion in their work. This is crucial because it is the claim that professional practice is not just about expert knowledge or confidential relationships, but, in addition, it is the application of professional judgement to the particular situation. Professionals come up with solutions that, in information systems terms, are not 'programmable' – they are a mix of knowledge, existing evidence, experience, but also perhaps instinct and gut feeling. Such complex decisions are not easily captured in the terms that allow them to be replicated by machine – the relationship between decision and inputs is not always easily explained. As decisions get more complex and where the variables within them become more interrelated, the need for professional discretion grows ever greater. This has a range of implications for public managers.

First, it creates 'wriggle room' for the occasional public professional who wishes to try and opt out of management systems by simply arguing that his or her work is too complex to be assessed because they must be able to retain their discretion in order to be able to retain their professional identity. This chapter has already looked at several ways in which this difficulty can be overcome, but they will all involve public managers putting themselves in the position of having to ask question, which professionals may prefer not to answer. However, just because professionals have discretion, it does not mean that they do not have to be accountable. Some public professionals have used their expert knowledge and professional discretion to allow themselves to be unaccountable in their work (Marquand, 2004), but this position is getting harder and harder to sustain. Public managers have to find ways of ensuring that professionals are accountable without resorting to mindless target setting and bullying, or attempting to standardized their work to a point where professional judgement is no longer trusted. Professional work is difficult to measure and can occur in confidential settings through the application of complex judgements – but this does not mean that those decisions should be unaccountable.

Professionals are extraordinary

The next characteristic of professionals is their ability to often be able to do something extraordinary, or at least, because of their position in society, to be positioned so that certain tasks are only accomplishable with their help. The clearest case of this is that of the doctor – few other groups can literally save lives. Modern medicine can appear almost magical at times, being able to bring sight to the blind and to intervene to bring people back from the most horrendous injuries and illnesses to have reasonably normal lives again. This means that doctors often top opinion polls measuring the most trusted groups in society. Equally, however, other professionals gain considerable power from their ability to be the only ones who can make particular things happen. It is extremely difficult to pursue a legal case without a solicitor or barrister (although not impossible) and businesses may find their future plans hanging on the decision made by a town planner.

Professionals often hold considerable power; be that over life and death, or over the future. They can therefore do extraordinary things. The role of public managers in this relationship is, again, to try and make sure that accountability comes with this power. Many readers will have come across doctors who have perhaps become a little too aware of their power over life and death, and have so become rather arrogant and patronizing. Academics sometimes seem to want to judge student work in a cursory way, and react angrily when their grades are challenged. It is perfectly possible to have the powers of a professional without needing to belittle others who do not hold them. Public managers need to get professionals to keep their feet on the ground, and despite their extraordinary powers, to remember that they are dealing with the hopes and fears of human beings. The very best professionals, no matter how exalted in their standing, tend not to lose sight of this. For the cases where professionals believe they have become a law unto themselves, managers clearly need to find ways of intervening.

Professionals are self-regulating

Finally, professionalism is often associated with self-regulation. This means that professionals often regard themselves as being held to account in the first instance by their professional association rather than the organization they happen to work for. Doctors will be allowed to practise as the result of their membership of a professional body, which can refuse them their right to practise if they are found to be dangerous or incompetent. This decision is not taken by the organization employing the doctor, but by a separate regulator such as the American Medical Association or the General Medical Council of the British Medical Association. If a doctor is removed from the list of practitioners, his or her employer will probably also have to sack the member of staff concerned because they will be unable to carry out their duties, but it is unusual for the organization concerned to take permanent action against a member of staff before their own regulatory body has met to decide their future. An organization might suspend that member of staff, but not dismiss them until the regulatory body has made its recommendation. Were a professional to be sacked by a public organization and then subsequently cleared by their professional body, it would probably lead to a claim of substantial damages by the member of staff affected.

Self-regulation allows professionals to settle their disputes 'internally', but can also cause problems. Where a professional is cleared of wrongdoing by its own regulatory body, but there are numerous user complaints about that individual, should managers side with the regulatory body and support their member of staff, or side with the users and still attempt to dismiss them? In this situation, it is not unusual for further investigations to be made and for issues around professional competence to drag on for very long periods of time indeed, often with the member of staff suspended on full pay. This may be occasionally necessary, but it is clearly not a good use of public money to employ an expensive professional and to not allow him or her to fulfil his or her duties.

Given the many difficulties that professional status seems to cause, this leads us to the question – if professionals are so difficult to control, who should manage them?

Who should manage professionals? Should managers manage professionals, or should professionals manage themselves?

A recurring problem in the above analysis is trying to work out who should be in charge of professionals. There are three generic answers to this.

Putting managers in charge of professionals

Option one is for public managers, trained primarily as managers, to be put in charge of professionals. This means that management takes place independent of the professionals present in the service. The advantage of this is that managers will be able to bring a different set of priorities to the process of organizing the public service, being grounded in different thinking, and creating the opportunity for a wider discussion of the issues before the organization than is likely to otherwise take place. Managers may believe that they can better act on behalf of the public interest if they do not come from the same background as the professionals they are placed in charge of (but professionals will often dispute this – who speaks for the public is an extremely contentious topic), and be better able to represent the public interest than professionals who may have a vested interest in preserving the status quo.

However, this approach has the potential to lead to conflict. If managers are being brought in especially because they have a different background to doctors, and because they are there to represent users to create changes to services, then they are creating the potential for disputes over who is best placed to run public organizations. Professionals may regard managers as being ignorant of the complexities of their work, not fit to be placed in charge of them, and refuse to co-operate with managers or even campaign to have them removed. Managers may be left wondering after every meeting with professional groups exactly what it is they have done wrong to be so roundly attacked when all they wanted to do was to try and make things better.

Putting managers managing alongside professionals

The alternative logic of putting managers into public organizations is that they work alongside professionals rather than trying to be in charge of them, in line with the professional support role envisaged by the public administration approach. The irony in that approach pointed out by some of the leading British writers in public management (Harrison *et al.*, 1990) is that it positions managers in what, according to management theory, is a remarkably contemporary, facilitation-type role, at exactly the time it became unfashionable in the public sector. In the coach or facilitator role of public management, a distributed leadership approach is taken by attempting to get behind those that deliver services to users rather than get on top of them (Conger & Kanungo, 1998). This is not to say that public managers adopting this role is not without its problems – a brief review of the problems of managing professionals will make clear that this is far from the case (see above). However, it does suggest that management thinking can often be as much a function of prevailing fashion as it is about 'what works' (Greener, 2005c).

Professionals managing professionals

The alternative to managers managing professionals is that professionals take over the job. Perhaps the clearest expression of this came in the National Health Service (NHS) Management Inquiry of the early 1980s where the Chairman of a successful supermarket was asked to examine how the NHS could be better managed, and went as far as suggesting that doctors were the 'natural' managers of the health service (Department of Health and Social Security, 1983). If professionals can be persuaded to see the problems of their organizations from perspectives other than their own, placing a high priority upon financial responsibility and user responsiveness, and can be persuaded to become accountable for their decisions, there is no reason why this cannot work.

The difficulty is that the transition to this position can often be a difficult one, with many professionals believing that thinking in a managerial way undermines or compromises their professionalism. This is unfortunate and unnecessary. There are clearly flash points around which services will always have to navigate (professionals having to navigate the problem of providing services within fixed budgets for the collective rather than according to the need of the individual client before them, for example), but these problems are unavoidable, and surely it is better they are thought about and confronted rather than being labelled as being about either managerial or professional intransigence?

Where professionals are able to understand perspectives other than the one native to their own training, however, they can find the process of 'selling' change to their professional peers to be rather debilitating, being seen to have 'gone native' as a manager by the professionals and regarded with some distrust by other managers as a former professional. In these circumstances, it is hardly surprising that many professional managers regard themselves as professionals first and managers second, and that in situations of conflict between the two roles, professional identities tend to reassert themselves.

In all, when managers attempt to tell professionals what to do, even though they may have the authority on paper, this is likely to lead to conflict. Professionals may spend their entire careers working for a particular organization and regard newly appointed managers as underqualified and ignorant of the realities of running public organizations. The administrative approach of supporting professionals has much to commend it but may fail to hold professionals to account, and this lack of accountability detracts from the legitimacy of public organizations and may lead to public managers being positioned so that professionals are forced to report to them. Finally, there is the option of professionals managing professionals, but the danger that professionals taking on this role will be isolated from their peers, or that they will simply side with them whenever a conflict situation appears. Given the lack of clarity over who should manage professionals, is there at least an answer to the question of to whom they should be accountable?

To whom should professionals be accountable?

The question of accountability is a key for public services. To whom should professionals be accountable? Several answers suggest themselves, but perhaps the four most likely will be discussed here: to managers; to service users; to their peers; and to politicians.

Accountability to managers

Holding professionals accountable to managers does not necessarily mean that managers have to be placed in line-control relationships with the professionals. It does mean, however, that professionals are required to report back on their activities and to be scrutinized in relation to them. Because of the specialist and confidential nature of professional work, its results are often easier to examine than its processes, and, Chapter 9 make clear, it is often difficult to find appropriate measures on which to base these results. Even so, given the huge amount of information now connected in relation to public sector performance, identifying professionals who are outliers (both good and bad) and expecting them to account for their results seems to be reasonable. It is also possible to examine feedback results from users and to ask professionals to account for poor feedback ratings, or for poor results from peer-review processes.

Examining performance and feedback results for statistically significant deviations from output or outcome measures allows managers to argue that they are not victimizing particular professionals but are instead using objective measures to identify good and poor performance and requiring professionals to account for their activities. Capturing both good and bad performance is still political in that the boundary of the category labelled as 'bad' will still need to be decided, and will be open to contestation, especially activity is primarily linked to financial measures (Broadbent & Laughlin, 2002) instead of elements professionals might regard as more important, such as public service.

Once it has been established that particular professionals' outcomes present a case that needs answering, both professionals and managers will need to work out an action plan to either try and avoid the problem from occurring in the future, or to provide an adequate explanation for the deviation that both professionals and managers can accept. Despite its contentious and difficult nature, the process can at least give managers some legitimacy for asking professionals questions about accountability, and give them a route into a more regular dialogue that has often been missing in the past. Managers can try and position themselves as being part of a multidisciplinary team put in place to examine unusual outcome results, and who take the lead in organizing a response to the findings of reviews, as well as putting forward action points, hopefully with the support of professionals, for how the difficulties will be resolved.

Accountability to service users

Making professionals accountable to service users suggests another different approach. In this situation, accountability systems will attempt to try and achieve direct or indirect accountability. Direct accountability is where professionals regularly meet the representatives of service users face to face to discuss their concerns, and to attempt to agree in consultation with users what needed to be done as a result. This is most common perhaps in local government where representative hold open meetings for the public to attend, or in education where teachers or lecturers will meet regularly with student representatives, as well as inviting them to committee meetings so that they can contribute directly to the running of their university. Indirect accountability is where professionals are required to respond to the feedback taken from service users through surveys or complaints. In this case, an intermediary will be necessary to record the professionals' response and to pass it on to user representatives to make sure that, where necessary, something is done in response to user concerns.

In either case, making professionals accountable to users means a different form of responsiveness compared to the outcome approach where professionals are accountable to managers. In the latter case, user feedback will be one aspect of the way that professional performance is measured, but will be combined with other outcome measures that are appropriate to try and get a fuller view of performance. In the case, where user accountability is favoured, different elements are likely to become more important such as politeness and friendliness (nurses sometimes complain of face pain from smiling all day in this type of regime (Bolton, 2001)), with the inherent danger that incompetent professionals with nice dispositions can be favoured over their brilliant peers with fewer social skills. Good public service requires a mix of both professional and personal skills, but most of us would still probably prefer to be cured by a surly doctor than made more ill by his polite colleague.

Balfour and Grubbs (2000) suggest that, when made accountable to individual service users rather than collective publics, civil servants become focused on a continuous quest for change and innovation rather than providing good services. They suggest that the 'values of the marketplace must be balanced with other values such as equity, justice and human dignity' (p. 581), reminding us of earlier debates about public service values, but also pointing to the difficulties of identifying exactly who public professionals should be accountable to.

Accountability to other professionals

Making professionals accountable to other professionals has been the means most often taken in public services. In this model, professionals are accountable through disciplinary mechanisms that come through self-regulation, through professional development and updating, through internal promotions procedures, through anonymized case reviews, or through peer review.

The disciplinary mechanism model usually only applies to cases where allegations of incompetence have been made of a professional, and the regulative body responsible for that group has decided that there is a case to answer. This is a form of accountability designed to prevent incompetent practitioners from being allowed to practice, but does little for the vast majority of practitioners that are between the extremes of competent and brilliant. Where professions have development commitments they must meet to re-register to show they are keeping their skills up to date, this puts in place some basic safeguards that appeal to the professional's sense of pride, but clearly attending an updating meeting is very different from understanding all that goes on within it. If disciplinary hearings are meant to address incompetent practitioners, personal development and skills updating are meant to try and prevent practitioners from becoming out-of-date in the first place.

If the emphasis moves away from incompetence and its prevention, then there may be an attempt to try and reward good behaviour through promotions procedures. In this case, professionals will often review the work of other professionals to see if they are worthy of better pay or more elevated position. The academic world offers itself as a model here, where tenure or promotion to a higher grade is usually based upon the member of staff being able to demonstrate expertise to his or her peers. This may be through high teaching scores (often measured through student feedback, but also through peer review) but is more likely to come through achieving grants and peer-reviewed journal articles in prestigious publications. Peer review of grants and research means that work is scrutinized by other academics, and it is then other academics that judge the importance of the publications – a kind of double academic review, or double accountability. Promotions are given to staff judged to have achieved good publications in highly rated journals, and those that do not achieve this asked to try again. Staff graded as poorly performing by these criteria may even have to face performance reviews where they fail to meet minimum standards of achievement.

Professional to professional accountability can also be achieved through case reviews. Professionals here, often brought in from outside of the institution, or at least the department, under review, come and go through the anonymized notes pertaining to a particular case to try and see if there is anything to be learned from them, or at worst, whether there were failing in procedures or judgement from the professionals involved. In hospitals, particular kinds of death are subject to this kind of review routinely, with a panel being convened made up primarily of other doctors, although other professional groups and managers may also be involved, to try and work through the circumstances leading to the death. There are good reasons for this activity; it can foster learning and try and improve handling of difficult cases for the future. But in addition to this, it can also protect the institution from subsequent legal claims against it by demonstrating that the organization is serious about reviewing its processes and procedures, and that it is taking action to try and achieve the best possible outcomes for service users.

Peer review is perhaps the most common form of professional to professional accountability, and can take a number of forms. Peer review of work has already been mentioned in relation to academic promotions criteria above, but any professional work that produces work that might be assessed can be reviewed in this way. Where it is more difficult to assess a final object, peer review will typically take the form of assessing process; so for academics, their research can be assessed as an object in terms of their research papers and books, but their teaching will usually be peer reviewed as it happens as it does not produce as clear an end object.

Political accountability

Finally, there is political accountability. Politicians are elected in order to represent their citizens, and to represent their views. As such, political accountability is a kind of democratic accountability, albeit an indirect one. Most public organizations have a strong political element in that elected politicians may be given the specific role of overseeing a particular service, or in some states there may be elections held to decide who runs particular public services. In the first case, the aim of the politician may be to improve the service, but according to public choice theorists, it may also be to maximize the opportunities for both public managers and politicians (Boyne *et al.*, 2003). Reasoning that public managers often progress by showing they are effective, and politicians become popular by demonstrating they have improved public services for the better, the public choice view suggests that public managers will be trying to demonstrate effectiveness, even if what they do is not necessarily in the interest of the service they are managing. Equally, politicians will want to demonstrate improvements in public services in order to achieve a bigger and better portfolio to try and get a more important job.

The public choice view presents a rather cynical view of the motivations of public managers and politicians, but gets at a human universal in that we are all prone to responding to the incentives we find before us. Public managers may be as much interested in creating the illusion of success (engaging in gaming or even misrepresentation, see Chapter 9) as success itself, and politicians may be keen for them to do so, as this might mean, in turn, that they too are judged to be performing well. What the public choice view highlights is that political accountability can lead to a range of perverse incentives for managers, politicians, and professionals if those incentives are not designed well.

One of the main perverse incentives affects the time horizons of both public managers and politicians. In cases where officials are elected to run particular public services, the electoral cycles will mean that they will often want to make as much difference as possible, as quickly as possible. This can lead to an incentive structure in politics where periods of frantic change occur, followed by periods where services settle back down (perhaps also punctuated by an attempt to secure quick improvements before the election, in-line with the theory of the 'political' business cycle). Similarly, public managers may face some difficult choices between short-term maximization in order to satisfy their elected official leaders, and long-term maximization, which they might deem to be in the best interests of the service. If they adopt the second view, they risk being portrayed as having 'gone native', and may come to regard themselves as the guardian of the service, attempting to shield it from the whims of political masters.

As such, there are a range of different means of achieving greater accountability for public professionals, but they all carry with them particular problems. The question of how professionals should be accountable is not quite as difficult as the one of who should manage them, but is still far from straightforward.

Public professionalism
after the financial crisis

The discussion above makes clear that managing professionals can often be a central part of public management, but one which is extraordinarily challenging.

The financial crisis has led to two clear tendencies that are relevant to this discussion – large reductions on expenditures on public services and closer scrutiny of how money is being spent. Let's deal with each in turn.

First, the financial deficits described in Chapter 5 have led to countries having to come up with deficit reduction plans. These plans impose, from above, cuts in public services. In the United Kingdom, around 700,000 public sector jobs are being lost and inevitably, some of those will fall on public professionals. Professionals therefore face challenges to the idea of having a lifelong career in public service, and certainly will have to be rethinking assumptions about job security. This has to change the dynamic of relations between professionals and other public groupings such as managers.

Secondly, public professionals are facing themselves under even greater scrutiny. In a time of financial austerity, savings must be made and efficiencies are being demanded. In the United Kingdom, for example, a £20bn efficiency saving is demanded from the NHS, which puts local managers and clinicians under pressure to look at their processes and find ways of saving considerable sums of money whilst minimizing disruption to patients. Economists' studies of cost-effectiveness, productivity and efficiency are being discussed in the newspapers and wider media as demonstrating either improvements or the need for reorganization. Professionals are finding themselves having to engage with these views in public forums to defend themselves in ways that would have been unthinkable 30 years ago.

In either case, however, the main reorganizational challenge to professionals comes through the continued roll out of market mechanisms into public services. Markets challenge professionals because they position service users as customers who are to be given choices and anticipate their expectations about service levels to be met or exceeded. If the essence of professionalism is autonomy and judgement, then consumerism suggests that it is not professionals who should be sovereign, but those they are providing services to. Regardless of whether the increased marketization of public organization leads to improved efficiency or productivity, and the evidence on this is very mixed, the lasting challenge will be in the way it recasts relationships between professionals and service users.

Conclusion

The central paradox of dealing with professionals in public management is that professionals often don't regard their primary responsibilities to be the organization that employs them, but to their clients and to their professional grouping. However, we need professionals to take decisions within a resource context that takes account of decision making within a collective frame, and to be democratically accountable to the collective public as well individually accountable to their users and to their professional organizations.

Professionals are a distinctive part of a great deal of public service provision, but there are significant problems in answering both who should manage them, and to whom they should be accountable.

The nature of professionalism means that they have expert knowledge, that they are socially powerful, that they are autonomous, that they often have confidential relationships with their clients, that their outputs are difficult to measure, that they have discretion in their work, that they are capable of extraordinary things, and that they are self-regulating. All of these aspects of professionalism create particular challenges for public managers as it means they are often dependent upon professionals to deliver the service, but may find it difficult, without the professional's co-operation, to influence the way the service is delivered directly.

The question of who should manage professionals has three generic answers. Managers can try and take on the role, but professionals have often strongly resisted this, and because of their autonomy and self-regulation, they have often been able to insulate themselves from managerial reforms. If managers work alongside professionals, this provides a compromise answer, but this goes against contemporary ideas in public management based around managers being the leaders of their organizations. Finally, professionals can try and manage other professionals, but stepping outside of their professional role, especially in times when managerial and professional agendas conflict, can be extremely difficult.

The question of to whom professionals should be accountable is also a difficult one to provide a straightforward answer to. Accountability to managers can possibly be best achieved where managers and professionals work together, but this can be seen to be working against contemporary new public management ideas. Making professionals accountable to service users has much to commend it, but carries with the danger of confusing popularity with high professional standards, when the two may not at all be the same. Achieving accountability to other professionals can be achieved through a number of means, but with the concern that professionals will tend to protect their own rather than conform to management reforms where a potential conflict occurs. Public professionals are all politically accountable in some way or another as their salaries are often paid for by public funds, and carry with it the problem of the public choice critique that combining self-seeking professionals with self-seeking politicians is a recipe for public services being run badly.

Public management of professionals

As the main concern of this book is with public management, some kind of conclusion about the relationship between public managers and professionals is needed. The dynamics of the likely relationships can be summarized in a grid that considers the possibilities where the status of managers and professionals are strong and weak, respectively. This will be, to some extent, culturally specific as the standing of managers and professionals varies between countries, but some generalizations can be made. The combination of the strength of professional and management groups gives a situation a 'situational' logic (Archer, 1995) that does not determine what happens, but does create a tendency towards a particular kind of relationship that may be difficult on either side to overcome. These logics are summarized in Table 6.2.

Where there are weak management groups and weak professional groups, neither will find it straightforward to challenge the inherited organizational

Table 6.2 Relationships between managers and professionals

	Weak professional group (poor organization, gender bias, e.g. nursing)	Strong professional group (highly organized, highly educated, e.g. lawyers/barristers)
Weak management group (low status, low qualifications).	Inertia – neither group able to challenged inherited organization.	Professionals dominate and self-organize.
Strong management group (higher status, higher professional qualifications).	Management able to challenge professional power and organize professionals around their agenda.	Two scenarios. Conflict – where neither group able to back down. Protection – where both groups acknowledge their mutually dependent status and work together.

form. This will tend to result in inertia, and tends to occur where professional groupings are not well regarded in the organization, and management is poorly organized. A situational context with weak managers and strong professionals will tend to mean that professionals dominate, with it being difficult manage them, or to make them accountable. This has often been the case within public management and is illustrated by the public administration approach that dominated for much of the post-war period. Where managers are strong but professionals are weak, then this will mean that professional expertise can be challenged and managerial agendas become dominant, unless the professionals become better organized. Finally, where there are both strong managers and strong professionals, this might lead to either continual conflict where neither group is prepared to back down, or to a situation where both groups seek to protect themselves, recognizing their mutual strength. In this situation, a kind of mutual respect can be possible where managers and professionals are prepared to work alongside one another.

Professionals often have high status for good reason – they have expertise that means that they are able to do things that those without their training, knowledge, and accreditation simply cannot. Professional power can lead to abuse – we will all have met lawyers or doctors who seem to have forgotten they are there to provide the public with a service, and instead regard their clients with disdain. It is, therefore, necessary both that public professionals are managed and that they are accountable.

There are, however, no simple answers as to the best way to achieve either of these goals. The answers most likely to work will depend on the context within which professional work occurs, how well organized and respected managers and professionals are, and the extent to which relationships can be recast into ones of mutual respect rather than suspicion and opposition. Managers have to understand that professionals need to exercise their judgement, and that professionals' decisions cannot be broken down into simple input–output measures of performance, but professionals understand that if their practice suggests they are statistical outliers, then they must be prepared to account for the reasons why that appears to be the case. Public professionals also have to respect the fact that they need, in the final analysis, to be accountable to the collective public that they serve – public organizations, to hold legitimacy, need to achieve democratic accountability, and where a public service depends on its professionals to provide a service, then those professionals have to be expected to be held to account. Holding public professionals to account democratically is more complex and difficult than assuming they are providing a service to a consumer but is surely a more constructive way of casting the dilemmas of managing professionals in public service than to lose the defining features of professionalism – autonomy and judgement – in the name of marketization.

Case study – Managing doctors

As has already been mentioned in the chapter, the archetypal professionals are doctors and lawyers, and in the public sector, the growth in state provided healthcare in the twentieth century means that doctors have become hugely important public professionals.

Managing doctors presents a number of challenges for public managers. They belong to highly prestigious professional groupings such as the American Medical Association, or UK Royal Colleges and British Medical Association, meaning that they have access to peers in elevated social positions holding significant power. Winston Churchill's doctor, Lord Moran, was not only used to occupying the corridors of power but also of being in charge of doctor organizations. The organizational details present in the NHS Act of 1948 were largely the result of informal negotiations between Aneuran Bevan, the first post-war Minister of Health, and the Medical Lords, in the period leading up to the NHS Act (Rintala, 2003).

The relationship between the state and the medical profession in the United Kingdom has been characterized as a 'double bed', in which mutual dependence exists because the state needs the doctors to run the NHS and make difficult decisions about who gets cared for and in what order, and the doctors need the state because, with the creation of the NHS, it effectively became a monopoly employer of medical expertise (Klein, 1990). Although in other countries the state does not have the monopoly employer status, the double bed is a powerful metaphor for the way politicians and medical leaders have often worked together.

Managers enter the hospitals, the bastions of medical expertise, characterized as being 'corporate rationalizers' (Alford, 1972, 1975), put in place by the state to challenge the dominant interest, the doctors, to achieve greater efficiency and effectiveness with public funds. A variety of management tools and techniques have been employed by healthcare managers and the state to try and give them greater leverage. Management information systems have been used to scrutinize clinical performance, and ever more elaborate coding systems employed to try and measure clinical activity in greater and greater detail (Bloomfield & Best, 1992, Bloomfield & Coombs, 1992). Budgeting systems have been put in place to attempt to make clinicians aware of the resource implications of their decisions (Buxton & Packwood, 1991). HR practices have attempted to become more proactive to find ways of removing medics who do not conform to reform agendas or are shown to be poor performers through the new measures.

At the same time as this, however, managers have also found themselves increasingly scapegoated by the state for poor organizational performance (Greener & Powell, 2003) and come to regard the state's need to frequently reorganize health systems as 'redisorganization' (Smith & Walsh, 2001) in which they find managing increasingly hard as the parameters and structures they have to work in are continually changed. Instead of being rather one-dimensional figures, put in place by the state to act upon its agendas and close implementation gaps, healthcare managers are far more interesting figures, often having clear ideas of what needs to be done in their organizations out-side of central agendas, and having to make choices about what their priorities will be. They may even come to identify more with their local health organi-zation than with the national targets and goals set for them, and so become, in the state's eyes, as difficult to control as the professionals they were introduced to challenge in the first place.

At the same time as this, healthcare managers have found that the difficulties of managing professionals have led to them using a range of tactical behaviours that mean they are able to take decisions and implement government agendas where necessary, but avoid direct confrontation with medics. To this end, they may attempt to shape meeting agendas so they are able to carry votes over decisions unlikely to be popular with their clinician colleagues, and engage in other forms of 'negative power', where they try and control what is spo-ken about (and not spoken about) rather than trying to argue face to face with doctors. By doing this, they are able to restrict arguments to times and places where they have a chance of getting their own way (Greener, 2005a). Equally, the framing of many public management techniques as being objec-tive by the state means the use of performance management and budgeting can be presented by managers as being outside of their control and necessary evils rather than being attempts to move power relationships away from clinicians. Whether doctors accept these limitations, however, is open to question.

Doctors have also faced pressures from their patients to improve services, asking difficult questions of the nature of professionalism in even its most elite settings. Worryingly, Dent (2006) suggests that this can lead to a situa-tion where consumerism, because it leads to some patients becoming more demanding and less deferential to doctors, and to a situation where they may try and impose their own interests upon medical relationships, can lead to an undermining of trust in doctors more generally. Giving patients more choices over healthcare can therefore not to them being more satisfied with their care, but to greater disaffection (see also Bauman, 2007). In this situation, public managers have to find ways of challenging professionals to improve their services, but also accepting their expertise and not undermining public confidence in their ability to deliver it.

The extent to which government health reforms have created change over the last 20–30 years is difficult to assess. In the United Kingdom, budgetary pressures have led to hospital managers having to drive health reform faster than at any time in the NHS' history, and this has led to doctors rated as poor performing or surplus to requirements losing their jobs. Whether healthcare managers hold any greater power in the long term, however, remains to be seen (Peckham *et al.*, 2005).

Further reading

The classic studies of the relationship between healthcare managers and doctors in the United Kingdom are those conducted by Stephen Harrison, David Hunter, and Christopher Pollitt (Harrison, 1982), (Harrison, 1988, Harrison & Wistow, 1992, Harrison *et al.*, 1990, 1992). Equally, there are numerous studies of medical power, with perhaps those by Turner (1987), Illich (1977), and Ehrenreich (1978) offering the most powerful critiques.

7

The role of users in public services

Introduction

This chapter considers the roles the public can play in public services, linking particularly with Chapter 8, which considers the extent to which markets can be used in the public sector, and Chapter 6, which considers the role of professionals. It proceeds by first presenting the approach that has perhaps most influenced the New Public Management (NPM) – that public organizations should become more market-oriented, and by doing so, achieve accountability to individual service users in the same way that goods and service providers in the private sector are accountable to their customers. It then explores what a customer service-oriented approach would mean for public sector organizations, being especially concerned with the difficulties this raises for public service accountability.

The chapter then moves on to public participation, a more collective approach than the individualized, customer-service approach, considering the various means by which this is often attempted in public organizations. It considers the most recent attempts to influence user behaviour by incorporating insights from behavioural economics, often summarized as 'nudge' strategies, but suggests that the most successful ways for service users to participate in the running of public services might be through co-production or through 'collectivized individualism', where user voice is collected and acted upon rather more routinely than is often achieved at present. It concludes by considering the implications of the analysis for both marketing and public participation for public services.

Different individual public service user roles

To begin, it is worth reflecting on the different roles that users can take, as individuals, in relation to public services. These roles can be changed, and indeed it may be government policy to attempt to change them. However, the way that the service is organized, and the relationship with professional groups, both have a significant influence on the way that users are likely to be positioned in relation to public services.

As Table 7.1 suggests, when considering professional power and market provision, three positions reasonably straightforwardly arise. Users can be clients, which often puts them in a relatively passive relationship with professionals where the professionals set the standards for the interaction. This is likely to occur where the professional is working in a monopoly (so that the user has little choice in respect of whether to use the professional's services or not). Where professionals are strong, clients are effectively dominated by them, but even where professionals are relatively weak, in situations where they face a monopoly provider user voices might be very weak. An example of strong professionals in a monopoly might be senior doctors in a government-provided healthcare system (such as the UK NHS, at least until fairly recently), and weak professionals in a monopoly those working in a public benefits office. In the last case, the public professionals will largely have their agendas and work practices set by others so can be labelled as weak relative to senior doctors, but as they work for a monopoly they may still appear strong to their clients.

Where market provision exists, things begin to change. Users now, by definition, have choices. In this situation, they can expect their professionals to behave in a way that treats them differently from the passive client role – the professionals will show respect and courtesy, but still have expertise that the

Table 7.1 User roles in relation to professional power and type of governance

	Strong professionals	Weak professionals
Monopoly provision.	Users as clients of professionals (passive, professional-led).	Users as clients (passive, lack of discretion).
Market provision.	Users as customers of professionals (more active, can choose and change, but user may not be informed).	Users as consumers of professional services (active, choosing informed).

user needs. In a monopoly situation, the professional will treat the service user as a customer, being there to provide both advice and a service, but offering a standard of treatment and care probably above that of the passive client, expecting the user to have an opinion, which needs to be factored into the decisions that are made, and also with the user having the ability to choose another professional if they believe their needs are not being met. An example of this might be where the state provides legal advice to those who cannot afford it themselves, but with the state paying the bill on behalf of those clients, and so professionals having a monetary (as well as professional) incentive to provide good service.

Where professionals are not as strong, but market mechanisms exist, users may position themselves as consumers instead of customers. The key difference here is that the user will often be informed (or believe themselves informed) about the service, and may even be paying for the service themselves. In this case, with the consumer being both informed as possibly even paying, the professional is in a weaker position, and so the relationship has moved in favour of the user, or consumer. Professionals become far more required to provide the user with what they want, and, even though the professional may have expertise beyond that of the user, users are making decisions not only about which professional they want to use, but also believe that they can decide whether or not professionals are doing a good job. An example of this relationship can occur where an individual is receiving personal care at home. Here they may have the choice of several agencies or several care workers within a given agency, as well as specifying what services they require they will also be able to choose who provides them. The care workers that provide the service will often have expertise more than that of the user (and so, still occupy a professional role), but it is the user who decides whether or not to make use of that expertise. Whereas a care worker might think what is best for the user is to do some exercise, the user may overrule them and say they wish to be taken to the shops instead.

The public sector and customer focus

The common sense regarding user roles in public services with which this chapter began suggest that, as we move to more market-oriented modes of delivering public services, and as the population have grown more used to being consumers in other aspects of their lives, they increasingly position themselves as consumers of public services as well, demanding choice and greater flexibility from the service in terms of appointment times and speed of service. However, many of these principles run up against both profession-alism and the lack of expert knowledge in many public services means that users may not always be best placed to be making choices in relation to them, or even want to make those choice.

There may be good reasons for services being organized around a profes-sional focus rather than a user focus; doctors are a scarce resource as they take so long to train and their times is often in short supply when they have qualified. From an efficiency perspective, it may be better to organize patients around the doctor rather than vice versa, as this will allow more patients to be seen, creating a benefit for the system as a whole, as well as getting patients seen more quickly. Where the service professional represents the bottleneck or scarce resource in a system, there is certainly a case for the service to organize around him or her rather than the service users.

However, organizing services around professionals may require service users to have to wait for long periods, to find themselves turning up for appointments, which they share with several other users because this allows the professional to see more people. This can lead to service users feeling that their time is being wasted and that they are receiving disinterested, almost rude service from the professional when their turn eventually comes. What profes-sionals may regard as giving objective, efficient service may be interpreted by users as disinterested and rude. There seems to be at least something of a clash between an objective, efficient service, and an engaged, user-centred service (Newman, 2002). These can be made more apparent by considering the impli-cations of taking a consumer-led approach to organizing public services more generally.

It is also the case that professionals often have knowledge that the users of their services simply don't possess. One of the defining characteristics of professionalism is the expert knowledge it claims to have, and from which self-regulation and autonomy flow. The danger of consumerism is that it sug-gests that users are able to choose the right professional on their own terms, and this may simply not be the case. If I am asked to choose the best doc-tor, I may be able to look up data about user satisfaction or data concerning readmission rates after treatment or even mortality data (if I am able to find such data) but have little idea of how to interpret that data to make the best choice.

However, it is perfectly possible for public professionals to take a market-based attitude to service users, treating them as customers (in the terms presented above), even if there is no market structure in place. In such a sit-uation, the professional will be expected to make use of their expertise and experience, but the user also to be consulted, and for a joint decision about the best course of action to be taken. This treats both professionals and users with respect and leads to the idea of a customer-led one public service.

Taking a customer-led approach to public services

A customer-led approach to public services leads to a reconsideration of the way that professionalized, monopoly-based services are conceptualized and delivered. Instead of starting with the question 'how best can services be delivered to secure maximum possible efficiency from the professional?', instead 'how can services be organized to place the needs of the service user first?' is the guiding principle.

Table 7.2 shows the tension between services organized around professionals and those organized around a customer-focused approach. Public services are often associated with the attempt to provide a service that it is objective and fair, but often taking place under considerable time pressure, and with standards of service being assessed by the professional's peers. A customer-focused service, however, is geared towards the needs of service users instead, where professionals are expected to engage with them in a friendly and personal way that makes professionals' expertise available, but on users' terms. Appointments take place at a clearly defined time chosen by the user, and with users having a strong say in whether the service was delivered successfully or not. In many respects, it is a complete inversion of the public administration approach described in Chapter 3.

Amongst the tensions in Table 6.1 perhaps the most contentious is the last, whether professionals should have their work peer reviewed, that is assessed by other professionals, or whether the users of their services should be the arbiter

Table 7.2 Professional-organized services versus marketing-organized services

Professional-organized service	Customer-led service
Need of the professional (to be efficient within a scarce time resource)	Needs of the user (to receive high-quality professional service)
Objective service	Engaged service
Impersonal service	Personal service
Time pressure (because of the need to move on to next case)	Clearly defined appointment time (to allow full discussion of issues)
Peer review	User feedback

of what counts as good service. This debate is particularly important as it can lead to services being performance managed in entirely different ways. A professional who is acting in line with codes of conduct and standards drawn up by his or her peers may behave towards users in an entirely different way than one who is attempting to achieve the best possible feedback from end users. Teachers in the first instance, for example, might want to demonstrate depth of knowledge, evidence-based pedagogy, and class control, but if attempting to secure higher feedback might find themselves attempting to gear classes towards exam performance rather than learning, reducing complex ideas to bullet points, giving lots of handouts (usually electronically in today's classrooms) so students don't have to take notes, and allowing students to disrupt lessons for fear of reprisals that might come from criticizing them.

Of course, many good teachers are student-centred as well as excellent professionals, but there can be very definite conflicts that can come from the competing demands of trying to be both peer- and student-centred. Taking a customer-focused approach involves the considerable redesign of public services. Two examples will hopefully demonstrate, around a hospital and the home visit for an elderly patient from social care.

An X-ray appointment

A patient visiting a hospital for an X-ray is a useful case study. If this is designed from the professional's point of view, something along the following lines would tend to occur. First, the patient would be given an appointment time that fitted with the needs of the radiographers, and which would be regarded as offering only a generalized, one-way commitment from the hospital. The commitment would be for the patient to turn up at the time suggested, or risk not being X-rayed. However, this would not be a commitment from the hospital to X-ray the patient at that time – patients would be expected to wait if services were running behind schedule where emergencies had arrived, or if professionals felt that more urgent cases required earlier treatment. Next, patients would be required to wait in a shared area so that they could be called when their time came, and probably would have to change into hospital gowns upon arrival so that the radiographer did not have to wait for patients to change their clothes once the time came for them to be seen.

Changing areas would typically be very basic, as funding high-quality areas would be seen as an unnecessary waste of money that took away funds from the most important part of the service – the X-ray itself. When they were eventually seen, patients would be treated quickly and efficiently, but often without much courtesy, and patients who required reassurance and patience might find it in short supply. Where children required X-rays, they would expect to receive much the same service as adults, with it being up to parents to provide appropriate distractions both before and during the X-ray process to make sure that children did not disrupt the waiting facility or take up the radiographer's time by crying or refusing to have their X-ray taken.

After the X-ray was taken, the patient in either adult or child case would be told to get changed, and not given any feedback on the result, even if it was obvious to the radiographer, because this would take up more of the radiographer's time. Results would be communicated formally through a letter or by the patient seeing a doctor later on, often after having to arrange another appointment with another wait attached to it.

In contrast, a customer-focused approach would reverse most of the logic described above. Patients, upon needing an X-ray, would be able to ring the radiography department, expect to be seen at their convenience rather than the radiographer's, and to be able to turn up at the agreed time and be seen immediately. Appointment times would be adjusted to suit patients and extended or reduced, leading to the need for a far more flexible system for booking them within the department. Patients would expect to wait in a high-quality area with distractions for children if necessary (perhaps video games or at least non-broken toys and children's magazines). Patients would be given high-quality, private changing areas as it would be acknowledged that their dignity is important to the overall provision of the service. The X-ray itself, although the most important part of the service, would be seen as one component amongst many that leads to offering patients an excellent service. Patients might be pre-seen by a nurse to assess their needs, to explain what their X-ray composed of, and to provide reassurance and any other additional information as required. Children would probably be seen in a separate room, decorated to appeal to younger people, perhaps with a television showing something appropriate in a corner to distract the child from the X-ray itself.

After the X-ray was taken, a nurse would escort the patient back to the changing area and be on hand to answer any questions. The radiographer would then make him or herself available to give preliminary results and refer the patient on to whichever healthcare professional was appropriate for further care. Where patients required hospital transport to get home, this would also be organized as soon as the patient's appointment finished (or perhaps even earlier, in order to make sure that the patient was taken home without a delay).

The contrast between the two approaches is considerable. Individual readers will be able to consider which is closest to their own experience. The key point, however, is that it is the responsibility of the public manager to work out which model their service is currently providing, and to work out what its problems and drawbacks might be. There may be good reasons for favouring the professional-led model, but that will have trade-offs and tensions with the customer-focused view. Most X-ray departments, in practice, will produce parts of each version, but this does not detract from the tensions present within each element of the service delivery when considered from competing perspectives.

A home visit

A second example, this time from social care, will support this further. A home visit (in the case of an older person) can be a valuable support mechanism as it allows people to stay in their own homes for longer rather than being relocated to a home specializing in care for the elderly, and therefore allows greater independence and can be a valuable way of preserving dignity. This is not to say that elderly homes do not provide this, but that many people, given a choice, would prefer to remain in their own home if they are able to receive support to allow this happen.

A visit organized around a professional would occur at a prescheduled time with little or no consultation with the service user, and with no guarantee that it would occur at exactly that time. The user would be expected to be ready to receive the visit, which could cause stress and concern that sleeping or visiting the toilet might mean the visit is missed. The carer would not have telephoned again to let the client know they are on their way. The home visitor might never have met the older person before, as professional carers might regard their work as being substitutable for one another.

The visit would then be organized according to what the professional believed needed to be done, probably in line with standardized best practice, and would be efficiently organized to make sure that work is done in an accurate and clinical fashion. The visit would end when the home visitor needed to move to the next appointment, and a further appointment scheduled according to his or her professional expertise. The home visitor would then leave after making sure that their client is safe.

A customer-led view of the home visit would be where the visitor has been booked according to the schedule of the older person. This may have been at short notice, with the home visitor's organization making sure that spare capacity is available from their staff to make sure that this can happen. The home visitor would be expected to turn up at the agreed time, but with an open agenda as to what the visit will cover. The older person and home visitor will agree what needs to be done together, and there may be elements of care delivered by the visitor, but also more mundane tasks performed, such as a shopping trip or a visit to a friend, neither of which might be possible for the client alone if they are relatively immobile. The appointment might therefore need to be more open-ended, and the home visitor work organized flexibly on a 'pool' basis with appointments met by trained staff, who expect to fit around their clients' needs. Where clients require particular members of staff for continuity of care, or where they have specifically requested them by name, they may have to wait a little longer, but when the home visitor sets off to visit they will ring the older people to let them know they are on the way and be given an estimated arrival time. The visit ends when the requirements of the older person have been met, and when he or she is back safely in his or her own home, having had the agreed goals for the visit met. A further appointment might then be arranged at a mutually agreeable time, or via a telephone call at a later date to the home visit organization.

Again, the contrast here is great. Home care delivered by professionals will be more flexible if user-led, both in terms of time and in terms of the type of care delivered. Professionals may feel that supporting users to go for shopping or to visit friends is demeaning to their skills, but if that is the type of support the user needs, then a marketing view would dictate that this is the type of care that should be delivered.

The customer-focused view of public organization then places the needs of the user at the centre of organization, rather than the needs of professionals (be they doctors, social care workers or managers). It becomes the role of managers to make sure that services are reorganized on this basis, and to survey users to make sure that their needs are met.

Difficulties with the customer-focused perspective in public organizations

There are a range of dilemmas that come from the customer-focused view that public managers need to find answers they are comfortable with.

First, where service users demand an unreasonably high level of service, what should managers do? If public managers are responsible for refuse collection, for example, and users suggest that daily collections are most appropriate as that level of service would remove the need for them to store unhygienic and unpleasant rubbish outside of their homes, should they go along with this request? The subject of how often rubbish should be collected from people's homes is a universally contentious one. In the United Kingdom, attempts to move rubbish collection from a weekly to a two-weekly basis have proven unpopular, even when local authorities have attempted to justify the service on the grounds of persuading users to recycle more of their waste, and the coalition government, apparently in response to media pressure, have attempted to force councils to revert to weekly collections.

A sensible alternative might be for households (as is done in other countries) to have their rubbish weighed and for them to be charged in line with the volume of waste they are producing, but this again will not be popular as it requires households to change their behaviour and to take greater responsibility for recycling – and it may also lead to the public attempting to put their rubbish into one another's bins! A customer-focused refuse collection service would be very different from a socially responsible one. Where end users are demanding high levels of service, it might require a considerable investment in educating them to substitute the values of responsible disposal of refuse for those of high customer service, and even then, some individuals may not accept that the local authority has any right to tell them what to do with their rubbish. Refuse collection is an area dogged particularly by the free-rider effect where individual service users may believe that recycling rubbish is not their problem because someone else will do it on their behalf.

The problems of what appear to be as mundane an issue as refuse collection were illustrated in the Simpsons episode 'Trash of the Titans', Homer Simpson is put in charge of refuse collection for his home town of Springfield with an agenda of offering extremely high-quality service, but ends up spending the entire annual budget in one month. His answer to the problem is – allowing other cities to dump their rubbish in Springfield's empty mines in return for cash to pay the public workers, end up with the entire city having to be abandoned and relocated.

As public services are often offered within a fixed budget, the spectre of funding always has the potential of limiting the level of service available. A possible way of offering a higher standard of service is to offer weekly or two-weekly collections, but charge for additional collections if they want a higher standard of service. Where this is economically viable it may square the circle of cost and service, but at the price of allowing those with higher incomes to be less responsible with their rubbish, which may go somewhat against the grain of social and environmental responsibility. Placing the needs of local users at the heart of delivery can mean that other important agendas are missed out.

A second potential tension is between safety and user need. If local park users want their local council to set up an adventure playground for their children then the children themselves might want climbing frames that go very high, swings with long chains on them to allow both greater speed and height, skateboard areas with big ramps, and slides going from the tops of trees down to the floor via ropes and pulleys. If examined from a health and safety perspective, however, the local authority may feel that these proposals are likely to result in children being injured and so want less exciting facilities. But if the users, with the support of their parents, want more risky, more exciting playground rides, should this override the safety concerns of the local authority, even when they know the proposals are likely to result in injured children?

A third difficulty, and a variation of the tension between safety and user need, is where evidence and user need appear to work in opposite directions. Healthcare providers are good example of this. Where a patient demands an untested treatment, perhaps one from homeopathy or another alternative therapy, should this be funded from public funds, or the more conventional version given instead? Should public funds be used to support treatments that cannot be shown to have a scientific base, or which do not have randomized controlled trial data to support them?

Many writers argue that using public funds for unproven medical treatments is a waste of money, using up funds that could be used to help patients scientifically (Tallis, 2005). Many medical practitioners seem to be taking a more view that what supports and helps patients should be paid for by the state even if the treatment itself does not meet the same standards of evidence as other funded treatments. A good example of this comes from a patient approaching a local health authority or insurance company to be treated for HIV entirely using complementary medicine. According to a strict evidence-based regime, the patient would be refused public money for this. But several patients appear to have managed to prevent his HIV from developing into full-blown AIDS for several years by using a complementary medicine regime, and so, even though there is little scientific data supporting this treatment, they have been funded through the UK NHS on the grounds that it seemed to work for that individual. Whether this decision could be generalized across a population is, however, rather more open to question.

Who is the public service customer?

There are also situations where it is not clear who the customer of a particular public service is (Christy & Brown, 1996). Do the police serve the public as a whole (in which case, how is this even possible?), or do they serve the members of the public who have been victims of crime specifically (which would exclude crime prevention as being part of their role) or, if they have a member of the public in custody, is he or she their customer? In a blood transfusion service, are the donors customers, or are they the recipients of the blood donated instead? Giving simple answers to these questions never really works – almost invariably public organizations must treat all members of the public as customers or potential customers, but this does not mean they always have to do exactly what the customer wants. Some clear thinking needs to take place in each service as to what the public generally should expect from it, as well as to what specific interactions with particular public groups mean.

The clash between need and resource

Last in terms of the problems of utilizing customer-focus in the public sector, there is the clash between user need and resource, perhaps the most pervasive dilemma of all. The case of refuse collection already begun to explore this issue, but there are more specific cases that illustrate it. One resource in short supply, as noted above, is public professional time. Doctors take time to train, and are expensive to employ. As such, requiring doctors to be available to see patients at the patients' convenience, funded from public monies, would appear to be unreasonable as this would suggest a great deal of doctor time is presently redundant, and this is simply not the case. Another good example is the 'places' available in high-quality higher education institutions. If choosing University was based entirely upon user preference, then the most prestigious sites of learning would become overrun with students whilst those less well known might struggle to fill their places. Given a choice, wouldn't most US and UK students prefer to go to an 'Ivy League' University or to 'Oxbridge'? However, these universities simply could not take everyone who would like to go to them, and their prestige may well be tied up with them being able to be extremely selective in their intakes. Allowing everyone to attend would reduce the quality of the student experience for everyone, as facilities would become over-crowded and standards fall as a result, as well as meaning that the badge of being a graduate of those institutions would not carry the status it held before as far more students would be able to claim it.

In these circumstances where user wants and capacity clash, other ways of organizing services need to be found. In the case of doctors, most people would agree that patients with greater clinical need should be seen first, and in the case of universities, the ability of the student (or at very least the potential ability of the student) would seem to override the demand that users in each service should get what they want. Hospitals and universities will still want to market their service to attempt to make clear what distinctiveness they offer, but will also want to preserve their ability to make decisions on criteria other than user need.

Making a customer-focused approach to public services work

There are many cases where public services appear to be organized excessively for the convenience of professionals. The key task for public managers is working out whether services that are less user-friendly are in need of reform, and if so, how professionals can be brought on board to reorganize services. Public managers often have the tricky task of representing user voices against professional groupings whose training and practice are grounded in a very different view of how services should be organised and delivered

Many of the problems highlighted above with using the customer-focused approach in the public delivery or services are based on tensions between what is good for the individual, and what is good for the public as a whole. When wanting an improvement in a service being delivered to me, thinking as an individual, I may not take into account the need to deliver that service to the rest of those needing it. If I am prescribed an expensive new drug, it might mean that there are insufficient funds to treat patients with other conditions (or even the same condition). If my bins are collected weekly, it might mean that those in more remote locations are unable to have their rubbish collected more than every month. Public services, as they tend to occur within relatively fixed budgets, have to deal with the tension of the individual versus that of the group.

Vigoda (2002) suggests that treating citizens in a customer-focused way has worked for the benefit of bureaucracies by forcing them to take greater responsibility towards citizens (in the sense of customers collectively), increasing public service accountability and transparency, and has emphasized that government must be continuously monitored to ensure high efficiency, effectiveness, and good economic performance. It has also, according to Vigoda, made clear that government power must depend upon citizen support, especially with regard to the services they receive. However, in line with Fox and Miller (1995), Vigoda suggests that citizens are 'unwilling – perhaps incapable – of becoming practical owners of the state even if they are the real owners by all democratic and business criteria' (p. 538). Members of the public seek 'practical flexibility' between the role of citizen and client, and that public managers must foster greater collaboration and partnership with the citizenry in order to increase the authenticity of their relationship, turning the 'they' view of customers into 'we', where service managers, politicians, and service users work together. Market-type modes of governance increase the potential risk of 'citizen alienation, disaffection, scepticism and increase cynicism toward governments' (p. 538) and will require a high level of co-operation that fosters mutual effort. Similarly, Clarke suggests that it may also be the case that many of the public resist considering themselves customers or consumers of public services, explicitly rejecting this language because they favour alternative discourses about public provision based on partnership between providers rather than competition (Clarke *et al.*, 2007).

The risk of the alienation of service uses through the use of market-type mechanisms in the public sector comes because organizing public services around a customer-focus view risks them being accountable to individual users only, with the collective needs of the public disappearing as a result. In this circumstance, individuals may find services unresponsive or unhelpful and be unable to understand why their needs are not being met, when public managers are simply trying to make provision fair to everyone. Where services refuse to collect rubbish more frequently or to prescribe the latest drugs, individuals may feel aggrieved, but there may be good collective reasons for them not receiving the level of service they are demanding. But, as seen in previous chapters, public service accountability can be achieved not only through customer-type relationship alone, with them also needing to be democratically accountable as well. Organizing public services on a customer-focused basis alone makes them accountable to individuals, rather than accountable to the public more generally as democratic accountability attempts to achieve.

Given the problems associated with attempting to make services accountable to individuals, or making them democratically accountable, what other means can be found for public service users to participate in the running of services?

Achieving greater local accountability for public services

A first method of getting greater local accountability for public services is to get users involved in the running of services themselves. User representatives might be appointed to work with public managers in making decisions, and to give the 'user' view when required in the planning and management meetings to which they are invited.

However, it can be difficult to get users to volunteer to be involved in the running of services, and those that volunteer may not be representative of the public as a whole (if this is, indeed, even possible). Equally, user representation can sometimes become tokenism where users in decision-making meetings have one or two votes compared to the 20 or so assembled representatives of professional and management groupings. Lay membership (as it is often called) does, however, lead to professionals at least having to listen to user views in meetings, which is no bad thing in itself, and may lead to support for managerial initiatives to change services more in line with the needs of the public.

The difficulty with getting local people involved in public organizations comes in achieving membership that is at all representative of the public at large, especially with regard to groups that may find dialogic debate difficult, and so could be marginalized by it. Even those members of the public that are comfortable with participating in the running of public services can become effectively incorporated or institutionalized into them, risking losing the point of bringing in members of the public in the first place (Barnes *et al.*, 2003). However, few public organizations (I hope) would suggest there is no role for user representation within their decision-making structures.

A second approach to public participation is for groups of users (which again ideally should be representative of the public as a whole in some way) to be empowered to make decisions that affect their public services. A panel of local people might be given two or three days of briefings from interested groups and professionals, and then be asked to make a decision for what happens next. In social housing estates, user groups (or 'citizens' juries') have sometimes taken control of the future of their housing by working out strategies for dealing with social problems in their areas and working collaboratively with the police and social services to try and come up with innovative new ways of tackling long-standing problems where conventional approaches have failed. Equally, many local authorities ask local people to prioritize what public funds should be spent on by involving the public in decisions about local amenities by inviting them along to local halls and explaining the possible decisions, and giving them the opportunity to vote on the options available.

This kind of initiative, however, is not without its difficulties. Where users take decisions on behalf of their local communities they may enter the decision-making processes with particular prejudices, with the end result be based more on the pre-existing views of those that are able to organize themselves to participate in the decision-making process than of the views of the public that have to live with the decision more generally. Tenants might have opinions that are racist or sexist, or which even involve illegal acts. The idea of 'community' can be an empowering one that asks us to think at a level other than ourselves, but it can also be a source of intolerance and elitism.

In the circumstances where users' views are illegal or even dangerous, some limits might have to be placed on the ability of the decision-making body to come to the conclusions it wishes to, but this, in turn, might be experienced as an attempt by managers to prevent the popular will from being carried out.

Equally, holding decisions in local halls that decide priorities for expenditure may be dominated by groups that manage to organize to attend the meeting, crowding out other opinion, or users may feel that the decision delegated to the local level are too trivial and so not worthy of their attention. Local meetings may become dominated by discussion about the relocation of bus stops within a 20-metre stretch rather than more important issues such as crime or the availability of other public amenities.

Equally, public participation can be extremely expensive. Irvin and Stansbury (2004) present a range of 'ideal conditions' when citizen participation in agency decision making might work, and when it might not. They ask key questions such as whether citizens care enough to actively participate in particular decisions or service areas, or would resources devoted to participatory processes be better directed elsewhere? They ask if participation offers the opportunity for economically motivated special interests to dominate decision-making processes, and whether public managers can indeed avoid some level of interest dominance over public decision-making processes. They emphasize that 'talk is not cheap – and may not even be effective' (p. 63).

The role of public managers, if it has been decided that decisions will be delegated to local people, is to make sure that the decisions delegated are meaningful and that the solutions created are legal, safe and viable. This last point may involve extremely careful work in trying to steer users away from particular solutions and creative work in attempting to come up with alternatives. Equally, public managers will also have the responsibility for making sure that the decisions are carried out and that successful implementation occurs. If local people have made a decision, which has cost them time and energy, but nothing is seem to come of it, then they will be reluctant and understanding suspicious of becoming involved again.

Co-production

A third approach attempts to steer a middle path between professionals and users towards achieving a 'co-production' model. Co-production can mean a number of different things, depending upon the exact public context where it is being used, but usually means that the service users takes responsibility for some aspect of the delivery of the public service him or herself (Pestoff, 2006). This can be done in a number of ways. At the minimum, professionals might be required to demonstrate that they have had meaningful consultation with users before decisions have been made, with users given the opportunity to scrutinize the decisions made by local professionals and to have their say.

In local authorities, co-production might mean that decisions about the allocation of land or local authority budgets are made recursively, as decisions made by professionals might be passed for consultation with local people, and then passed back to the professionals to see how they respond to the problems or criticisms made. This clearly requires local people to be extremely engaged with local decision making, and for their views to be taken seriously by professionals rather than simply rebuffed or ignored. Bovaird (2007) suggests that co-operation between public professionals and service users needs to be proactively managed to the point of appointing a 'coproduction development officer' (p. 858) to oversee it. Achieving a high level of public engagement can be extremely difficult, but the increased use of on-line consultations and of local authorities having to justify their budgetary decisions to their local populations points to possibilities where it can become more widespread, especially in a context where local authorities find their budgets frozen.

Alford (1998) takes a slightly different approach to co-production, presenting techniques such as web-based tax assessment as an example of co-production, but also including definitions more in line with those of Pestoff in his discussion of tenants' councils on high-rise estates – a far more collectivist and activist model of co-production.

If involving local people in decisions on an occasional basis represents the minimum end of the scale of time and effort in terms of co-production, a far greater role is also possible. In childcare, co-production models have led to parents becoming more involved in looking after children, brought in as a source of additional labour and expertise by the state (Pestoff, 2006). As such, parents become the deliverers of childcare as well as the clients of it, with childcare coming to represent an employment possibility as well as a need.

Co-production can also take place in a more intimate setting where professionals are encouraged to consult with the users of their services on a one-to-one basis, such as when they visit the doctor. The conventional model of doctor diagnosis and prescription is one where the doctor fires off a series of questions and then informs the patients what is wrong with them, and what the doctor thinks should be done about it. A co-production model attempts to give the patient alternative treatments, along with their possible advantages and disadvantages, and to involve the patient more in decisions such as where they should be referred for further treatment (if necessary) or how the patient might go about making changes to their lives required by ill health. The co-production model in these circumstances should lead to greater patient compliance with the diagnosis and treatment, as it has been decided together, and so clearly has advantages from an implementation perspective. However, it also means longer consultations between doctor and patient, and so a greater resource commitment, which again is difficult to achieve at a time of budget cutbacks.

Nudging service users

Recent research from US behavioural economists has had a significant role in shaping the debate around the role of users in public services across the world (Thaler & Sunstein, 2008). In this work, the public generally are considered not to be the highly rational individuals of economic models, but instead to have a range of behavioural irrationalities that need to be taken into account when designing policies, but which also offer insights into how policymakers who want to improve the lives of their publics can make what appear to be subtle changes to great effect.

These strategies, perhaps most pithily summarized as 'nudge' approaches, aim to offer policymakers and public managers the means to intervene to gently push ('nudge') service users towards the best result for them. Rather than making rules or passing legislation, the approach suggests a complementary approach where, by changing the way options are presented to people, they can be led to better outcomes.

This requires an example. One of nudge's successes comes in getting people to enrol in pension schemes that will hopefully lead to more comfortable retirements for them. If we ask people to enrol in a pension scheme, many will not get around to it, or become used to the level of pay without a pension deduction being made, and so argue they cannot afford it. If, however, we enrol what is ostensibly the same group in the pension scheme by default, upon joining an employer, they will tend not to leave it. They have been 'nudged' to a choice that will probably benefit them in the long run.

According to economic rationality models, people should rationally assess when joining a firm whether they want to be enrolled in its pension scheme, and it should make no difference if we are enrolled by default or not. But the initial state of enrolment in a pension scheme seems to make a considerable difference – the default option (around which much of nudge's ideas are organized) is important.

Nudge clearly includes a strong element of paternalism in that either politicians or public managers, in the way they design their organizations, are seeking to lead people to particular answers that they regard as being right. For this reason, many commentators find the approach distasteful. Nudge advocates, however, make clear that they allow people to take other options open to them, but are simply thinking carefully about which option a particular organizational form or programme appears to be the default, and trying to make it the best one, conscious that people are rather more inclined to accept it than conventional economic theory would suggest.

Nudge positions service users neither as consumers or citizens, nor as co-producers, but instead in relatively passive positions where they can be steered towards goals that those in charge of policy and organizational design believe best. This raises ethical issues about which options are set as defaults, and so are regarded as being 'best', but it is surely better to be conscious about how our organizations and policies inevitably lead people towards some choices rather than others to imagine such processes do not exist. When it comes to setting defaults, however, they should surely be made openly rather than covertly, and through as democratic as means as possible.

Collectivized individualism

The above approaches attempt to try and bridge the gap between the individual user and the general public, through public organizations incorporating individuals or groups of individuals into their decision-making processes. However, there is another possibility. This is where individual user feedback is 'collectivized' and patterns sought in order to try and find lessons through which services can be improved for everyone.

User complaints are often regarded by public managers with a sense of dread because they can mean having to investigate professionals who may feel they are being deliberately targeted by both users and managers because they do not go along with organizational reform. Equally, in an increasingly litigious world, complaints can be attempts to try and extract money from public organizations where no wrong has been done. There will always be a small minority of people attempting to claim compensation fraudulently.

However, complaints also have the potential to provide public managers with detailed feedback about user experience of services offered. It can, therefore, be a valuable means of finding ways, which those services might be improved. If this feedback is routinely collected and analysed by public managers responsible for the delivery of that service, then it can at least give them a clear idea of what is going wrong with their service.

An alternative to managers reviewing feedback is for it to be passed on to citizen advocacy groups. This allows individual complaints to be effectively combined and for the citizen groups to lobby public organizations for improvement. Individual patients are often unaware that patient groups exist that can represent them and drive for service improvement, and may also not want to be bothered themselves to complain as they may never need the particular public service they are unhappy with again.

If public feedback can be collected and passed to independent patient organizations, this would allow recurring problems to be identified, for providers to be held to account for it and for opportunities for service improvements to be made. Complaints are a powerful source of feedback about what is going wrong with particular services, and public organizations are often extremely poor in dealing with them. Of course, where the public write to congratulate public organizations for their high standards and good performance, this can also form the basis for working out what is being done well, and how to achieve more of it.

In either system, where public managers collect complaints or where public advocacy groups utilize them, this allows the possibility for individual responses to be collectivized, patterns examined, and services, which are experiencing systemic difficulties (or successes), investigated further to see what can be learnt from them, and what can be improved. This 'collectivized individualism' has the advantage of being potentially a routine part of service delivery, requiring no additional work on the part of service users, who do not have to attend additional meetings or have to confront professionals with problems directly, which they may find intimidating or difficult. It cannot work in all areas of public service but can be viewed as a potentially fruitful way of bridging the gap between consumerist, individualistic notions of service delivery, and the collective need for public services to be accountable to the public more generally. Table 7.3 summarizes different approach to local involvement in public services along with their advantages and drawbacks.

Conclusion

The paradox of user involvement is that we usually only experience public services as individuals either through own use of them or through the reports of our friends, families, and peers, but to understand their quality, efficiency, and effectiveness we also need to understand them from a collective perspective. We need to be both customers and citizens – customers to demand better services for ourselves and our loved ones, but at the same time understanding what our own demands are doing to the provision of those services for everyone else.

This chapter began by asking how the public are generally conceptualized in relation to public services, and moved on to the question of how they could become more involved in the running of public services. The two questions appear separate, but are related to one another. When considering a marketing view of public services, the central problem is how to meet individual

Table 7.3 Different ways of achieving local accountability

	Advantages	Drawbacks
Get users involved in the running of public services.	Potential for public to be directly involved.	Can be difficult to get individuals to volunteer.
		Individuals who volunteer may not be representative of public.
		Users on committees may be treated as 'tokens'.
Empower users to make decisions.	Informed, sensitive decisions can be reached by those that have to live with their consequences.	Pre-existing prejudices might inform decisions.
		Limits may have to be placed on scope of decisions and public resent this.
		Representativeness of those making decisions.
Co-production.	Collaborative approach between professionals and users stressed.	Users may feel that they are not able to participate on equal terms and defer to professionals.
	Public may provide extra capacity by providing services themselves.	Public may become cheap source of poor-quality services.
'Nudge' approaches.	The state is still able to influence how service users respond to public services to guide them to the approach desired, but no coercion is involved – users can do otherwise.	Concerns that nudge approaches may simply not work in many areas, and where they do work they may have a lack of transparency in selecting the 'default'.
Collectivized individualism.	Routine feedback is acted upon and service change occurs as a result.	Does not engage public deliberatively and this may create a different result from individual-only responses.
	Has some sense of collectivity as all feedbacks can be examined.	

service user's expectations within the resource constraints available to public organizations, without sacrificing the needs of the public to the needs of the individual. Where particular individuals demand very high standards from public services that mean significantly increased resources will need to be deployed, should they receive a much higher level of service, even if it means services reductions for other members of the public? What about the needs of the public collectively?

It is hard to see how a customer-focused approach can be taken without regard to resources, especially given the context that public services face in the years ahead. Public managers will struggle both to provide good customer services to everyone individually, and meeting the needs of the public collectively in providing efficient and fair services. To deal with this dilemma, managers need ways of engaging with the public in order to make their services accountable to them collectively as well as individually. Various mechanisms for getting the public involved in services exist, with the two least problematic being the co-production and collectivized individualism models. In the first, the public themselves become more involved in service provision. This covers a wide variety of positions from the public running the services entirely themselves (as in childcare) through to professionals being required to demonstrate adequate consultation with service users has occurred, as might be the position in healthcare. Nudge-based approaches attempt to give the public choices about their lives, but with a defined default that the state has picked as being the best option, and around which they must orient their choices. The collectivized individualism model attempts to find ways of collectivizing individual feedback, either by public managers or by citizen advocacy groups, and that services are required to find a response to systemic problems identified by it. This has the advantage of being potentially a part of everyday feedback collection by public managers (whether they analyse the results themselves or not), and so does not require members of the public to attend specific meetings or confront professionals themselves. It cannot work in all circumstances, however, and will not engage members of the public with the dynamic of negotiating their views with others. It therefore does not get users involved in the process of deliberative debate that other means of public involvement can achieve.

Case study – Co-production and benefit fraud

One of the most controversial examples of co-production comes in attempts to extend co-production methods to the reporting of benefit fraud. It spans a range of issues regarding individual and collective responsibility, as well as being located in bigger narratives about welfare change.

The way we view benefit recipients has changed considerably over the last 30 years. As unemployment rates rose in the United States and United

Kingdom in the 1980s a new language emerged, which suggested benefit recipients such as the unemployed were not unfortunate victims of changing patterns of work or economic recession, but instead were choosing simply not to work. Unemployment went from being a social issue to a behavioural issue.

In such a situation, the state began to ask members of the public not only to work if they could, cutting back on benefit payments, putting in place more robust eligibility criteria before benefits could be claimed, or initiating 'workfare' approaches where benefit claimants had to earn their payments by carrying out work in their local community, but also, where they knew of people who were engaging in benefit fraud, to report them.

The scale of benefit fraud in any given economy is a contentious issue. Right-of-centre media take great delight in finding claimants living in apparent luxury, and work out the often extraordinary amounts those claimants have managed to extract from the state over their lifetimes. However, because of the very nature of the act (it being illegal) it is extremely difficult to know how much fraud takes place – if we knew, we could stop it.

Asking the public to report benefit fraud is interesting both in terms of what it reveals about the dynamics of user involvement, but also interesting in what it reveals theoretically about the way we are being asked to effectively police public services ourselves. From a user involvement perspective, giving people a telephone number or email address and asking them to report fraud positions potentially any member of the public as a co-producer of fraud detection services. Where cases are reported and found to be examples of fraud, they are often widely publicized to show the efficacy of the scheme, as well as being a warning to those continuing to fraudulently claim benefits. It is equally as possible to imagine, however, a great deal of time and effort being wasted as people take out grudges against neighbours by leaving anonymous tip-offs that lead to unnecessary investigations.

In addition to encouraging service users to be co-producers, benefit fraud reporting also says a great deal about changing attitudes amongst the public. Attempts to explore the dynamics of contemporary politics, such as Gould's *The Unfinished Revolution* (Gould, 2011), suggest that the US and the UK public are often surprisingly 'strong' on issues such as crime and benefit fraud, even if they are 'soft' on the rights of those who are genuinely in need to claim benefits. User reporting of fraud is a viable policy because, as citizens, we are increasingly intolerant of those who engage in it. It is also very noticeable that, in an era of tighter budgets and public austerity, public attitudes to fraudulent claimants appear to be hardening still – in the Winter of 2011 the BBC broadcast two documentaries, one led by the 'Today' show presenter John Humphrey asking whether those who choose not to work should receive benefits, and another investigating benefit 'cheats' – especially those who claim incapacity benefit but were filmed riding on bicycles or sailing on their private yachts.

Finally, asking service users to report on fraud has interesting implications. Foucault's concept of 'governmentality' suggests that the most effective way of getting the people to manage themselves is to influence their mental concepts so that their common sense reflects what the state requires. This is applicable in two ways here – first, in successfully getting the public to report those that might be fraudulently claiming we are effectively policing ourselves, rather than asking public managers (or the police) to do the job. Second, in publicizing cases where this strategy is successful, we may reduce fraud by getting those who believe they will be caught to stop engaging in it. If the policy achieves these two goals, it will have achieved a state of governmentality indeed.

Further reading

One of the earliest books fully exploring the use of marketing and asking questions about how public organizations might become more user focused was by Rod Sheaff (1990) in his examination of marketing concepts to healthcare organizations. More recently, I have co-edited a book on the 'consumer in public services' that extends the work above in a number of ways (Gillies, 1978), and Catherine Needham has published the widely cited work looking at how we have come to refer to service users as citizen consumers (Needham, 2003). John Clarke and Janet Newman's work has taken up this subject further, exploring the contradictions that treating service users as consumers holds for public services (Clarke *et al.*, 2007). The 'nudge' approach is explored in Thaler and Sunstein's book of the same name (Thaler & Sunstein, 2008).

8

The use of markets in the public sector

Introduction

The majority of the services now provided by the public sector were once delivered via the private market in some form or another before the creation of welfare states. Healthcare systems, for example, developed through doctors being able to charge patients for care, and those patients who could afford to pay navigated themselves through a market of competing services, and unemployment benefits had their precursors in mutual associations where members paid to insure themselves so that they would receive a payment should they become unemployed.

Recent public reforms have tended to try and reintroduce the market dynamics into public services on the grounds that it will make them more responsive and user focused. The questions this chapter seeks to answer is how markets change public management, but also asking what conditions need to be in place for a market to work for public delivery? When do markets work and when do they not? Before these questions can be explored, however, it makes sense perhaps to begin by trying to be clearer as to what is meant by the term 'market' in the first place.

What is a market?

For a concept that is so widely used in economics, business and management, it is surprisingly difficult to define exactly what a market is. Economics textbooks present enticing frameworks showing how supply and demand interact to deliver equilibrium prices and quantities available for purchase in a cut-throat world where firms enter and exit at a moment's notice and consumers are ruthless and supremely well informed in their purchasing decisions. Economists have always claimed that they are describing the way markets work, but in more recent years criticism from sociologists have suggested that instead they are providing elaborate theories that prescribe how markets should work rather than reflecting any empirical reality (Callon, 1998). Sociologists examining buying and selling in settings such as stock and commodity markets have suggested that, even where conditions exist that are close to the preconditions specified by economists for their efficient operation, the economic theory of the market bears little resemblance to what is actually happening. Instead, they suggest, it takes a huge amount of regulatory effort and organization to get buyers and sellers to behave anything like the way economists say they should be, and that the term 'market' is therefore both a theoretical ideal advocated by economists and our experiences of exchanging money for goods in everyday life that will probably be very different (Aldridge, 2005). It is therefore important to separate the economists' ideal of the market from the exchange experiences we come across in our lives, and to be careful not to mix up the two. The influence of economics-based ideas on public markets has been huge, but that does not mean that they actually resemble the theory much in practice.

The preconditions for a market to work

Given the ambiguity over what a market actually is, it is important to try and say that component parts need to be in place before we can say a market mechanism is both in place and working. One way of doing this is to think about the configurations of buyers and sellers that markets require. Markets are often contrasted with monopolies, with the latter form being where there is only one provider, or only one dominant provider. Monopolies are not well regarded by economists because of their potential for sellers to be able to exploit their selling positions and achieve high levels of profit while offering poor customer service. It therefore makes sense to suggest that one precondition for the functioning of a marketplace is that there need to be enough providers in place to prevent them from organizing themselves into a collusive monopoly, and so that they are in a competitive relationship with one another. On the supply side then, a market needs a minimal number of providers (perhaps say five, to pick a figure out of the air). However, it is important that there are not only a minimum number of providers but also that they are in a competitive relationship with one another. This means that they must be striving to improve their quality or lower their price (or both) for fear of losing market share to other providers.

On the demand side, a situation where there is one dominant purchaser (a monopsony) also needs to be avoided as this will skew relationships in favour of the purchasers of goods or services. A dominant purchaser will leave sellers of goods or services in the position where they go out of business if they fall out of favour. Supermarkets in the United Kingdom are sometimes accused of having achieved this position, because, having purchased the entire output of particular farmers, they can then force them keep lowering their prices or face the threat of the supermarket taking their custom elsewhere.

To achieve some kind of balance, there must therefore be a reasonable number of purchasers, again with none dominating the marketplace, and where those purchasers are attempting to achieve the best use of their resources.

In addition to the relationship between buyers and sellers, purchasers also need information about the goods and services offered by the suppliers, and to be able to understand it. There is little point in having a competitive market for a service that is so complex no one understands as any choice made by buyers will be arbitrary. Equally, providers need information about the potential customers in a marketplace so they can inform them of the goods or services they are offering. Markets cannot function without good information circulation, and both buyers and sellers being able to understand it.

Finally, markets need at least a little renewal or destruction from entry and exit into them. Where providers have been in a market for a number of years, their form of competition may have settled down into a structure where each has found a comfortable place with little threat or drive for improvement any more. There needs to be some means of preventing this from happening, but without providers in markets changing so frequently that there is no continuity of supply, and purchasers seeking other markets to spend their money in.

A market therefore exists where there are a minimum number of suppliers of a good or service organized in a competitive relationship on the supply side, and a minimum number of purchasers who understand the offerings of the suppliers, on the demand side (Le Grand, 1991). These elements are summarized in Table 8.1. Being clear about what is necessary for a market to function is not simply a definitional issue. Defining the prerequisites of a market allow an analysis of how markets have been constructed to deliver public goods will work, whether they will favour the supply or demand side, and what challenges

Table 8.1 The basic preconditions for a market to be able to work successfully

Precondition	Reason for precondition
Minimum numbers of supplier in a competitive relationship with one another.	Without a competitive relationship not clear what the purpose of a market is.
Minimum number of purchasers who understand providers' offerings.	Without understanding of providers' offerings, purchasing will be ineffective, and contacts will have significant transactions costs. Minimum number needed to prevent purchasers from having too much power.
Some means of entry and exit.	Without entry and exit, danger of market stagnating and becoming uncompetitive.
Sufficient information so that suppliers have to compete with one another, and purchasers spend their money effectively.	Without good information, purchasers will make choices that keep poor suppliers in the market, and good suppliers will not be rewarded for their efforts.

public managers face in the particular market environment in which they find themselves.

Markets and public goods and services

Having specified the preconditions for markets to exist, we can begin to consider what happens when those preconditions are not met. Where competition is not practical, public provision might relieve concerns that exploitation might occur by allowing a private monopoly to occur or exist (Bozeman, 2002). Equally, where a particular good or service is regarded as being essential to the people or to the country, then competition may also not be the best way of proceeding. A government might decide that the provision of water, for example, is too important to leave to competitive forces, and so risk members of the public potentially losing their supply where they are in uneconomic locations for private firms to supply them, and so the state becomes the monopoly provider to guarantee supply or minimum standards.

Which industries particular governments decide are essential for their economy or public, however, will vary from place to place and are value-laden decisions. In many countries, industries including coal and steel have gone through cycles of nationalization and privatization, depending upon which government has been in power, whereas in others the idea of nationalizing industry would be unthinkable. Arguments about which industries should be within the public sector are not only a function of which country is being considered, but also which time period.

The number of prerequisites for markets to work well suggests that they may not always be the best way for goods or services to be delivered to the public. Transport by train is one example; there is likely to be only one train line between two points (or where there are many possible routes, one that is likely to be the shortest or most convenient), and, as most travellers are concerned first and foremost with the time of travel, it is hard to create a competitive environment easily (Greener, 2008). Train travel may then be a case where competition does not appear particularly relevant to those who require the services, as well as being difficult to achieve on the supply side; it may well be a natural public monopoly. When we have goods or services that appear to have substantial problems being delivered through market mechanisms, we sometimes refer to them as 'public goods' or services.

Technically, public goods or services are either non-rival or non-excludable, so we need to define what these terms mean.

Non-rival goods and services

Non-rival goods and services are those whose consumption does not reduce their availability for others. Non-rival goods have gone from being relatively unimportant economically to of serious concern because of the widespread use of computers. Twenty years ago, if I wanted to read a book, I had to buy or borrow a physical item and carry it around with me. If you wanted to read it, I was prevented from doing so. Now I can purchase a book in a sharable format from an electronic book store and (provided it is not digitally protected in some way) send you a copy too so we can both read it as the same time. This has most obviously affected the music industry, where I can make a digital copy of a CD (or even just download the music), and if I wish to break the law, circulate it globally using file-sharing software in seconds. Music and books (and film, and anything else that can be stored electronically) have become non-rival goods.

More generally, provided I do not live in a polluted area or one where air is made artificially scarce, air is a non-rival good – there is so much oxygen available that me breathing it does not prevent you from doing so.

The economists' argument is that non-rival goods are necessarily public goods – unless I impose clever restrictions on digital sharing (as Amazon do using their 'kindle' e-reader) or ration air and charge for it in some way (as Ben Elton did in his play 'Gasping'), then it becomes impossible to have a market in non-rival goods because they are so easily shared. This is clearly a huge challenge to those industries that have become 'digitalized', even if this category of goods, as yet, is less of a threat to public services, which tend to be predominantly delivered by human beings.

Non-excludable goods and services

Non-excludable goods are those that, because of their nature, cannot be charged to people individually. Streetlighting is the classic example – if a person decides, in the absence of an alternative, to put a light outside of their house, then they cannot prevent others from sharing it. As such, despite not having paid for the lighting, others can receive its benefits without having paid for it themselves. Areas such as streetlighting create a problem in that some people might decide to try and rely upon others rather than spend any money themselves – they might try and 'free ride'.

Where goods are non-excludable, it makes sense to them to be publicly provided because in the absence of public provision, they may be underprovided or not provided at all, as markets and private provision cannot charge effectively for them. Again, streetlighting is a good example – where it is not provided for the public sector, there is a danger that it may not exist in some communities, and this, in turn, might lead to an increased incidence of social problems such as crime, as well as lead to more accidents.

Public managers and public goods

Public managers, according to the idea that some goods are intrinsically public in nature, are those who are in charge of goods or services that are either best organized out of a competitive environment, or are non-excludable. This distinction is perhaps made most forcibly by the US Economist J.K. Galbraith who noted that, whereas the private sector has a tendency to produce goods of increasing triviality (electric toothbrushes being a favourite example), the public sector produces far more important services such as education (Galbraith, 1958). Galbraith was also extremely concerned that, because public goods tended to be underprovided in the United States, this would lead to 'private affluence and public squalor' with terrible effects upon society such as increasing inequality between the rich and the poor. This is a particular problem where public schooling does not allow individuals to achieve, to a significant extent, equality of opportunity compared to those attending private schools (see the example at the end of Chapter 5).

Public goods in practice

As noted above, both the ownership and the means of delivering services vary tremendously from time period to time period, and from country to country. In the United States, there is a thriving private healthcare sector with the public one being a source of much debate in terms of its scope and cost (with up to 50 million Americans not having health insurance, this is a major issue), whereas in the United Kingdom there is a large and established public sector, with the private sector struggling to gain a foothold and dependent on funding from the public sector for its services for around 25 per cent of its revenues.

In the present era, we have been in thrall to the idea of making public services more like private ones, and attempted to introduce private-sector style competition and incentives even where they seem entirely inappropriate – as in the case of railways in the United Kingdom. It seems conceptually obvious that achieving competition on train lines is a futile task, but that hasn't stopped governments from attempting it, creating elaborate structures of charging and countercharging in the name of increasing efficiency, even though there is little logic in the argument of trying to create competition for competition's sake.

Non-excludability seems to work better as a barometer of which services are provided publicly and which note that non-rival criteria are able to offer, with the latter more applicable to the digital economy. When non-excludability is added to the preconditions for markets to work, this gives a framework for considering when a good or service might be better off provided through public rather than market means.

To recap, market-based provision of goods or services would seem sensible where we have rival goods or services, enough suppliers or purchasers to make a competitive marketplace, where there are sufficient means of entry and exit to refresh providers suppliers or purchasers to keep them on their toes, and where information is not good enough information for purchasers to buy the best good or service, giving an incentive for suppliers to compete with one another to improve.

This kind of outline is fine in theory – it represents a clear statement of what markets ought to be like. However, few markets in public or private sectors are able to meet these standards. Given that the common sense of public reform has meant that, regardless of whether they can achieve the goals set for them, markets are being introduced, it is important to explore what happens when we relax different assumptions from our ideal. From this, we can explore three generic types of market; a balanced one, close to the ideal; one where purchasers tend to dominate; and one where suppliers tend to dominate. What happens in each case?

Different kinds of public markets

A generic model exists where the conditions for a market are most closely met; there are a reasonable number of purchasers and providers, they understand each other's offerings as information about the market is clear and understandable, and goods and services are non-rival. Then there are simple variations on this; where there are relatively few providers compared to purchasers; where providers are organized in more of a collaborative than competitive relationship; where there are relatively few purchasers compared to providers; and where purchasers have little understanding of the market when they are working within. By working through these variations it is possible to see how the role of public managers varies in each situation. A good starting point is to examine the generic model of the market and how it might apply in a public service setting.

The 'balanced' market

In a balanced market there are rival goods, a minimum number of suppliers organized competitively, and a minimum number of purchasers with an understanding of the suppliers' offerings. There are likely to be public managers on both the supply and demand side, so it is necessary to examine both perspectives on the market. In this situation, the criteria for a market have been met, and so a first question is why we are thinking of public involvement at all? Despite the conditions for a functioning market being met, politicians and policymakers (or the general public) may want a service to be publicly provided or funded where it meets a national need of importance and so there is a need to guarantee supply (as many countries believed their 'core' industries such as steel and coal represented after the Second World War), or where the good or service is deemed too important for individuals to be denied access to it (such as education or healthcare). In each case, market mechanisms may work if designed well, but the state or public do not want an entirely private market to function.

Managers on the supply side

On the supply side, a competitive relationship means that managers have to be aware of what others are offering within the market, and to try and improve upon it. In line with business theory more generally, there are several possible sources of advantage they might seek. Managers might seek to gain an advantage over their competitors based on the quality of the services they offer, the

Table 8.2 Sources of competitive advantage

Source of competitive advantage	Benefits	Problems
Quality	Allows users to choose best providers and drive up standards.	Quality can be difficult to measure and assess, and selection on arbitrary measures instead.
Cost	Drives up efficiency.	May creating skimping on service quality and to public-funded services having to provide expensive services where new entrants will not enter markets.
Niche	Allows focus on a single core service.	May need public-funded services to provide cover for gaps in provision.

cost of those services, or by providing a niche product that is presently not being provided by the market (Porter, 2004). These sources are summarized in Table 8.2 and discussed in detail below.

Competing on the quality of public services

Measuring the quality of public services comes with particular problems. In education, exam results might be seen to be a good index of quality as the most measurable outcome for students, and these can be used in national or international rankings of schools and Universities. As rankings and ratings have become more significant, it has become an important part of public managers' jobs to attempt to drive up the elements of their provision measured by rating systems. This can create difficult tensions where rankings fail to capture (as they almost invariably do, because of the difficulty of measuring the output of public services) the nature the service. Exam results do not really capture fully whether schools are doing a good job or not, even if they are clearly a very important factor.

Systems that attempt to get around the problem of measuring complex public sector outcomes can have perverse effects upon public institutions. In higher education, for example, rating systems might measure student opinion and the proportion of students receiving 'good' degrees from a particular institution, or those that rate themselves as being satisfied by the service they have received from their university. This seems sensible on the surface of it but can create problems where managers encourage lecturers to simplify teaching and not challenge students in order to try and achieve better student feedback. Pressure can also be brought to bear at exam boards, where student marks are approved, for lecturers to give higher marks than they believe should be awarded in order to achieve particular proportions of degree classification awards and so increase student satisfaction or performance measures as a result.

Any performance measure or rating system risks creating perverse incentives for providers of services, getting them to focus not on the service as they believe it should be delivered, but on whatever variables are currently being used to rank organizations in those areas. The problems of performance measurement are explored in greater depth in Chapter 9 and are clearly a significant part of being a public management in a market environment, especially where 'league tables' of performance are constructed, and which the public might use to make decisions.

Where there are very strong central performance management systems in place for public organizations they will not only have to try and compete with other providers based on the measures they use, but may also be required to conform to a whole range of measures imposed by the state as well. In this situation, managers may have to choose which targets are most important, or even whether they believe that the targets and measures are so unreflective of the goals of their organizations that they will focus their energies on other areas of their organizations instead that may be less easily measurable. Those designing performance management systems for central government have sometimes expressed incredulity that managers are unable to both conform to central targets and provide what they believe is a good service to the public (Barber, 2007b), but there is a real possibility that managers might be so disillusioned with targets and measures from outside-rating bodies or from the central state that they begin to work on an entirely different basis, meeting only the targets that might lose them their jobs, and judging for themselves whether their organizations are a success or not (Greener, 2005a). Where this happens, the market environment is in danger of breaking down as it no longer carries the support of those working within it, and the state perhaps needs to think again about its use of markets and measures.

Competition on cost grounds

Depending on how markets have been set up, competition may also be possible within them on cost grounds. In some cases, the state may have explicitly removed this option, trying to force competition to be on quality grounds only, by setting a standard price to be paid for a specified service, but cost competition still exists in many services.

The choice of provider when contracting out what are regarded as non-essential services is often decided largely on cost grounds. In this situation, services are put out to tender, and the provider who is able to offer the level of service specified in the contract at lowest cost will often secure the contract. This offers the chance for public services to be offered at the lowest possible cost, and so to drive up efficiency.

The problem here is that what falls into the category of essential and non-essential is inconsistent across both different countries and time. In the 1980s, it seemed to make sense to contract out cleaning services for hospitals, and politicians pointed to the money that was saved as a result. However, when infection rates went up in the 1990s because of unclean wards and poor standards of service, many services were brought bank 'in-house' so their quality could be monitored more closely once more, and services made more flexible than contracting out services often allowed.

Equally, there may be some areas of public provision, which are simply so complex and subject to variation that providers may not be interesting in entering a market for them. Social care services that are provided for long periods of time may require an almost open-ended commitment to supporting particular people with special needs, and may make it extremely difficult for private or not-for-profit providers to guarantee service into the future. It is no coincidence that one of the largest providers of such care, Southern Cross, fell into bankruptcy in the United Kingdom in 2011. In these kinds of cases, public provision may have to be offered to guarantee that the service takes place not irrespective of cost, but without it being a focal point for concern.

Equally, where services require a considerable initial investment (or 'sunk cost') before competition can occur, smaller providers can be squeezed out as they are unable to make the large investment required. As a result, this can competition, leaving one or two big providers to compete, being the only ones able to afford the initial investment, and effectively carving up supply to the market between them.

Competing through niche advantage

Finally, niche advantage can be sought where provision focuses on a clearly defined product or service where the market is not meeting the needs of a particular group well at present. Because most public provision is in the area of services, there is huge potential for them to become more individual and tailored to meet the public's needs. Niche providers entering the market may mean that the group that they service have their needs particularly closely met, so providing a very high level of service that publicly funded providers may not be able to achieve.

The problem with providers seeking niche advantage is that, by definition, they are not interested in serving the market more generally, and if all providers pursue this strategy then it will leave gaps which, if serious, may require further state intervention to serve. Public transport can fall into this category – private firms may be very happy to provide buses and trams at peak times in cities, but less happy to run buses out to rural locations at mid-morning or late evening. The state can attempt to subsidize certain routes and times in order to make them attractive, but this is really an acknowledgement of the need for public intervention rather than allowing a market mechanism to work.

A second example is the 'pupil premium', where children measured as being disadvantaged (perhaps those who qualify for free school meals) receive an additional public subsidy to schools that admit them. This is meant to lead to schools wanting to make themselves attractive to children and parents from disadvantaged groups, and if the pupil premium is set correctly, could lead to schools putting on additional services (breakfast clubs, after school clubs and additional tuition) for students from those backgrounds and effectively niche marketing to them as a result.

Promoting market-based environments

In a balanced market environment, public managers on the supply side must try and make sure not only that their organizations are performing well according to the measures currently in place to assess them, but also that the purchasers of services know about their performance and understand what is distinctive about their organizations. This is an often overlooked aspect of public management. It is one thing for public managers to know that their organizations are performing well, but quite another to be able to demonstrate it to the users and purchasers of their services. What this entails is for public managers on the provider side to try and construct a 'frame' for explaining the performance of their organization, which has a straightforward message, and which shows their organization to its best advantage. This is extremely hard – the frame chosen must be straightforward enough for non-specialists to understand, but complex enough to capture the performance of their organization and be representative of it. This is the role of promotional marketing in the public sector – not only to miss-sell or confuse potential purchasers, but also to portray their organization in such a way that both represents it and explains its strengths.

On the supply side, public managers are responsible for ensuring that their organization is performing well (as they will always be), and they also need to demonstrate it is performing well compared to its competitors in a form that the purchasers of services can understand – the two are not the same thing.

Managers on the demand or purchaser side

A balanced market environment means that no purchaser is dominant, and that purchasers cannot exert a greater influence over the market than suppliers. Purchasers in a public markets might be individual users on whose behalf the state purchases a service (by paying for it directly), or by giving them funds or vouchers to purchase services themselves. The state may also fund organizations specifically tasked with asking as purchasers on behalf of the public. This approach can lead to the state being able to achieve considerable purchasing power, and so good deals for public services, but at the same time risks creating monopsonies (single purchasers) and so unbalanced markets, while at the same time giving individual users little say in what services are purchased on their behalf. There is therefore something of a tension between efficiency in purchasing (which means large-scale public purchasers) and responsiveness to user need (which means small-scale public purchasers, or giving individual users the budget or money to buy services themselves).

Assessing contracts

Where public organizations are acting as purchasers, one of public managers' key roles is attempting to assess the needs of their particular public, and to make sure that the services that are purchased meet those needs. This is the case whether the managers themselves are purchasing the services on behalf of the public, or whether they public are purchasing them through some kind of voucher or devolved budget system. It is incumbent on public managers on the demand side to make sure that providers are held to account for quality of the services they provide. A market-based system means public services are accountable through contracts, and so it is vital that those contracts are monitored and assessed in terms of their value for both money and quality. Where a particular provider is not meeting the required standard, managers need to make sure that corrective action is taken. Because of the difficulty in measuring public service outputs, it is possible that purchasing managers may even need to override the opinion of service users in their decisions about the level of quality service providers are offering. An example will illustrate this.

Where a university is allowing (or even encouraging) staff to teach material that is not challenging, and then overmarking student papers, the students themselves, if they are primarily focused on exam results only, may be delighted with this. However, managers on the supply side of the marketplace are plainly failing in their duty to provide an education by focusing on elements of their service that are easily measured rather than dealing with the underlying idea of education – to get students to learn. As such, it may be left to managers on the purchasing side to intervene, acting against student wishes if necessary, to drive standards back up by either sending their students to other institutions, or by demanding that educational standards improve at the university that is under-teaching and overmarking.

There may be other means by which both purchasing and providing institutions may be held to account, with democratic accountability being the most obvious. Political representatives might attempt to hold public organizations to account, or they may even be elected to run public organizations, particularly at city level. Where public managers elected democratically make use of markets, however, they clearly have the responsibility of ensuring that both contracts are monitored to give the public a good standard of service, and that the measures of success in those contracts are not so crude as to fail to capture, or at least acknowledge, the complexities of measuring public outputs.

Again, as noted in the chapter on paying for public services, arranging public–private partnerships (PPPs) have become an increasingly important part of public managers' roles. However, PPP contracts have highlighted the relative lack of experience of public managers in writing and negotiating complex legal documents compared to their private counterparties and has sometimes led to the private partners often getting the upper hand and putting in place terms that have given them substantial advantages over the course of the contracts (Asenova & Beck, 2003). It has not helped that public partners in PPP agreements have often effectively been told that they are the only route to securing much-needed capital funding, and so they have been given little or no choice in entering into such agreements, also making them vulnerable. It seems extraordinary that there has been little or no democratic accountability for the worst PPP contracts that have been signed from either the public managers who signed them, or the politicians who allowed them to go ahead.

Designing contracts

Before contracts can be assessed they must be brokered, and so public managers will be responsible for the decision of which services will be purchased, how much of them, at what standard, and from whom. In the chapter on public financing, research suggested that budgetary allocations tend to be largely a function of decisions made in the previous year. In many cases, contracting decision tend to be subject to the same pressures. Once particular providers have received public contracts to provide services, it can be politically difficult to withdraw them. Where public organizations lose public funding, their future may be jeopardized, and the state must make a conscious decision because the removal of public provision in a given area might mean it loses direct control over all provision in that area. Where public services effectively act as a provider of last resort, guaranteeing that services will continue even if all private and not-for-profit providers decide to exit from the market, putting limitations on the extent to which the market mechanism might be allowed to operate.

Equally, however, the state might deliberately favour private providers by giving subsidies and better rates of funding than those available to public providers in order to attract new entrants into public markets. Attracting new entrants might be justified on the grounds of dissatisfaction with existing providers, or on the grounds that in the long term, a larger number of providers will drive the price of services down and the quality up, and so paying a subsidy for new entrants might be cost-efficient in the short term. These kinds of arguments were made in the UK National Health Service in the 2000s to attempt to achieve a more 'mixed' economy of providers in the new market for care introduced then, by getting private and not-for-profit providers to compete with existing public hospitals and clinics. The row over the coalition government's Health and Social Care bill of 2011/12 focused around whether a further extension of this competition could turn the National Health Service (NHS) into a US-style healthcare market, and led to considerable opposition from many medical groups.

Costs and benefits

Decisions about which public services should be contracted for have led to the development of a range of increasingly complex techniques since the 1980s, with economists particularly prominent. Complex models of the benefits and costs of services have been compiled that then attempt to list services into rank order of which achieve the greatest benefits at least cost. Health economics has become an industry with both academics and consultants constructing indexes of possible treatments and advising governments how their money can be best spent to achieve maximum returns on their investment in healthcare. Quality-adjusted life year (QALY) tables, for example, attempt to examine the cost of treatments in terms of the health benefits they give, adjusted in turn for the quality of life they might deliver.

In the United States, experimental attempts at local democracy have been made where those responsible for purchasing healthcare services have consulted with citizens to attempt to draw up a list of which services should be funded using public money, and which should not. The difficulty this raises is that the services economists advocate worthy of funding may be very different from those that professionals in the service believe are important, which may be different again from those that the public would like to see receiving funding. In these circumstances, it is difficult to see how public managers are meant to make purchasing decisions. They have a duty to purchase services according to what represents best value for public funds (which is likely to follow the advice of the economists), to take into account the views of the professionals that often have to deliver public services (which would favour that group), but also to serve the needs of their local population (which would tend to favour their views). Where these different groups produce very different priorities, making final decisions is a very political exercise as it attempts to incorporate the wishes of these possibly competing voices, but decisions also need to be justifiable. Given these tensions, public managers responsible for purchasing decisions appear to be in a near-impossible situation.

Lotteries

One response to the dilemma of what the state should do where there is a shortfall of public funds to provide a particular service is to fund them through the use of a lottery. In the United States, states have conducted experiments in allocating government funding that first works out how many people meet the eligibility criteria for potential funding (such as severity of illness, for example), and then allocates funds according to a lottery system with only a limited number of those meeting eligibility criteria subsequently receiving state funding.

In the United Kingdom, there were experiments in allocating school places by lottery to try and avoid parents of children from more wealthy backgrounds taking up all of the places at schools rated highly. In this case, every child who requires a public school place in a given year is given a place within a local area randomly, with the hope that this will mix up ability levels and social classes to the extent that no school will have a built-in advantage because of where parents live, or because of previous school results. The upside of this is that it should be possible to judge schools entirely free from 'input' considerations such as the educational abilities of their intakes and the wealth of their parents. The problem is that many parents, fearful of their children being allocated a place at a school they do not like, have taken their children out of the public schooling sector and chosen a private school instead, leading to the potential for the area as a whole to suffer from a lack of 'voice' (see Chapter 5). Such systems have also been successfully subjected to legal challenges by parents. Lotteries highlight the tension between trying to work out a fair system between the public as a whole, and individual members of it. They may work well in providing a fair chance for everyone, but that may not be consolation for the individual member of the public that feels he or she has lost out as a result.

Intermediaries

A further complication (if one is needed) is that intermediary bodies often appear where markets are created in public services. Intermediaries appear where markets have reached a level of complexity that some kind of brokerage, or information-based role, is required. Healthcare again represents an example of this. Insurance companies might be licensed by the state to oversee funding arrangements for the provision of healthcare, often receiving funding from the state to supplement payments made by individuals and their employers. These insurance companies then might purchase case, using a mix of public and private funds, from both public and private providers, or even from their own organization if they provide as well as purchase care, but may themselves not be public organizations.

Where non-public intermediaries are an important part of the process of delivering services, this creates an additional level of complexity as public managers may be responsible for overseeing the performance of the service in question, but depend upon intermediate organizations to deliver and purchase care on their behalf. In these circumstances, their responsibility is to attempt to hold these intermediate organizations to account on behalf of the public they are serving. Issues of accountability and blame come to the fore, as it is crucial that public managers don't simply blame these intermediate organizations where problems occur, but that they do scrutinize their performance. Policymakers need to make sure that there are clearly defined roles and responsibilities so that where a public service failure occurs, which at the worst could be a disaster such as a train crash, it is important that the response of every organization involved in the network of provision is to not to try and blame someone else. Sadly, this appears to have been the case in the period since rail privatization in the United Kingdom, with track companies attempting to blame subcontracted maintenance operators, no one being prepared to take responsibility for lives lost. The creation of intermediaries must not take responsibility out of the system.

A similar range of problems can also occur where public managers purchase services from private providers. The danger in these circumstances is that problems are not learned from, as they instead degenerate into cycles of mutual blame with no organization prepared to take responsibility. The contract environment can make this worse as admitting to error can mean a threat of withdrawal of the contract in the future for providers, or for allegations of incompetence in purchasing for managers involved in errors on that side. In either case, where a contract exists it carries with it the threat of legal action where errors are made. This can provide a strong disincentive for collaborative working between purchasers and providers, which public managers have to work hard to overcome, as they will have to find ways of resolving disputes in a way where learning can take place, but accountability is still in place.

The balanced market – An assessment

In practice, balanced markets, those not dominated by providers, purchasers (or intermediaries), presents a model of distributing resources based upon a 'governance' approach. Here, a regime of organizations is established in which no organization is able to dominate any other, and so must form relationships with other organizations based on either trust or contract for the system as a whole to work. The extent to which this is the case varies considerably from service to service and from nation to nation.

In centralized parliamentary systems, the state will tend to retain a stronger role in the policy process and the management of public systems because of the strong sense of central accountability and the continuing temptation to get more involved in the everyday running of public organizations. One of the defining features of the United Kingdom is its centralized political system and its first-past-the-post electoral system, leading to whichever political party, so long as it is able to retain a parliamentary majority, being able to pursue policy change more or less as it wishes for its time in power. As such, the United Kingdom saw radical public reform under both Thatcher and Blair governments, and underwent a programme of nationalization and public service expansion in the 1940s under the first post-war Labour government under Attlee. In the United States, however, because of the more fragmented state system, radical public reform has been more difficult to achieve with presidents attempting radical reform, especially in contentious areas such as healthcare, finding their reform plans blocked in Congress, where a different political party may hold a majority, and far more power is passed to state-level government away from the federal centre. In the latter instance, where power is already far more diffused, the governance model seems more explanatory than in systems where central dominance persists.

Provider dominance

Having explored a 'balanced' view of the state as an analytical ideal type, it is now possible to explore the implications of variations of it in terms of provider and purchaser power. The first of these might be where there are relatively few providers compared to purchasers.

A situation where providers dominate a market, public management purchasers face a problem; each provider has several purchasers where they can secure contracts from, but each purchaser has only a limited choice of providers. Public managers on the purchasing side therefore face an even more difficult situation in the balanced market, as the threat of removing a contract from a provider because of poor performance is less credible where there are fewer providers to contract with, and the scope of competition reduced. Public managers therefore approach a situation where they may be trying to achieve a contestable rather than a competitive market – one where the threat of competition is used to attempt to drive improvements from providers rather than competition itself. In such a situation the threat of moving contracts to other providers is possible, but this may be more at the level of threat and theory than practice as much actual moving of contracts would quickly exhaust the available providers and undermine the credibility of the approach.

The main danger where providers have potential to dominate a marketplace is the phenomenon economists refer to as 'cream skimming' (Le Grand, 2007). In this situation, providers are able to exert their dominance by giving services only to members of the public that they believe will be the cheapest or easiest for them. In education cream skimming means picking the students most likely to score highest in exams and be the easiest to teach, and in healthcare it means providing insurance or health services only to those that suffer the least illness. If some providers are able, through their dominance of the market, to achieve this position, it has the potential to undermine the system of provision as those less educationally able may find it difficult to get into a school, and those who are really ill find it difficult to be treated. Cream skimming is a serious problem in public markets, and great care must be taken in organizing markets to make sure that it is minimized.

Cream skimming is especially problematic for public managers as it creates additional dilemmas for them; they clearly have strong incentives to get their organizations into a strong financial position in order for them to be able to keep providing services, but if they take this too far through cream skimming they might undermine the whole basis of public services.

In all, where providers are relatively few, this will tend to guarantee them at least some contracts from some purchasers, so giving public managers on that side of the market greater power, but the temptation to engage in cream skimming. Public managers must try not to do this and remember their duty to the wider public, and policymakers that are responsible for overseeing and creating public markets must try and take away the potential to gain from it as much as possible.

Purchaser dominance

The opposite case to producer dominance is where there are relatively few purchasers compared to providers. In this situation, purchasing public managers are likely to be larger in size than providers, but may want to spread their purchasing across several providers in order to give themselves or service users, the widest possible choice of providers, but also to reduce the risk of depending entirely upon one. Providers, on the other hand, will have to negotiate with purchasing managers who have considerably power in the contracting process than they have, and so will be keen to foster long-term relationships to try and reduce the risk of losing contracts. However, this carries the risk of providers becoming overdependent upon a particular purchaser, putting them in a vulnerable position should they lose that contract.

If providers split their activity across several purchasers, that may result in them asking for contracts of a relatively low volume, increasing the cost of contracting for them (raising their 'transaction costs', but making their future more secure as the loss of one contract will not automatically lead to failure). Purchasing organizations will decide, however, how the market is structured, as they hold not only the funds to drive it, but those funds are concentrated in a relatively small number of organizations' hands.

The problem most likely to occur where there are relatively few, dominant purchasers, is that they are likely to lose contact with the purchasing wishes of their public. The more people purchasing public managers are representing, the less representative of that public their decisions are likely to be, and the more difficult it will become to consult with them.

Table 8.3 The market in conditions of provider and purchaser dominance

Provider dominance	Purchaser dominance
Contestable market because of lack of competition.	Competitive market because several providers available.
Purchasers have strong incentive to form long-term contracts.	Providers have strong incentive to form long-term contracts.
Danger of cream skimming.	Danger of purchasing not being representative of public its serves.

Table 8.3 summarizes the market situation in conditions of provider and purchaser dominance.

Additional difficulties in getting markets to work

There are additional difficulties in getting market mechanisms to work in public settings. The first is where providers organize themselves not competitively, but instead into collaborative relationships. One of the confusing tendencies of public policy is its tendency to revert between requiring providers to compete with one another to create cost saving and drive up quality, and requiring providers to collaborate with one another to provide new service pathways and to provide a seamless 'joined-up' service for users (Newman, 2002).

Where collaboration becomes the norm, so that providers find themselves offering more and more services in concert with one another, this increases the chances for service users to move between interlinked contracts, but this risks competition being effectively driven out of the market. Equally providers may take the opportunity in collaborative situations to specialize in particular services, making themselves indispensable and to occupy points in the networks of provision where, for a particular service to be delivered efficiently, the contract must be negotiated through them. In this situation, there is a danger of the provider creating an effective monopoly for itself.

Contracting can present problems because it can result in public managers becoming less democratically accountable as a greater stress is placed on contractual performance instead, and it may also lead to a reduction in the opportunities for democratic involvement for citizens or consumers in the administration of public services as organizations become more concerned with commercial confidentiality and meeting the thresholds specified in their contracts than on meeting the needs of the public more generally (Kirkpatrick & Martinez Lucio, 1996).

Practical examples of specializing in collaborative relationships might occur where a particular organization owns much of the local infrastructure, for example, in waste disposal. Although they may not provide services in relation to it directly, all the providers of waste disposal services in the local area have to make contracts with the infrastructure provider in order to be able to provide a service to end users. In this case, the infrastructure provider insulates itself from the local economy and effectively becomes a monopoly. Where public markets have been constructed in areas considered 'natural' monopolies, this phenomenon is more likely to occur. Where railways are privatized for example, the problem of who should own the track remains a difficult one as all the providers of trains will have to contract with the body, which therefore has little competitive incentive to improve the service it offers to the train companies. This problem has the potential to undermine the entire basis of the competitive market, but might work well if providers are positioned collaboratively with one another.

A second problem occurs where purchasers have little understanding of the offerings of providers within the market. This might occur where the offerings of public organizations are complex and not easily reducible to simple league tables or performance measures. In healthcare, organizing hospitals to compete with one another to improve standards and reduce costs appears to make sense, but this is only the case if the performance of the hospitals can be compared and purchases be able to tell which would be the best to purchase on behalf of the end-users, local patients (and the public more generally). If the job of choosing between providers is difficult for healthcare managers, this may be doubly the case for the users of services. In this case, it will be the job of healthcare managers to attempt to produce information that will allow users to make informed choices, but this, because of the complexity and specificity of health services will be very difficult.

Health decisions are complex because they can involve professional judgements not only about how patients should be treated, but also what is wrong with them in the first place. It is no accident that doctors take so long to train. Expecting patients to be able to acquire detailed medical knowledge and decide which treatment is right for them is plainly unrealistic. The nearest many patients come to being able to make informed choices is where they have long-term, chronic diseases and so acquire considerable experiential and theoretical knowledge about their own condition, and so possibly exceed medically trained staff in their knowledge of their own specific situation. For many other medical conditions, providing patients with information to allow them to make healthcare decisions is extremely difficult. At present websites and patient information leaflets exist to attempt to provide patients with what they need to know when making healthcare decisions, but necessarily have to simplify the complexity of the decision process. Should the choice of healthcare provider be made on the basis of who has the shortest waiting list, or the longest? The former might indicate that no one else wants to go to that particular provider, and the latter that everyone else agrees this is the best provider but will mean a longer wait. Should patients choose the provider with the lowest death rate or the highest? A low death rate would appear a good choice, but could simply be driven by the doctors at that particular hospital only admitting patients who do not really need treating. A high death rate might be excusable where the doctors treat only the most difficult cases, and may indicate that those doctors, because of their experiences at dealing with difficult cases, are likely to be extremely proficient at simpler ones. If healthcare managers and even other healthcare professionals struggle to interpret health data, it seems unrealistic to ask patients to attempt to try to.

In other public services, however, the decision may be easier to make. Where the decision is less complex and less specific, users or managers might be better able to examine the relative performance of providers. In secondary education (high school education) the results of exams taken at the end of schooling give at least some indication of the success of schools. Of course, they are not the only indicator worth considering, but the average experience of a student in a school is far more likely to be representative of the average patient in a hospital. Students are expected to attend similar classes and take similar exams at the end of their time at school, but patients may be at hospitals for a range of different conditions at very different times of their lives. In addition to this, in contrast to at least 'one-off' medical services, students can move schools if they find the one they are going to doesn't meet their needs.

The decision of which school to attend is less specific to the individual than the choice of hospital – the experience the school providers is more concerned with classes and other groups rather than individuals. Equally, the choice of school is probably less complex as parents are able to visit schools before choosing them, speak to parents of children in the local area to find out their experiences of their children attending the school, look at independent inspection reports of the school, and also examine school exam results. The decision of which school to send a child is not an easy one, but parents can generally understand the choice before them and are able to combine the available information into a form that allows them to choose.

Whether the purchasers or end users can understand how they are meant to be making choices is an overlooked but extremely significant part of a public market. Just because it is possible to combine providers in a competitive relationship and put in place a number of possible purchasers, it doesn't mean a market will work well. The simple provision of information by providers is not enough – it must also be understandable by potential purchasers and enable them to make informed decisions. Without this, there is a danger of purchasing decisions in the market becoming arbitrary or incoherent.

Equally, positioning public service users as individual consumers through the use of markets runs the risk of creating problems that require collectivist responses; public managers have to find answers to serve whole communities, whereas the answer that is more convenient or best for any individual member of that community might be rather different. Aberbach and Christensen suggest (2005) several tensions that can emerge between the individualism of markets and the collectivism of the political aspects of public management (Table 8.4):

Table 8.4 Consumer and citizen roles of users in public services

Consumer role	Citizen role
Individuals have preferences acted upon through market mechanisms.	Communities have preferences acted upon through collective voting and political action.
Consumer sovereignty and authority.	Authority and accountability of political leaders.
Consumers satisfied individually.	Citizen needs met collectively.
Profit incentive.	Equitable provision goal.

The tensions above lead to a significant problem in that, Aberbach and Christensen suggest, it is often extremely difficult to identify exactly who the consumer or customer is in public services, and even if they are identifiable, should public managers be focusing on meeting individual user needs or the needs of their communities as a whole?

Conclusion

The paradox this chapter suggests is that those introducing the use of market structures into public services have tended to forget that the very definition of 'public' means that introducing markets into these areas is likely to be fraught with difficulties. Public services are 'public' because they operate in areas where we either suspect market failure might occur, or where it has actually occurred comprehensively in the past.

This chapter has shown that the notion of a market, especially in public services, is problematic. This is an important point as it is a term that often claimed it is obvious what markets are, and how they should work, when in practice markets can mean a number of different arrangements, and present a range of difficult problems. For markets to work in the public sector, a number of preconditions need to be in place; there needs to be real competition in place with sufficient purchasers and providers to make this happen; choice must be informed in that it must be based on criteria relevant to the market, which is understandable by both purchasers and providers; and market imperfections such as cream skimming must be avoidable (Le Grand, 2007). These preconditions are outside the control of public managers, but if any of them are breached, then it will have significant implications for them.

If competition is not real, then providers can form cartels or partnerships and a more collaborative system of provision might occur. This may not be a bad thing, as it might be easier for managers to arrange a seamless service provision where providers are not in direct competition with one another, but does take the dynamic of relationships present away from those expected of a market. Equally, where purchasers dominate the marketplace a whole range of different problems occur because of the different asymmetry of power this causes, and because purchasers are likely to have become so large that they have lost touch with the needs of their local publics. A common way of dealing with the problem of markets becoming overly complex is the use of intermediaries such as insurance companies, but these bring new problems as the interests of the intermediaries may not reflect those of the state or of the public managers required to work with them, and because of the difficulties of accountability their use can cause.

If choice is not informed, then there is a real danger of markets producing perverse outcomes. Purchasing decisions, be they made by individuals or by public managers, need to be based on good information, and for that information to be understandable. Neither of these factors has been especially easy to achieve. Good information depends upon good information systems, and the record of investment in public sector management information systems, especially where they involve complex information technology, is not happy one, with huge amounts sometimes being spent and very little tangible benefit generated. Even if good information can be captured, it then must be communicated, and it cannot be assumed that it is always straightforward to show what good public sector performance looks like, and what this means in terms of the use of league tables or other performance data.

Finally, cream skimming is a problem that can potentially undermine any attempt to set up a public market. If providers become dominant in the market, they may attempt to narrow the range of public they provide their services to in order to minimize cost or disruption to themselves, and this goes against the principle of public service, as not all the public will be served. In practice, because public organizations tend to have professionals in place who have at least some autonomy in their decision making, public managers will struggle to cream skim unless they are able to put in place incentives for professionals to deliberately act against their own codes of conduct. Doctors might be told to treat only particular groups of patients, and not to attempt to help all their potential patients. Schools might deliberately put in place exclusionary admissions policies to make sure that they get the best students only. Undoubtedly this either explicitly or implicitly goes on in a number of public organizations. The job of public managers wishing to serve the public as a whole is to try and minimize it while at the same time accepting that they work within considerable resource constraints that mean they often cannot provide a service to everyone.

Bozeman (2002) provides an excellent checklist of the situations where markets in the public sector might fail (what he terms 'public value' failure). Bozeman suggests that markets tend to fail when (1) mechanisms for value articulation and aggregation have broken down; (2) where imperfect monopolies occur (particularly where government monopolies would be in the public interest); (3) where benefit hoarding occurs (where public commodities and services have been captured by particular providers or interest groups); (4) there is a scarcity of providers; (5) a short-time horizon threatens public value (particularly where longer term horizons give very different behaviours to short term horizons); (6) where the conservation of public resources is threatened; and (7) where market transactions threaten fundamental human subsistence (perhaps leading to man-made famine, political imprisonment) (Bozeman, 2002). Bozeman's list provides a good way of ending this chapter; where his conditions have been breached, then the thoughtless imposition of a market could lead to very significant problems.

Case study – The creation of markets in the National Health Service and the UK public schools

The NHS in the United Kingdom is often presented as being the archetypal public service organization in that, for the majority of its history, it has been almost entirely publicly funded and publicly provided, and insulated from the pressures and disciplines of market competition. Public schools (taken in this case to be schools funded and provided by the government) have been in much the same position. However, since the 1980s, there have been repeated attempts by the government to introduce competition into both healthcare and education – there have been an attempt to create markets in each.

The drive for market-based competition in schools has come from two reforms. The first is giving parents the right to choose (or more accurately, to express a preference of choice) for which school their child should go to. Prior to the reforms, Local Education Authorities were effectively responsible for deciding which child attended which local school, with it usually being a simple matter of where a child lived deciding which school they attended. The introduction of choice meant that parents could choose a school that was not the nearest to their home. Parents were usually asked to rank schools in order of preference, with the Local Education Authority or schools then trying to find a place at the school at the top of the list, and working their way through parental preferences where their places at their first choice school were not available.

The first problem of school choice is that popular schools are often over-subscribed, and it is difficult to expand them as this will mean having to add to infrastructure and increasing teaching staff, which may not mean standards can be preserved (even if there is space for expansion). Equally, it is politically difficult to allow those schools graded as poorly performing to close as it may mean some children have long journeys to school, especially where the school is in a rural area, and even that some communities might lose their local schools completely.

Allowing funding to follow the choices of parents of where to send their children allows good schools to receive more funding, but only if they can expand to meet need, and often only after they have expanded will they receive additional funding, leaving a financial gap until then. Whereas parents might feel qualified to judge which school to send their children to, being able to visit schools, look at their exam results, and remove their children from them if things don't work out, they may have little choice in practice if the most popular schools in a local area are already oversubscribed.

Where popular schools are oversubscribed, some of the children who choose them must be disappointed, leaving the problem of how to decide who should get in, and who should not. This can be settled by allowing children nearest the school first call on places, but this tends to result in good schools becoming hot spots for rising house prices as parents who want their children to go to a good school move into the area. This can act against children from less well off parents, who may also have less understanding of how to make sure that their children attend the best school in a choice system (Ball et al., 1995).

Alternatively, places could be allocated on a lottery basis, which means that the process for the system as a whole is fair, and that schools can be judged on their ability to teach children from right across the ability range. However, children who are assigned schools believed to be poor will believe the system is working against them, and their parents, where they can afford it, will want to remove their children and put them into private schools instead. Again, this has the potential to act against the children of less well-off parents.

In schooling then, there seems to be a theoretical ability for many parents to be able choose the school for their children, as they understand how such a choice might be made, but there may be problems in making the school infrastructure follow the incentives of the market, and it may work against children from less well-off parents.

In healthcare, the problem may be the other way around. In most urban areas there are likely to be many places where most patients can be treated for health problems. Specialist care aside, there are likely to be several hospitals or primary care doctors who can treat a particular problem, and, as long as an information system can track who is treating which patient, and funding can be made to follow the patient, there seems to be the infrastructure to make possible the development of a market for care.

The problem is how patients are meant to make informed decisions. Medical knowledge is specialist, and may take several years to acquire. Despite claims that it is now possible to research most conditions on the internet (Nettleton & Burrows, 2003), an awful lot of inaccurate of biased information exists, and it is sometimes difficult to separate quackery from fact (Tallis, 2005). Many medical interventions are also likely to be one-offs, so unlike schooling, where children can be moved if things don't work out, choices may not necessarily allow the chance for learning. Equally, as many medical treatments are invasive and even dangerous, the penalties for choosing the wrong place to be treated might be considerable.

Given the difficulties of patients making informed choices their choices might instead be based upon non-clinical factors, such as the proximity of the treatment centre to home, the availability of car parking or public transport, or the attractiveness of its buildings. These are important in the decision, but surely not as important as the level of care offered, which is often very difficult to measure or assess. In healthcare markets, the opposite problem to schooling may well be in place. There may be the infrastructure for a market to take place, but patients may not be able to make informed decisions about where they should be treated.

In education, managers face less of an infrastructural problem from competition as they are less likely to lose all applicants for their schools. Risks must be taken to expand schools as funding will not follow until additional students can be admitted, and it may involve considerable expense to put up new buildings and employ new teachers if the school is already at capacity. If schools are not attracting students, the challenge will be finding ways to avoid laying off staff who may be needed if applications rise again, and trying to keep infrastructure fully deployed through the use of community programmes or child care, for example.

In healthcare, public managers face greater risks from competition, but patients may find it very difficult to choose between providers. This means that public managers must actively use promotion strategies to make sure that their provision is well regarded. This may involve advertising to reassure potential patients, as well as investment in non-clinical aspects of provision such as car parking or building appearance, both inside and out. This clearly has tensions with the logic of public service, as it could mean taking funds away from patient care. The consolation is that patients might get better more quickly in a well maintained and presented environment.

This analysis carries significant implications for the use of market in the public sector. It implies that, instead of, as often appears to be the case in the United States and the United Kingdom, that markets are the automatically preferred way of organizing public services, it is a false premise that the relationship of state to citizen is that same as between the private enterprise and its client (Larson, 1997). The use of widespread marketization would make state bodies more responsive, but strip them of their public legitimacy. Both public managers and public policymakers must instead find ways of safeguarding their role as guardian of the public interest. There is a need for a 'portfolio' approach to management of public services in which some services might be suitable for marketization, but for others this may not be appropriate at all (Greener, 2008).

Further reading

My own work has tried to explore the implications of markets generally (Greener, 2008) and in the contexts of healthcare and education specifically (Greener, 2003a, 2003c, 2005b). The work of John Clarke and Janet Newman has examined UK public reforms introducing markets from critical perspectives that make for fascinating reading (Clarke & Newman, 1997, Clarke *et al.*, 2006, 2007). Equally, important is the work of the US psychologist Barry Schwarz, who suggests that giving the public choices in areas where they don't feel able to make them can be hugely disempowering (Schwartz, 2004).

Julian Le Grand has been examining the potential for markets to be used in the public sector for several years, and his recent work uses economics-derived frameworks for exploring their benefits and drawbacks (Le Grand, 1997, 2003, 2007), although Le Grand clearly believes they should be more widely used. To some extent this is mirrored in the work of Britain's most famous sociologist, Anthony Giddens, who in recent years was a prominent policy advisor to the Labour government in the United Kingdom. The UK government, in turn, has increasingly shown a strong preference for the use of markets in the public sector (Minister of State for Department of Health *et al.*, 2005).

Performance management

Introduction

Previous chapters have shown how, along with the growth in the use of markets and market mechanisms, performance management has also become an increasingly central issue in the public sector. There is something of a paradox in this. On the one hand, markets are often used and invoked as a means of decentralizing public service delivery. Their advocates claim that markets take the politics out of public services by forcing them to become more responsive to user need, rather than being the product of political design. On the other hand, however, performance management is often a strongly centralizing force in public service delivery. It is often used as a means of getting local organizations to be more accountable to central or regional government bodies. Performance management is often portrayed as a neutral set of tools for planning and monitoring public service activity, but is inherently political in that it makes public organizations accountable to government for a range of goals, which government has itself set (Spicer, 2004). The chapter asks the question 'what is the role of performance management in public organizations?'

The chapter proceeds as follows. First, a brief section outlines the importance of performance management in today's public services, and gives some reasons for its increased usage. Next, the chapter explains the difference between performance management and performance measurement before discussing the problems that result from performance management in the public sector. After giving examples of how performance management plays itself out in specific services, it explores the implications of performance management for professional groupings in public services, especially in terms of the role of the HR function. It concludes by summarizing the tensions found in the chapter and discusses their implications for public managers.

Performance management in context

There are a number of reasons why performance management has become so important in public services. A few of these are presented in Table 9.1 and summarized below.

For much of the history of public services central or federal government has struggled to measure or control what happens at local levels as the organizations responsible for the delivery of services can be hundreds of miles away, and policy can be mediated heavily through the activities of public professionals. Performance management has been seen by many in government as a means by which the stronger implementation of central policy can be achieved through the active measurement and the rewarding of local performance that meets centrally designed targets. Performance management can be seen as the solution to the 'implementation gap' between the ideas of policymakers in central governments, and the delivery of public services on the ground.

Attempting to bridge the implementation gap is not the only reason for increased significance of performance management in public services. First, there is perceived failure of democracy as a means of achieving accountability

Table 9.1 Reasons for the growth of performance management in the public sector

Fiscal and financial crisis and concerns about lack of public service measurement.	As public budgets got tighter, especially in the 1970s and from 2008 onwards, performance management became a more relevant tool for scrutinizing public organizations, especially in relation to finance.
Implementation gap.	Policymakers became increasingly concerned that the plans were not being carried out at the local level – performance management gave them a way of trying to bridge this gap.
Failure of democracy.	If public services were not directly democratically accountable to the people, then a greater central accountability through performance management might provide an alternative.
Concerns that decentralization will mean loss of control for government.	If markets and decentralization are being carried out, how does the state continue to guarantee quality standards and accountability without greater use of performance management?
Wider availability of information technology.	Wider use of IT means that more complex information systems can be constructed upon which performance management systems depend.

(Fox & Miller, 1995). This results in a deficit that stronger performance management can narrow by making sure that services at least correspond to the standards prescribed of it, standards that are monitored ultimately by politicians, making public services at least accountable to democratically elected figures, if not the public itself. Second, in an era where public policy advocates have argued for the greater decentralization of public services (Osborne & Gaebler, 1993), governments have felt the need to try and retain some central control whilst decentralizing through the use of market mechanisms. They have decentralized the allocation of public services through markets, but tended to simultaneously centralize the accountability of their delivery through performance management systems. There has been a simultaneous decentralization (of allocation) and centralization (of accountability measurement) (Peckham *et al.*, 2005). Third, performance management systems depend on high-quality information systems. Public sector information systems have often struggled to meet the needs of their users or of central governments, but the wider availability of IT more generally has led to the potential for far greater information collection and analysis than in the past, and so to a far greater potential for some degree of performance measurement.

Performance management is not an entirely centralizing force – this is only the case if performance standards put in place are decided centrally and local organizations are penalized if they do not meet them. It is equally possible for performance standards to be delegated to the local level, and so for them to become a means by which services might become more decentralized. However, the temptation has always been for central policymakers to use performance management as a means of achieving greater control over public services rather than delegating greater responsibility.

Performance management and performance measurement

Performance management is often equated to performance measurement, when the two are not the same, as the measurement of performance is only one aspect of its management, even if it tends to become the most contentious. A basic performance management feedback loop suggests a first stage where a plan for what needs to happen is constructed. Second, measurements are taken against that plan to establish whether performance is developing in line with the plan or not (the performance measurement stage). Third, corrective action is taken where performance is falling short of targets (negative feedback) or perhaps to push it even further from the target where the target is being exceeded (positive feedback). Finally, the cycle starts again, with a new plan being drawn up as necessary to reflect changes in the situation within which the service finds itself, such as the introduction of new policies or a change in the service's environment.

Management theory based on a systems approach, such as the performance management loop, treats performance as a control mechanism, suggests that learning can occur as adjustments are made to the organization if its measured performance falls short or exceeds the standards of the plan (called 'single-loop' learning, as it occurs within the standard feedback cycle in the manner of a simple closed system like a thermostat and radiator). Further learning can also occur as planners look to see how realistic their expectations were in the light of actual performance and changes in the wider environment of the organization called 'double-loop learning' as it means that the plan upon which the performance plan was based is itself called under question (Argyris & Schon, 1995).

As such, performance measurement is an important part of the cycle of performance management, but it also involves planning, taking action to deal with good or bad performance, and making sure that plans are still relevant. As such, it can be regarded as a strategic process in which all of these elements must be considered. Strategy is a term that is much used and abused and needs to be treated with caution because it has been somewhat 'naturalized' in the management literature as representing an objective series of processes when, especially in the public sector, strategies will fall upon organizational actors (especially public professionals) in different ways (Llewellyn & Tappin, 2003). Where it falls on actors who are inexperienced in strategic processes or represent 'uncultivated ground' (p. 978) there is a danger of a lack of debate over the meaning and purposes of strategy occurring. Bearing this in mind, how does performance management work in the public sector?

Performance management in the public sector

Planning

In order to performance manage, a plan is necessary. The first question is establishing actually how a plan should be put together, and who should contribute to it. One obvious answer is that it is for the government to put together plans for public organizations – in the past this has often been how things worked. In order to try and achieve a unified hierarchy of control, government put together plans that were then worked out in greater detail at each level down the hierarchy, being broken down into more specific and precise goals.

However, the view that central policymakers are solely responsible for the setting of plans has come increasingly under question. The role of the user has become more important as consumerist agendas have become more significant in public organizations, and the public more generally have demanded the politicians to pay closer attention to their needs and aspirations. Politicians have increasingly found themselves engaged in consultation and 'listening' exercise before constructing plans, having to show that they are not simply constructing plans according to their own understanding and prejudices. Equally, there are several other bodies that have had considerable influence over the policy process at various times in the history of public organizations. Trades unions have sometimes demanded inclusion where plans for public services significantly affect their members, with corporatist models of policy-making more common in Europe than elsewhere, but attempted at various times in the United Kingdom as well. Strong professional groups in public organizations have also demanded inclusion in policy formulation, particularly those with high prestige and status, such as the doctors. The influence of professional groups often goes beyond their expertise and to a level where they may have attended the same schools and universities as policymakers, so creating an administrative 'elite' where understandings are reached outside of the formal policy process itself (Wright Mills, 1956). This means that the plans that finally emerge for public services might be the result of informal discussion and consultation that is not at all transparent to the public at large. This is a more pluralistic view of policy than the assumption that politicians alone put together plans, but not one that is particularly democratic or very accountable to the public.

The fact that many societal groups are interested in being a part of the plan setting for public organizations is because their scope is often so wide, and because their activities have so many implications for so many people. School provision does not just impact upon parents of children of school age and their children, but can also significantly affect property prices in the area, meaning it potentially affects all householders, has the potential to cause planning issues because of traffic problems when children are arriving or leaving, can reduce crime (by taking young people off the street) or increase it (creating a concentration of young people who might try and 'bunk off' or 'shirk' classes), as well as creating a potential market for local business suppliers and local businesses themselves, who may come to rely upon school children spending money in their stores. The knock-on effects of public organizations are considerable, leading to local communities and businesses wanting a say in how they are run as well as the service users and general public.

As public services have so many interested parties (or, in contemporary parlance, 'stakeholders'), any plan must attempt to work through the competing interests of those parties to attempt to create goals and targets that as many as possible can sign up to. This requires public managers to be able to work across several different groups, to listen to their concerns and to show that they are being treated seriously, even if they cannot all have what they want. This also means that long-term relationships must be formed as not all the goals put forward by interest groups can be achieved quickly – patience and mutual understanding are important virtues in public service planning (Stoker, 2006).

Most recently, ideas such as 'The Big Society' (Norman, 2010) have attempted to introduce more 'bottom-up' approaches to public service by encouraging the public to get involved in co-production or even new service provision. Such an approach still requires planning – first at the local level to make sure that services are coherently provided – even where a community takes over a library, for example, it must still have opening times. Second, some planning will be necessary to co-ordinate the activities of community groups to make sure that the coverage of public services has some coherence at the higher level – so that some communities don't end up being over-served and others excluded completely. Making public services work from the 'bottom-up' can work, but may also require, where services will not otherwise run, interventions from planning bodies at a higher level to try and encourage local people to get involved.

Plans and measures

Planning is a complex process, then establishing reliable measures that can assess the success or failure of the plans is perhaps harder still. There is now a considerable literature on the difficulties of performance measurement in the public sector (Greener, 2003b, Pollitt, 1986, Sanderson, 1998, Talbot, 2000), and within which is a recurring theme about how difficult it is to measure the outputs or outcomes of public organizations. This problem is clearly a part of both the planning and measurement elements of performance management – it relates to planning as plans must be broken down into objectives, at least some of which need to be measurable – but also to the measurement element of performance management as actual performance needs to be compared with the plan in order to measure progress.

Boyne and Gould-Williams in one of their studies of local government planning (Boyne & Gould-Williams, 2003) found that plans can work well where favourable perceptions of the planning process are already held within the organization but that a 'proliferation of precise quantitative targets is associated with poorer performance' (p. 130). Their claim, however, is that planning does lead to service improvement overall, suggesting it has a valuable role in the performance management cycle.

The measurement of public organizations is difficult because finding variables that capture their activities can often prove elusive. Nicholson-Crotty and his collaborators (2006) found, in an examination of educational organizations in Texas, that managers' perceptions of their organizations depended significantly upon the choice of performance measures that they used. An example of the difficulties of finding appropriate measures in the public sector should make this clear.

Road planning and performance management

Road planning is usually carried out in urban areas by members of local authorities. Planning departments will work to try and deal with the problems of increased traffic flow through towns, at the same time trying to make sure that people are attracted into urban areas because of the increased commercial opportunities this affords businesses. They, therefore, have to balance the needs of commerce (and often tourism) in local areas, which want as many people as possible to visit, with the need of local residents, who probably just want to get to and from work as quickly as possible. Road planning also doesn't happen without regard to the road infrastructure of the past – today's planners inherit the decisions of previous planners and cannot simply rip up all the roads and start again. Some cities have heritage landmarks that may mean that the road infrastructure is very limited in where it can or cannot go, as demolishing buildings of historic significance is clearly off-limits.

The measure of the effectiveness of road planning is therefore a function of several factors. Clearly traffic flow is important, with higher volumes being better for business (up to a point where traffic simply stops moving or pollution get very bad, perhaps deterring people from visiting) and lower volumes better for residents (but not to a point where towns become so empty that property prices start falling and local amenities move away). Coming up with an agreed level of traffic that planners should be aiming for might therefore be a highly political, or even arbitrary exercise. Equally some areas of town might be traffic blackspots with either exceptionally slow-moving traffic or a number of accidents, but road planners unable to do much about this because the causes are the location of an historical monument (that means there is limited space for roads) or a school (which may be the responsibility of the education department and so outside the scope of their influence) or an employer with a large workforce all trying to arrive and leave at the same time (which might be the result of decisions from the local authority's commercial department).

As such, the road planning department might find themselves having to come up with highly contested measures of traffic flow the achievement of which are thwarted by decisions made in other departments (with tourism bodies and local residents representatives perhaps preferring lower flows, but business-oriented sections wanting higher ones). This highlights the need for public managers to be able to work across areas of their organizations (and even to work across organizations), but if each department or organization has its own performance management goals, then this may become impossible as the relationship might become competitive and insular rather than collaborative and outward looking.

Measurement

Moving on to the measurement stage of the performance cycle, a range of additional problems become apparent. These are summarized in Table 9.2, and again, discussed at greater length below.

Measuring what can be measured

One problem that overlaps with the planning process is where planners find it impossible to find a variable that measures the performance of their organization, and so instead of trying to find innovative ways of measuring activity, instead base their planning decisions on what they can measure. It may seem odd planning on the basis of what can be measured rather than on what the public organization really does, but this is surprisingly common. Healthcare is a good example. Working out how healthy a person is can be a remarkably

Table 9.2 Some problems with performance measurement

Measuring the measurable only.	Instead of attempting to capture the complexity of outputs of public organizations, over-simple measures are put in place that do not really represent them.
Target focus.	Managers become so concerned with meeting particular targets that they do not manage the service for the good of the public any more.
Gaming.	Managers manipulate systems in order to try and present their performance as being better than it is, even giving fraudulent returns of their activities.

difficult thing to do. Many doctors will ask 'healthy for what?' if confronted by the question as the standards required by a regular exerciser will be very different from those of a dedicated fast food consumer. In the former case not being able to run for an hour because of joint pain might be seen as a major problem, whereas in the latter this would hardly impinge upon the individual's daily activities, which might be more about being able to consume particular types of food without feeling sick. Objective measures can be constructed in terms of blood pressure and heart rate, but these again may simply not apply to many people, so long as they are able to meet their home and work needs they may not care if they are a little overweight or if their cholesterol level is too high.

How we measure how healthy we are is a function of our expectations and the environment we find ourselves in. If working this out for an individual can be hard, then working out how healthy a whole local population is can border on the impossible. However, there are a range of simple indicators that can be used to measure the health of both individuals and populations. The body mass index (BMI) can measure a person's weight to height, and give an indication of whether they are obese or not. However, the weight part of the measure does not differentiate muscle from fat, and so, famously, Hollywood stars such as Brad Pitt appear obese according to the index. Equally, finding a baseline from which to apply an index to assess healthcare can be very difficult, as much of the data upon which these baselines of healthiness are based are by their nature historic, and so may not be relevant in a world that has changed considerably since those measurements were originally taken. Attempting to measure health based on these variables might be deeply flawed, but public managers may find they have no alternative where they are faced with governments demanding that increased state investment in their service delivers an improvement in the area required, and that improvement is measurable.

Target focus

A related problem is where public managers become focused not on improving their service, but instead upon the variables used to measure the improvements in their service. To continue with the example of healthcare, doctors might be told, for example, that they must see a patient within 30 minutes of their arrival for an appointment. This seems sensible – patients should not be kept waiting for unreasonable amounts of time. However, it also creates space for public managers to 'game' the system. Within the wording of the target, doctors do not have to treat the patient, but merely to 'see' them. As such, an easy way of meeting the target would be for doctors, in-between treating patients, to periodically (every 30 minutes) emerge from their treatment rooms, greet all the patients waiting, and then to return to their room again. They will have 'seen' the patients, and so met the target. If this sounds far-fetched, then readers should be assured that I didn't make it up.

A second example might be where policymakers become aware of the 'seeing' patients ruse, and change the target to say that all patients should have their treatment begun within 30 minutes of arriving for an appointment. A devious public manager might again look at the exact wording of the target, and put in place a system whereby, because the new target does not specify a doctor will treat the patient. Instead, the target can be met by a triage nurse being tasked with meeting every new patient as they arrive, interviewing them, and where possible dealing with patient problems without the doctor. The hospital might argue that diagnosing the patient is a crucial part of treatment, and interviewing the patient is an important part of diagnosis. Although no doctor has been near a patient, the process of treatment therefore has begun as soon as the triage nurse sits down with the patient, and the target has been met. It may even be the case that receptionists might argue that upon being booked into the computer system a patient's treatment has begun, as their problem is entered into a computer system, which clinicians can monitor to see if urgent care is needed.

Performance gaming

Where public managers find themselves in a regime where they stand to lose performance-related pay or even their job should they fail to meet their required target level, the incentive 'game' performance measures increases. In these situations, blatant gaming of the system can occur. If patients cannot be seen quickly enough, bogus patients with very low waiting times have sometimes been entered onto computer databases to try and bring the average waiting time down. Where managers are responsible for several areas of a service and some are falling behind targets whereas others are well in front, there will be a temptation to try and 'reallocate' numbers to try and artificially bring up the performance of the poor areas where this might lead to sanctions against the managers or service. If public managers are on short-term contracts requiring high performance, or where promotions depend upon hitting particular targets, then there will be temptations to misrepresent data rather than deal with the rather more challenging task of improving service.

Where public managers do not expect to stay in organizations very long before moving on to new posts, the temptation to try and show improvements in measures may be even stronger. In these circumstances, public management performance literally becomes a performance (Talbot, 2000) – an attempt to present a view of the organization that may bear only a tenuous reality to its actual state, and to periodic crises before which managers attempt to move on before the underlying situation becomes apparent.

Hood (2006), in his summary of gaming problems coming from the UK Blair government's reforms, suggests that their extensive use of targets appears to lead to three classic gaming responses: ratchet effects (the tendency of target setters to fix next year's targets a little above this year's, leading to providers deliberately reining back on this year's production); threshold effects (where uniform target leads to no incentive for those that exceed targets); and output distortion (the deliberate manipulation of results). Hood also suggests that policymakers have been too quick to accept good news from their performance measurement systems uncritically, taking reported gains at face value, and having no coherent anti-gaming strategy.

Taking action

After performance measurement, the next stage of the performance cycle is taking action when measured performance appears out of line with reported performance. Where performance is less (or more) than hoped for, managers should be intervening to find ways of addressing the difference.

If too few patients are seen (or treated) by a hospital or if exam results in schools are below those expected, managers should be coming up with strategies to try and resolve the problems the performance system has brought to their attention. This asks a fundamental question of public managers – can they actually make a difference to the service they are responsible for? The limitations of what public managers can actually do to improve things can often be quite sobering.

The example of road planning above suggested that public managers might be held responsible for the results of decisions of other departments, and the only way for this to be resolved is for cross-boundary working and close collaboration across the whole of delivery. But what if the problems identified as preventing targets from being met go beyond the limits of local public organization? What if they are due to more general societal forces such as poverty or demography? A local manager might be held accountable for smoking cessation in the local area, or at least for persuading local people to enrol in smoking cessation programmes. The problem is that local people may not perceive smoking to be a problem – their social backgrounds might be such that their friends, relatives and parents smoke, and smoking might be a part of the fabric of social life. Cigarettes might be purchased in collective trips to the local shops, smoked together, and the habit becomes something regarded as a defining feature of a particular group. In this situation, if people do not regard themselves as having a problem, and they are not doing anything illegal, is it really the job of public managers to attempt to persuade them otherwise? What chance do public managers have in particular social settings where smoking is part of the embedded culture, compared to other areas, where it might be seen much more as an unacceptable act, and individuals come forward willingly to attempt to give up? The social setting a particular public manager might make a considerable difference for the measured success of his or her activities, as well as for the potential to change behaviour.

Equally, if a public manager is engaged in trying to improve services for older people in their local area, they are substantially more likely to be successful where a strong network of representatives for that age group are already in place and can be mobilized. A seaside retirement town is much more likely to back changes that mean more services for older people than a town where predominantly young people reside. Ironically, of course, the former town is likely to already be well endowed with facilities for older people, and the latter town having a shortage. Breaking through the existing infrastructure is difficult enough because of its very physical presence, but public managers will also have to deal with the vested interests that seek to protect it and persuade them, often in a situation where budgets are a zero-sum game (where an increase in funding for one service means a reduction in funding for another), that spending money in an under-resourced area is required.

In Chapter 7, the newest approach to trying to change behaviour in the general public, based around 'nudge' areas, which attempt to influence the public by using insights from behavioural psychology, was explored. To this end, Julian Le Grand has raised a number of possible approaches used in public policy and public management, including the idea of a licence to smoke (BBC News, 2008). Le Grand suggested that the inconvenience of having to get a licence to smoke would deter people from the habit, pointing out that 70 per cent of smokers actually want to stop, and so making it bit more difficult might make a big difference.

Applying this sort of thinking to public management problems does create new opportunities for trying to achieve behavioural change – thinking about the default option of a public service and making sure that it is the one that public managers really want to encourage. In the above situation, making it more difficult to smoke means that the default – that anyone can buy a packet of cigarettes – is changed to one where only licenced smokers can do so. Local resident parking is a similar idea – where streets are changed from a position where anyone can park to one where only local people can. This thinking is new and still untested but does give public managers potentially another tool to try and achieve change.

Interest groups and professional groups

Another performance management difficulty facing public managers, as noted in Chapter 6 especially, is that many public organizations, because of the nature of the services they deliver or the complexity of the organization required to deliver those services, have strong professional groups within them. Professionals will demand the ability to express their own judgement of what performance management standards should be put in place (if any) based on their specific expert knowledge. To achieve professional 'buy-in' to the achievement of higher levels of performance, those groups will need to be involved and engaged with the process, making such negotiations in which standards and measures are set extremely difficult. Where professionals are not engaged in this way, they may regard a deviation of measured performance compared to the plan as being irrelevant, and so no further action to be needed.

Public managers therefore have both a selling job and a telling job in relation to performance management. The selling is needed to show that conforming to the plan is necessary in order to secure the service's improvement, or even its future. A sense of shared destiny can overcome professional backgrounds remarkably quickly. In this case, public managers will have to show that they have the support of central or regional policymakers, and that there are sanctions for non-compliance (as well as hopefully, rewards for meeting the plan's targets), and to engage with public professionals to make sure that the plan reflects their views as well.

A telling job might be necessary where managers can find no way of persuading professionals that a change in their behaviour is necessary. This can be remarkably difficult, as professional groupings often have their own hierarchies and loyalties, may not regard public managers as holding any authority over them, even where this is, in fact, the case. Faced with the complexities of having to 'tell' professionals to change their behaviour, public managers often engage in a complex range of strategies for trying to achieve this goal without direct confrontation, such as scheduling meetings to give professionals minimum preparation time to oppose changes, setting agendas to conceal contentious items of business, and attempting to fill meetings with their own supporters so that professionals are bound by decisions taken collectively, but with the odds rigged heavily in their favour (Greener, 2005a).

These strategies of avoiding direct confrontation with public professionals are not exactly aboveboard but are a part of organizational life where change can be difficult to achieve. It is not entirely unknown for professionals to engage in similar kinds of behaviour to preserve their power as well. An interesting situation appears where professionals take on managerial responsibilities, and attempt to straddle the two roles. The evidence suggests that in a conflict-laden situation, professionals tend to revert back to their professional rather than their managerial role (Kitchener, 2000), but this will depend upon the particular professional in question, and some of the most evangelical managers of public organizations are former professionals who have become frustrated by the constraints of their previous identity.

Public managers and HR

The problems of the relationship between public managers and professionals can often be traced back to the poor development of the human resources (HR) function in public organizations. One of the differences between the old public administration and the new public management was that in the past, personnel functions were in place that were primarily concerned with making sure that legal requirements were met for the organization, and for dealing with any legal disputes that arose around employment (Boyne, 1999). These are clearly important roles within an organization but are rather passive uses of the organizational function responsible for overseeing and supporting those working within it.

Contemporary human resource management is a more proactive process, embracing the functions of the old personnel departments, but attempting to increase its range of activities across the organization. It takes a greater responsibility for the proactive recruitment of outstanding individuals into the organization, as well as their development once recruited. It tries to improve the productivity of those working within the organization by assessing their training needs and making sure that their skills and professional knowledge are kept up-to-date. Human resource management is regarded as one of the key ways that an organization can achieve a competitive edge over its rivals and to make the most of those working within it. It therefore corresponds with contemporary notions of achieving competitive advantage through the human capital of an organization, such as the resource-based view of the firm (Barney, 1996). Performance management is therefore a crucial part of human resource management.

HR and change dissenters

Faced with performance management pressures to deliver services at higher standards, public managers have increasingly called upon the human resources function to help them deal with professionals unwilling or unable to conform to the changing agendas. Professionals unwilling to change their practices have been requested to update their skills or acquire new ones, such as customer orientation, and have found themselves drawn into standardized employment practices from which they had previously enjoyed considerable freedom. Professionals might be required to attend a certain number of management development courses each year in order to show their commitment to improving the standards of customer focus. HR functions have taken a lead in developing standardized job profiles for professional groupings that specify the roles required of them, and once these roles have been standardized further, have developed the means by which the performance of individual professionals can be measured and assessed.

The promotion and development of professionals is no longer the exclusive concern of the professional groupings themselves, but instead involves public managers and HR professionals, who have become increasingly involved in making sure that professionals are meeting the roles required of them. Bonuses and merit awards, previously given by professionals to professionals through subcommittees that were based on professional expertise, have found themselves under the scrutiny of both public managers and user representatives in the name of increasing accountability and transparency. If they are to be promoted, professionals increasingly find themselves required to meet not only the standards of their professional organizations but also to have shown a commitment to their managerial development through attending organizational development courses and understanding budgets and marketing principles.

Where professionals repeatedly fail to come up to performance standards, or where they refuse entirely to co-operate with performance management systems, this might ultimately lead for public managers to be supported in a decision to dismiss them from their posts. Because of the high status of many public professionals and the prestigious professional support groups that they may belong to, this can be a time-consuming and difficult process for everyone involved. Challenging public professional performance can easily result in a legal case, with HR functions increasingly having to call upon in-house or external specialist legal services, as well as making sure that the cases public managers bring to them where dismissal is necessary are well supported by documentation and procedurally correct. The problem is that the sanction of dismissal is still relatively (compared to the private sector at least) underused in most public organizations, which means that public managers are still relatively inexperienced in dealing with it. They will therefore need a great deal of support and help from HR functions, which are themselves often under-resourced and ill-equipped to deal with complex cases. As HR in the public sector expands its role, it is becoming regarded as a service for public managers to utilize in their organizations, and it needs to raise its game to make sure that it is one they regard as valuable to them rather than as a central overhead that generates no useful return.

Completing the performance management loop

Having worked through the stages of agreeing a plan, measuring performance against it, and trying to change professional behaviour where necessary in order to meet performance standards, this takes us back to the beginning of the performance management cycle again, the process of reassessing the validity of the present plan amongst the many available stakeholders. At this stage, those responsible for planning have something of a conundrum. If they throw out the existing plan, opting for a range of new goals and targets, then they can be seen as acknowledging the problems with past plans and accepting the need for change. This may be embraced by public managers and those responsible for the delivery for public services as a positive step if the problems of the past have been overwhelming. However, it can also be seen as 'moving the goalposts' and a demoralizing process within which public workers have to constantly reset their goals depending upon which plan has been put in place this year.

Too much change can result in 'redisorganization' (Smith & Walsh, 2001) as reform programme comes after reform programme and little or no stability is ever granted for services. Equally, it is hard to measure whether a service is actually getting better or not if the variables used to measure them are changed every year, taking validity away from any claims of reforming services in the name of improvement because it becomes almost impossible to demonstrate such improvement has actually occurred. The argument for the stability of measures on the other hand is that allows continuity of measurement, and at least some indication of whether services are getting better or not. However, it will also be unpopular if poor measures, or difficult to achieve measures, are in place that lead to public managers being removed from their jobs for a failure to demonstrate success. Given this problem, it seems hardly surprising that politicians find it almost impossible to resist changing performance measures frequently, and that they may even want to try and revisit the entire basis of the performance management system in order to find a new solution to the many problems involved in attempting to assess how well public services are delivered.

Conclusion

The paradox of performance management is that, in order to know how well an organization is doing we need to be able to measure its outputs or outcomes, but any measure of an organization's performance is only partial, and so using measures can result in gaming and other unintended consequences.

A pithy summary of this problem is attributed to Einstein in a widely used quote – 'Everything that can be counted does not necessarily count; everything that counts cannot necessarily be counted.'

Performance management is based on the logical idea that you can't be managing an area unless you can know what you want to achieve, measure what is going on against your goal, and make changes as necessary. It is therefore about setting plans, measuring progress against them, taking any necessary action and then assessing the plan to make sure that it is still relevant. It's a simple process in principle, but its application in management generally, and the in the political environment of the public sector particularly leads to a number of difficulties and problems.

Agreeing a plan between multiple stakeholders is a complex process because it may lead to those with very different values and goals attempting to try and find ways of sharing sufficient common ground to come up with a plan of what should be done. The goals of business leaders will often be very different from the goals of local residents, and public managers must find some process by which an agreement can be reached that they all can respect. Where stakeholders are consulted and their views rejected, they may not wish to re-enter the planning process again, and so public managers will have to work extra hard to include groups whose views have been sought but not included in their present plans. Even if stakeholders can reach agreement, public managers must still work together to achieve their stated goals; middle-level managers may not share the same goals as those higher up their organizations, and often have a key role in modifying strategy rather than simply carrying it out (Currie, 1999).

Once a plan has been put in place, the problem will often come up with appropriate measures to determine whether or not it is being met. The difficulty of measuring public sector output is a recurring theme throughout the book because it can lead to some rather perverse outcomes. Good examination results are not the same things as providing a good education service (although the two are related) and high user ratings are not the same thing as a good public service (although, again, there is a relationship).

Public managers need to find the best possible measures of their service's success, and be flexible enough to realize that any measure is unlikely to do the job forever – as contexts and services change they must be alert to both 'hard' and 'soft' indications (Goddard et al., 1999) of whether their service is working. In addition to hard numbers of those things that are measurable, other softer forms of intelligence will be available that will be more opinion based, but may well be crucial in assessing how well organizations are performing. A distinction is sometimes made between outputs (the measures to be implemented) and outcomes (the end results of reform programmes) – the first are picked up by specific performance measures, whereas the second are often not, and performance management has both intended and unintended outcomes (Mannion et al., 2001). Public managers must also avoid the temptations of gaming their performance measures, even where policymakers put tremendous pressure on them to achieve results that may not be realizable.

If action is necessary because public organizations are underperforming, then managers often have to deal with strong professional groups and get them to change their practices. Where professionals believe that public managers have no authority, or that they lack legitimacy because they are not as well educated or as prestigious as them, this will be difficult. In this situation, public managers often employ a range of strategies to get professionals onside with change, but where these do not work, they may have to go down disciplinary routes. In these circumstances, the HR function of the public organization will become important, but it is still often the case that both managers and HR professionals are ill-equipped at dealing with low-performing professionals, making the problem of raising the performance of public organizations an entrenched one.

Finally, public managers must be resilient in that, once they have completed a cycle of the performance loop, little else remains other for them to have to start again and begin the planning process once more. They need to occupy a number of different roles during the whole process; facilitating between a range of stakeholders to get them to agree to 'buy in' to a plan, and so being able to both 'sell' and 'tell' it; being realists in the process of performance measurement by recognizing that some targets, if not met, might lose them their jobs; being able to support professionals who are prepared to work with new

Table 9.3 Public manager roles during performance management

Performance management stage	Public manager role
Planning.	Liaising between stakeholders. Finding ways of setting shared goals. Including all groups with a right to voice.
Measurement.	Ensuring targets are reflective of actual performance. Dealing with hard and soft information. Avoiding gaming.
Action.	Selling and telling. Utilizing appropriate change strategies. Working with HR.
Completing the loop.	Keeping the process going. Deciding between change or continuing with plans.

ways of working as well as trying to persuade and cajole that are not; being assertive and able to face up to professionals who are systematically underperforming; and having a considerable amount of stamina in the knowledge that once the performance cycle is over it must be begun again the following year. Table 9.3 summarizes public management roles during a cycle of performance management.

Public managers must therefore look to the future and be able to build long-term relationships that go beyond any particular planning cycle, but will possibly exist in an environment that encourages the meeting of short-term performance targets by any means necessary, with possible sanctions for those that do not meet them. Ackroyd *et al.* (1989) suggest that the imposition of prescribed managerial practices, of which centrally prescribed performance management systems are perhaps the most visible example, end up taking away discretion from public managers and reducing their autonomy and ability to manage their organizations. It is somewhat paradoxical that, at exactly the time the state has demanded that public managers take greater control of their organizations, the careless imposition of centrally imposed managerial strategies might actually remove their capacity to manage.

Behn (2003) suggests that performance measures are helpful in achieving eight different managerial purposes (evaluation, control, budgeting, motivating, promoting, celebration, learning and improvement), but that no particular measure is appropriate for all eight purposes. Public managers, therefore, need to think carefully about the managerial purpose performance management might serve in order to deploy measures appropriately, and to be aware that performance measures are not objective, neutral tools, but instead need to be treated with caution as each measure may fit some purposes well, and other purposes rather badly.

Case study – Performance management in hospitals and general practitioners

Throughout the 2000s the UK NHS introduced performance management into its hospitals and general practice surgeries. What follows, I think, offers important lessons however for performance management generally.

Performance management in hospitals has not been a success in the United Kingdom, and it is widely regarded as having led to widespread gaming and disaffection. In contrast, the introduction of the Quality and Outcomes Framework (QOF)in general practice stands as perhaps the most successful health reform, in its own terms, the NHS has ever had. What I mean by this is that it was designed to achieve a range of behavioural changes in General Practitioners (GPs)through the introduction of its linkage between funding and points, and met those goals extremely well.

The introduction of performance management in hospitals has had major problems. It has been based on government-set targets that hospitals have had imposed upon them in a top-down manner, with managers and clinicians not seeing clear links between the targets set and the improvements they believe their services need to make. The targets and the ways they are assessed have changed considerably, as an attempt to avoid hospitals becoming 'target-focused' and losing sight that they are meant to be providing high-quality care in the broader sense, but also as priorities for government and understandings of how the performance management systems have evolved.

The end result is that most research points to extensive 'gaming' of the performance management systems (Hood, 2006) with managers finding ways of 'playing' the statistical collection systems and often perverse behaviours resulting. Targets have changed the way hospitals operate to make them more focused on goals, but with significant questions about the reliability of the data collected and huge questions being asked about the efficacy of the system.

In GP surgeries, targets were set in a different way. Targets were agreed with national leaders, which were based not at abstract levels, but in concrete items of practice. GPs perceive the targets as being evidence based, and so they have been more accepted within the most influential professionals practising in primary care. At the same time, payments were linked to GPs achieving targets – effectively being held back from surgeries unless they met their targets (most, however, exceeded them).

Even more importantly, GP practices were given autonomy on how they met the QOF targets. Some made wider use of nurses or practice managers, in some cases GPs took on the work. Instead of saying how the targets would be met, practices had discretion and autonomy in working this out for themselves.

What all this adds up to is a process by which targets were pre-agreed, accepted as being legitimate, incorporated into the practice of care, and with local discretion on how they were to be achieved.

The result was that, as mentioned earlier, the GP targets (or 'QOF') were met, or exceeded. So why were GP targets so successful when hospital targets resulted in widespread gaming?

First, they were based on measures that those tasked with achieving them regarded as meeting the goals of their organization. People are more likely to try and achieve a target where they can see it is making a contribution to a bigger goal, and understand the linkages. In GP practices this link was made in the claim the targets were based on clinical evidence – but this can be recontextualized to any organization by thinking of it as a means of meeting a bigger public workers want to strive towards.

Second, the targets were agreed with representatives from the profession who would be responsible for meeting them. This meant that they were given legitimacy – they had been agreed by those within the profession, and so not imposed upon them.

Third, the GPs were given discretion in how they achieved the targets. They were told what their targets were (after genuine consultation), but not how to achieve them. They were given the discretion to adapt and find innovative ways of working to meet the new targets.

Finally, there were rewards available for meeting the targets. GPs often claim this was the least important element in meeting the targets – what they valued was the ability to work to a larger goals with their own discretion, but it certainly can't have hurt having resources follow their success.

What I think QOF shows is that it is impossible to come up with an approach to public management, which is sufficiently flexible yet rigorous to work in public reform. Sadly, the planned NHS reorganization of 2012 seems to pay little attention to the potential of this, with Secretary of State Andrew Lansley instead preferring to try market-based solutions where they seem to have little basis for working.

Further reading

Performance management and performance measurement have practically become industries in their own right over the last ten years. Amongst the earliest studies of the use of performance measures in the United Kingdom were conducted by Christopher Pollitt (1985) who has revisited the subject in his recent book 'The Essential Public Manager' (Pollitt, 2003). The strategic approach to performance management is presented in a number of contexts by Johnson and Scholes in their edited book 'Exploring Public Sector Strategy' (Johnson & Scholes, 2001).

A great deal of the work on performance management attempts to link it to variables that assess other aspects of public organizations, such as their organizational culture (Mannion *et al.*, 2004), and to try and find prescriptions for improvement as a result. The confusion over the use of performance management is perhaps best summarized, however, by Colin Talbot (2000) in his piece 'performing performance'.

10

Putting it all together — Managing contradictions in public management

Introduction — The context of public management in the 2010s

This book has concluded that there are a range of paradoxes in public management that public managers need to learn to live with, rather than assuming that the contradictions and tensions that they face can be made to disappear through better planning or the use of markets, or even wishful thinking.

The common sense public managers often face in the second decade of the twenty-first century is that public management as an idea is no longer really relevant as the boundaries between public and private organizations are being broken down through the use of competitive mechanisms and privatization, because we can no longer afford public organizations, which have in any way failed to provide a decent level of service, staffed by unaccountable professionals, and providing unresponsive and bureaucratic service to service users who regard themselves more as consumers than citizens. However, all these claims are based on one side only of the contradictory world that public managers face, and which also include the hard work of finding way to provide crucial services to society in extraordinarily difficult conditions.

There is, however, a crucial role for public services in the economy, providing a range of services which the private sector will underprovide and competitive mechanisms cannot adequately deal with, as well as helping the economy with an automatic stabilizer against the booms and bust of private, free markets. In addition, the financial crisis has surely meant that policymakers have to take a stronger role in making sure that private markets work efficiently and effectively in the interest of society rather than enriching a few only. Public management, however, is an inherently paradoxical enterprise, attempting to balance the need to be democratically accountable to the public as a whole as well as good individual service, meeting the demands of government as well as the needs of local people, balancing respect for professionals while demanding accountability from them, and allowing deficit spending when it is justified, but having the discipline to reduce expenditure in boom times when it is not.

As I write this conclusion, financial markets are undermining democratically elected governments in Greece and Italy. It may well be those country's governments have failed their people, but it is not for financial markets to change Prime Ministers and governments and public services, it is for the people of those countries. Speculative financial flows have come to dwarf investment in real goods and services, and the speculation in those country's debts involves no real long-term investment, nothing that is socially useful for the world. Italy and Greece (and Spain and Ireland) are democratic countries, and if they are prevented from being able to run their countries on democratic lines then something has gone very badly wrong. Speculative flows need to be slowed – the Tobin Tax proposed by the European Union is one way into this problem (and shamefully opposed by my own country's government), and countries made accountable to their people, and if this means that they have to learn to more live within their means (as there will be a fall in the debt they can raise) that is what needs to happen – but we must all stop imagining that more debt, either governmental or consumer is the answer to our problems, which are more fundamentally about the distribution of incomes in our society, especially in relation to what has happened since the 1970s.

At the same time as this, however, governments need take greater responsibility for making sure that markets work efficiently, and rewards from them are distributed more equitably – they have a legitimate role in the private sphere where markets do not deliver societal benefits except to the very rich, or where markets are skewed in favour of those that already have plenty, so that social exclusion is growing. We need a fairer society – but there is no reason why this cannot be more socially efficient as well (Hutton, 2010).

Public management after the financial crisis

Given the previous chapters the reader might by now feel rather confused. This book has not tried to give the right answers to the many problems

Table 10.1 Tensions in public management

Tension	Description
Public and private.	Public and private management are often characterized as very different, but are these differences narrowing?
Professionalism and customer focus.	Should public services be organized around professionals or customers?
Control and entrepreneurialism.	Should public managers be primarily concerned with control or with being entrepreneurs?
Provision for the public or provision for the individual.	Should public provision be concerned with serving the public as a whole, or individual users?
Services accountable to the public as citizens and services accountable to the public as consumers.	Should public services be accountable to the public at large, or to individuals as they receive the service?
Centralization and decentralization.	Should public services be controlled by government, or decentralized and allowed to become more locally diverse?

facing public managers in the contemporary world. Instead it has attempted to explore the kinds of issues they are likely to face with the view that being forewarned might not exactly forearm, but it might at least make clearer the nature of the challenges to be faced. This last chapter will attempt to summarize the difficulties and tensions present in public management to try and allow the reader to work through these issues and develop their own understanding of them. These are, by definition, difficult problems, but that does not mean they should be ignored or regarded as being too hard to deal with. Instead I hope that by encouraging readers to think about these 'disjunctures' (Newman, 2002) a deeper knowledge of the nature of public management might be achieved. This chapter asks the question 'how can we make sense of public management given the paradoxes contained within this book?'

The main tensions raised by the book are listed in Table 10.1, and then discussed each in turn below it.

Public and private

The first tension is between the public and the private. This is a neat division, but one that often crumbles under scrutiny in today's world. Public managers can be working for private organizations, and private managers working within the public sector. Does this mean that the terms are therefore meaningless? Boyne's work suggested that the differences between public and private management are not as widespread as is often believed, but also that many of the taken-for-granted assumptions about the nature of public management remain just that – taken-for-granted. They have therefore not been scrutinized, and it would seem an important job for research to be conducted that attempts to compare a range of factors between public and private management to better understand whether or not differences exist. In the meantime, however, some general tendencies appear to be present.

For much of the 1980s onwards, public management has been encouraged to be more like private management, to become more 'business-like'. Private management is regarded as entrepreneurial, customer-centred and efficient. This is, if you like, the taken-for-granted assumption about private management. However, how often is this actually the case? Business book shelves groan under the weight of case study style books traceable back to Peters and Waterman's *In Search of Excellence* and beyond (Peters & Waterman, 1982), but what seems to unite these organizations more than their business practices is their unerring ability to drive themselves into serious trading trouble almost as quickly as books celebrating their success hit the shelves. One of the most celebrated organizations (in the business press at least) of recent times also became its biggest corporate bankruptcy – Enron (McLean & Elkind, 2004).

This is not to disparage private management. There are extraordinary managers out there in both the private and public sectors. However, the important thing is surely to explore what works, where, how and when, rather than assuming there is an automatic fix-all for any managerial situation. Today's management theory is tomorrow's discredited fashion, be it organizational excellence, organizational learning, business process engineering, total quality management, or corporate culture or leadership. Instead of jumping on management bandwagons it would surely be better to try and form context-sensitive theories of what structures, incentives, practices, and policies seem to work, and to argue for extremely careful transplantation away from their original contexts. Both private management and public management have much to learn from one another; private management can be more dynamic and entrepreneurial, but public management can offer greater continuity and stability, and in a situation where lives might be at stake and futures risked, these values can suddenly seem enduring and important.

Instead of demanding that public managers become more like their private peers, it would surely make sense to ask what values we want our services to hold at their core. Public managers often argue they are there to preserve a public ethos, a set of values that are based around notions of public service and fairness. Many private organizations also seem to suggest they also hold these values. Values do make a difference, and instead of debating which organizational processes work best, perhaps it is necessary to start by asking what our organizations are for. It may well be that, in particular circumstances markets can deliver a fairer outcome than public bureaucracies. However, this cannot be taken for granted, and must be subjected to careful testing, and sometimes for policymakers and public managers to admit they have made a mistake where things are not working.

In sum, although the terms 'public' and 'private' both hold considerable explanatory power, perhaps when working out what needs to be done it is more important to analyse the values, context and goals of the circumstance rather than coming with a set of presumptions that either public or private methods are automatically best. There is something of a paradox here – despite the words 'public' and 'private' being so loaded in values and holding such emotion, neither may actually be that useful in working out what needs to be done or how. This book has written about public organizations and public managers because, at present, they are just about identifiable despite all of the change that has occurred over the last 30 years. It seems to me that there is a logical and empirical need for public services to continue to exist, but we need to get rid of many of the stereotypes about what constitutes public or private management practices and to think about what we want our services to achieve, and what principles we want them to hold dearest.

Professionalism and customer focus

A second tension present in the book is between professionalism and customer focus. Professionalism tends to lead to services having a producer focus and professional self-regulation, two of the enemies of many of those in positions of power who believe instead that customer focus brings individual accountability to public services, and requires professionals to rethink their approach to work to drive up standards and improve user responsiveness.

However, what often gets lost in this debate is that professionals are often self-regulated for good reason (that their job is so complex that only other professionals can often understand what they have done) and that producer focus may actually be an efficient way of organizing resource-poor services, as the professional's time could be the public organization's most valuable asset. It would be wonderful to be able to visit a doctor entirely at my own convenience, and to organize rubbish collection not once every one or two weeks, but when my rubbish bin is full. However, neither of these options, where public services are trying to achieve efficiency and have to operate on a large scale, are particularly efficient. To be able to see a doctor whenever I like, that doctor has to have a great deal of redundancy in his or her schedule, and employing public professionals on high salaries to wait for my convenience does not seem an efficient strategy. If I am not seen by a doctor until half an hour after my appointment time, this was probably due to a case appearing before me that was more urgent than mine, rather than because the doctor was sitting around drinking coffee.

This is not, however, to offer a universal apology for all the time public organizations keep their users waiting, or all the times that professionals seem rude to them. Public professionals often work under tremendous pressure and resource constraint. However, it does not seem much to ask that the dignity and privacy of service users is always kept in mind. It costs little for an administrator to monitor how far behind with appointments the professional is getting in order to be able to tell arriving users how long they are likely to have to wait, but this is still not routinely done. If it is necessary for queueing and waiting to occur, then those having to give up their time should at least have an indication of how long their wait is likely to be, and in what order they are being seen. This costs nothing. Practices such as booking users in for appointments at the same time in order to maximize professional time take the efficiency argument outlined above to the extreme, but clearly cross the boundary of common courtesy and so should be stopped. In return for users accepting that public professionals are busy and overworked, professionals must make sure that they are treated with dignity and courtesy in return. Professionalism and customer focus can appear to be contradictory where both are defined at the extremes, but they also have a great deal in common, and it is the job of public managers to try and find a meeting in the middle. However, policymakers must make sure that they do not stoke up expectations of public services delivery to levels that cannot possibly be met.

Equally, it is the job of public managers to find appropriate ways of scrutinizing public professionals to make sure that, where services can be redesigned to improve their service to users without diluting their professionalism, this should happen. Techniques such as business process re-engineering (McNulty & Ferlie, 2002) can be dismissed as management fads, but carry at their root an important message about services being designed around the needs of their service users. This can never be achieved completely within finite resources and with the safeguards necessary for professional work to be carried out safely and fairly, but public organizations should regularly ask the question of how they could better meet the needs of their users. This job seems a good one for public managers to have.

Finally in terms of the tension between professionalism and user focus comes the difficulty of what to do about complaints. Complaints are an important part of public management as they represent a situation where someone, for good motives or bad, has taken the time to go through a time-consuming process and instead of simply grumbling and walking away having received service they are not happy with, they have put pen to paper or been prepared to engage with the organization in some other formal way. The effort sometimes involved in making a complaint in public organizations should not be understated. Complaint procedures can be confusing, elusive and worded in obscure language. In Douglas Adams' book, *The Hitch Hikers Guide the Galaxy* a planning department required a ridiculous series of acts be performed for the local council to take user voice or complaints into account. Adams was parodying local government, but most parody contains an element of truth.

Complaints are an index of how well an organization is doing. Simply counting complaints can reveal very little – complaints may go up because new systems are in place that make it easier for users to make their voice heard, or go down because staff become efficient at intimating users into leaving before they have a chance to complain. The important thing is that complaints are treated seriously by both users and public managers, who will often have the job of investigating them. Public managers need to have robust processes in place to show that full investigations have occurred, and that they are able to explain clearly what action they have taken to service users at the end. There should be an assumption that users do not complain because they have nothing else to do, and their complaints treated, as a result, in good faith. Users, in turn, need to understand that wasting a public organization's time in an attempt to drive up a degree classification, which they do not deserve, or trying to achieve an unfair amount of resources compared to other users by complaining regularly, are not acceptable. Public organizations are universal in nature, and have to treat complaints seriously because of their fairness brief (private organizations, in contrast, can ban individuals from their premises relatively easily), but where complaints procedures are being abused, it surely needs to be possible to warn particular users that any further complaints are likely to strain credibility.

It is a sad state of affairs where the motives of user complaints have to be questioned, but where significant amounts of compensation and preferential treatment might be attained, there will always be small majority of users wishing to 'game' the system. The important thing seems to be that complaints are treated seriously and fairly by managers, but that users understand that complaints do not necessarily mean there is a case to answer, and that they do not abuse the processes in place.

Control and entrepreneurialism

A third tension present through the book is the one between control and entrepreneurialism. The standard critique of the bureaucratic organizational form is that its impersonality is a sham – all it does is legitimize and disguise pre-existing power structures under the guise of providing objective rules (Foucault, 1977). Feminists and disability rights campaigners were instrumental in showing how public policy and public organizations preserve pre-existing power relationship by making women dependent upon men for their welfare payments and how those with disabilities found themselves having to endure 'normalizing' policies that attempted to make them more like more prevalent members of society. If bureaucracies were not neutral and independent, what use did they serve?

Recent scholarship, however, has come strongly to the defence of bureaucracy, emphasizing the importance of control and the need for the objective administration of rules (Du Gay, 2000). Many public organizations' legitimacy depends upon them administering rules fairly, and if this is shown not to be the case, there also exists the possibility of making the bureaucracies work better rather than simply abandoning them. Equally Lynn (2001) has argued persuasively that the caricatures of bureaucracy often presented in critiques of it often fail to capture is complexities and that 'traditional' thought is far more sophisticated than painted by contemporary critics, exhibiting 'far more respect for law, politics, citizens, and values than customer-oriented managerialism or civic philosophies that, in promoting community and citizen empowerment, barely acknowledge the constitutional role of legislatures, courts and executive departments' (p. 154–155).

Entrepreneurial discourses, as Lynn suggests point, at their extremes, directly away from the bureaucratic form. They suggest that for public management to work better, managers need to be freed from constraining rules in order to give users the services they need and deserve. The term entrepreneurialism is commonly used in two ways. First, there is the notion of the dynamic entrepreneur creative new services and adding value to existing ones by being able to anticipate user need. This type of entrepreneurialism is strongly linked to market notions around placing the user at the heart of the organization's activities. Second, and more commonly in the social science literature on the subject, there is the notion of the entrepreneur as the filler of 'structural holes' (Burt, 1993), linking together the offerings of professionals and the needs of users, recombining professional services and marketing them to meet user need. This usage is distinctive from the first sense of the term because it focuses on entrepreneurialism as a structural phenomenon, as a process whereby under-demanded services can meet presently unmet user need through managers (and others) overcoming information or service delivery problems through their organizational abilities (Garud *et al.*, 2002, Hwang & Powell, 2005). The problem is that entrepreneurship is often used as a word in ways that empty of it of meaning – if it is to have value in public management, it must be clear exactly what usage is being evoked by the term.

The first sense of entrepreneurship, used effectively as a shortcut for the marketing approach, does clearly have tensions with notion of a bureaucracy. If the organization is driven to meet user need, this will tend to mean a more relaxed approach to rule interpretation. Advocates of the marketing approach often make the claim that customer-driven organizations need only two rules. Rule one is that the customer is always right. Rule two is for situations where managers believe rule one doesn't apply, and refers the manager back to rule one for reference. If the user is always right, it is hard to see how bureaucratic organization can work. However, the second sense of entrepreneurship does not necessarily conflict with the idea of the bureaucracy. Managers attempting to redesign existing services to overcome problems associated with a lack of information of problems with delivery might have to put in place bureaucratic oversight in order to make sure that a wide range of high-quality services are in place, or to make sure that existing services are publicized to users better. Publicizing services is often associated with a market environment, but this does not have to be the case – it could simply be about gaining additional referrals for a new medical service, or getting local authorities to make use of a pre-existing facility that improves service efficiency, but is presently being underutilized.

As such, the tension between bureaucracy and entrepreneurship depends on what is meant by the terms, especially with regard to its second, service combination-based usage. It also depends on those organizing services being careful enough not simply to dismiss notions such as bureaucracy because they are presently ill-regarded by many management theorists, as well as often by the public at large. There are circumstances where rules and regulations are important, and where bureaucracies might be the most efficient way to deliver services.

Provision for the public and provision for the individual

A fourth tension exists between the provision of services for the public, and the provision of choice for the individual user. This tension is based on the assertion that is what is good for us individually may not always be the best use of resources for everyone. The most extreme example of this occurs where an ill individual finds that a new, very expensive drug has become available, without which he or she feels might die. That individual clearly has a strong motivation to get the state to pay for his or her treatment with the drug, and whether or not that money could be better spent on treatments that provide bigger collective gains will not be a particular concern to the individual. As new drugs are developed, this situation appears increasingly regularly in healthcare systems across the world. Who is the right, the individual wanting potentially life-saving treatment, or the healthcare manager arguing that the resources could be better spent on activities such as getting people to give up smoking, or by testing people's cholesterol levels to try and reduce their chances of heart disease?

Inevitably, neither position is without its problems, but both are understandable. The individual in need of treatment has a pressing case to try and save his or her own life, and any healthcare system must have systems for dealing with this kind of need. The history of healthcare shows a bias towards acute medicine, treatments, which deal with the health problems of those suffering today, rather than fully utilizing treatments and promotional activity that might improve the health of the population as a whole tomorrow. This doesn't seem at all surprising – it takes a strong person to postpone the needs of those sick today in order to secure better care for others tomorrow, even if this will result in a net health gain in the long term. Those most in need clearly need to have public managers prepared to take up their cases and to try and find resources to allow their treatment. Equally, however, difficult decisions also need to be made about investing in services that are more long term in duration. It takes a brave manager to advocate and organize services that he or she might never receive the credit for, but it is also a necessary job.

The important thing is that the values of organizational systems are reviewed to make sure that the balance between the present and the future is justifiable, and that it reflects the wishes of sufficient members of the public to make it legitimate. Public services are there for both their specific users and the general public. If they become so focused on user views that they forget the public at large, they lack the legitimacy to continue to regard themselves as serving the population as a whole.

Public services accountable to the public as citizens, and services accountable to the public as consumers

This takes us on to the fifth public service tension, between services that are accountable to the public as citizens, and services that are accountable the public as consumers (6, 2003). Accountability to services users as consumers takes place primarily on the individual level, with users being offered choices and being able to say whether they have been offered high standards of service through feedback mechanisms. The most immediate mechanism for offering feedback where services are consumed frequently is through the strategy of 'exit' (Hirschman, 1970), through which they can choose another service provider if they are unhappy with the offerings or service levels of their present provider. Exit is an individual choice, but has collective implications – if enough users exit a service its future might be called into question. Public managers find out about exit by examining whether service users return, and by trying to work out why some leave and some come back. In addition to this, consumers also have 'voice' mechanisms through which they may try and improve services either for themselves or for others. Voice can, therefore, be either individual or collective, but at least gives public managers more information than exit alone. Of course, some users may exit with voice, or persist with their choice and try and achieve change by challenging their organization. In these circumstances, they are exhibiting a kind of loyalty, not exiting but instead trying to change things. This also brings service users closer to citizen-type roles in which they participate in services and try and improve them for all.

In public service delivery in the past, the primary means by which users have been involved in services is through voice mechanisms, as choices simply have not existed (except for the choice to use private facilities instead). However, voice mechanisms, such as complaints procedures, have often been weakly implemented in public organizations (Allsop & Jones, 2008).

The danger of relying too much upon choice to achieve accountability is that often gives public managers little idea about how good their services are, as exit information might come too late to change things. However, most people prefer exit to voice because it creates an easy way out without having to explain their decision. It therefore seems an important part of public management work to try and get voice from those that choose to exit a service, perhaps routinely attempting to capture a sample of all service users (some of which will subsequently exit). This may have the by-product of actually increasing the loyalty of service users, impressed that someone is asking for their views (but only if managers show that they are actually listening). Loyalty can lead to citizen-type behaviour by giving managers regular engagement with service users that can result in an improvement in services for everyone.

However, the term 'citizen' is more usually used in two other senses; in terms of the voice of the public more generally, and in terms of user representation specifically. Where 'citizen' becomes another way of referring to 'the people', it is used in the sense of attempting to make public services accountable to those they are meant to be serving collectively. This can be achieved through a variety of different routes but is most likely to occur during political election campaigns where politicians campaign, either locally or nationally, to improve services for all citizens. Using the word 'citizen' can, therefore, be shorthand for political accountability, with all of the strengths and weaknesses this can bring (see Chapter 9).

An alternative is to use the term 'citizen' in the sense of those users who offer themselves as representatives of other users. Citizens might be invited to give the views of others at government-held events where new policies are outlined, or even where which policies are to be pursued is decided. This mode of citizen representation has cycles of popularity and unpopularity. It is clearly useful in that it means that politicians or managers are being held to account directly to user representatives, and so this increases the engagement of public representativeness and the transparency of the running of public services. Citizen juries and other co-production methods can be empowering for local people who contribute directly in decisions about the future of public services in their areas. However, the issue of the representativeness of those that put themselves forward is always a problem. By definition, those that are able to attend frequent meetings and make a substantial time commitment to public service are not representative of most of those in a local area, and alternatives such as randomly selecting individuals, or using stratified samples to try and get representative groups together, often don't work where the majority of people in a local area are too busy, or simply don't wish to get involved. The notion of citizen decision making is also haunted somewhat by the danger that the majority of people in many populations might hold views that might lead to minority groups being ignored, or of decisions such as the wider use severe punishments such as the death penalty being taken, even though they may fly in the face of the best available evidence. Greater democracy and public accountability are clearly a laudable goal for public managers to pursue, but it is not a panacea that means that the public can make all the decisions from now on.

Centralization and decentralization

A final tension is one that has not been extensively covered in this book, but builds upon many of those described above. This is the tension between decentralization and centralization. Should public services be different from place to place based on local need, or conform to national standards, positioning public managers as implementers in a chain of command reaching to the centre? The former option gives public managers more responsibilities than the latter. In this case, they will be responsible not only for implementing plans but also for establishing what local priorities ought to be, and then producing plan upon which work is to be based. In a centralized system, public managers will also have to devise their own performance management system. A decentralized approach means that there is far greater scope for managers to innovate, but they will also have to confront the problem of users comparing what is on offer with other areas and feeling they are being short changed. Different local plans in different geographical areas mean different levels of service, and the potential for accusations from users that they are not receiving services they would receive elsewhere. In the United Kingdom, the language used by the media to make this criticism is that of the 'postcode lottery', the suggestion that where you live (your postcode) makes a lottery of the public services you receive. This goes directly against the grain of the public administration approach that suggested public services should be universal and uniform. However, following the logic of user responsiveness leads to locally differentiated services and locally differentiated priorities, compromising fairness in the name of greater responsiveness. Accountability is therefore primarily to local users and local people more generally, with national accountability less prevalent.

Centralization leads in the opposite direction. In this approach, public managers are responsible for the implementation of plans set elsewhere. As such, they are likely to have performance management systems imposed from the centre, and the system of accountability will be to politicians nationally. Local accountability will still be necessary, but public managers will always have the get-out of saying that their hands are being forced by nationally made decisions. Centralized systems more closely resemble the bureaucracies so resented by advocates of the new public management approach, with the need for local managers to occupy more clearly defined roles to fit within national frameworks.

Again, however, the differences between centralization and decentralization may be more theoretical than actual. What is centralizing from one perspective may be decentralizing from another; it depends on what you regard as being the centre of an organization, and from where in the organization you are looking. The centre of an organization moves whether you are talking about geography, resources or power. A geographical centre may be the hub of an organization through which all communications flows, but hold little power. The resource centre may be where money, head office staff or decision-making expertise resides, and may be entirely different from the geographic centre, but have little idea of what is going on in public organizations locally. The power centre of an organization may be something different again; in many public organizations, it might be where the dominant professional group have their headquarters, or there may be many local power headquarters where professionals organize and dominate. Whether the various centres are in the same place or not varies tremendously from organization to organization, but the more centres there are in one location, the greater overall centralization exists. A reform that is centralizing from the point of view of a user might be dencentralizing from the point of view of a public manager if the latter gains power or resource that previously resided with users instead. The issue of decentralization and centralization depends, to a considerable extent, exactly on what resource is being examined and from whose perspective.

Finally, recent reforms have attempted to square the circle of centralization and decentralization by creating new hybrid forms such as the one used in the United Kingdom of 'earned autonomy'. In the earned autonomy approach, public managers are promised greater discretion and the ability to locally manage, but they must first demonstrate that they conform to national standards set in areas policymakers regard as being necessary. This approach therefore attempts to balance the need of local managers with the needs of national policymakers. Local managers are allowed discretion but only if they first demonstrate their ability to meet national standards. How the dynamic of this works out will depend upon how many central targets are set, and how successful public managers are in meeting them. The more the targets, and the less the success of local managers, the more centralized the system will end up being. If, however, nationally set targets are minimums rather than maximums, they are more likely to be met and greater local discretion will be achieved. In the United Kingdom so far, it seems that earned autonomy has been more centralizing than decentralizing because of the number of targets put in place, but the rhetoric of government suggests that greater decentralization may still occur.

Conclusion

This book has presented a range of paradoxes that exist in public management, and this chapter has presented the tensions that result, in turn, from those paradoxes. Rather than considering these tensions as being resolvable through better planning or more rational thinking, its argument is that managers (and academics and students) need to learn to live with them because they are simply facts of live in public organizations. We need to rethink some of our basic categories – markets are not always right, neither is government. But we do need public services, and public management, and both have to be made more accountable to the people they are meant to be serving. There is a difference between individual consumers in markets and public services that need a collective accountability, and which need to be managed for the public good (but this doesn't excuse poor service to individuals).

The role of public managers has become increasingly more complex over the last 20–30 years. The criticisms that led to the decline of the public administration approach, that they lacked democratic legitimacy and developed unresponsive bureaucracies, do have some credibility. Public administration was based on principles of fairness, accountability, probity and service. These are fine virtues that form the centre of the public service ethic, and it is wrong to always assume that bureaucracies are self-serving and inefficient. The administrative role of mediating between professionals rather than trying to provide strong leadership can appear both simultaneously old-fashioned and able to correspond to a great deal of modern management theory positioning managers as coaches and enablers of others (Harrison *et al.*, 1992).

In the 1970s and 1980s, there was a strong suggestion from the state that public managers could learn a great deal from their private counterparts, that they should become more 'business-like' in their approach. In the views of politicians, public organizations had become too expensive, and economic difficulties led to demands for them to reduce their costs, whilst simultaneously, because the growing consumerist movement (Haug & Sussman, 1969), to improve the services they offered. Public managers were therefore, as well as facilitators, required to be corporation-style managers, running services efficiently and according to their customers' needs.

In the 1980s, managers were also told that their job was to implement government policy on the ground. They were the corporate rationalizers of Alford's model (1975), there to do the state's work and challenge entrenched professional groupings and make sure that the policy-implementation gap was filled. Managers who achieved this were to be celebrated, and those who did not comply were labelled as belonging to the past – dinosaurs who did not support reform agendas.

More recent reforms have demanded that public managers become more financially aware, having to gain an understanding of the complexities of contracting in the new market environments, and of working in public–private partnerships. Public managers therefore had to become competent accountants, able to balance their books (or even generate a surplus), as well as run a service that added value for the public.

In the era after the financial crisis, public services are under threat as governments struggle to find funds to pay for them, and privatization and marketization seem the most common strategies being adopted. But these approaches forget the reasons why services were made public in the first place. Assuming all public services can be equally well run in the private sector loses sight of what constitutes a 'public' service in the first place, and risks committing errors, which will add to the burdens of the poorest and most vulnerable, as well as creating opportunities for private profit, which are unjustifiable either theoretically or empirically. Markets don't always work, and where they don't, we risk replacing public monopolies, which are at least technically democratically accountable, with undemocratic private monopolies that exist mainly for their shareholders.

Public management has increasingly become about acting in an entrepreneurial manner. 'Entrepreneur' is a notoriously slippery word, but in the sense of acting as brokers to link together services, it is particularly apposite.

Public managers, however, must also be leaders. They are required to comply with centrally imposed government targets (as corporate rationalizers) but also to come up with new ideas for how services can be better run at the local level. They must then lead their organizations towards those goals, taking their employees with them. The leadership literature often has competing notions of what the term 'leadership' actually means, through from trait-based models to approaches that stress the transformational potential of leaders to delegate and empower those that work with them. The analysis presented here suggests that transformation leadership is a more appropriate model in public services because of the need to work closely with professionals, but it is still often unclear exactly what is required by policymakers.

Public managers are also required to be accountable for the service they are tasked with running. This means that they are often cast, not least by managers themselves, as heroes or villains (Greener, 2005c). When public organizations work well and are high performing by government measures, public managers become heroes, responsible for delivering high achievement. When things don't work out, where services have budget deficits or deliver service measured as being of low quality, it is the manager's fault. There are certainly good reasons for blaming managers when things go wrong – it is they are meant to be responsible for the governance of their organizations. However, it is also politically expedient. It is a lot harder to sack doctors than it is to sack public professionals. Professionals are often a lot harder to replace than managers, as they have expertise in short supply, and powerful professional bodies to support them in any legal action. Getting rid of a manager, however, is relatively easy, as a replacement can usually be readily found, and there is unlikely to be much public sympathy for the removal of a poor performing Chief Executive.

Then there is the role of being the public service guardian. Many public managers do not do their jobs for financial betterment or for career advancement, but instead because they wish to make a difference. They may closely identify with the goals of their public organizations, and regard attempts to reform them as crude and clumsy attempts by politicians to interfere in something they do not really understand. In many ways, they have a point. Public policy has a tendency towards being somewhat circular in nature, with periods of centralization and decentralization following one another, and the use of markets rising and falling in popularity. With all of this meddling it is often a wonder that public services work at all. As such, the role of public manager as guardian appears to be an important one, trying to keep the waters within an organization relatively still compared to the raging torrents that may surround it. Table 10.2 summarizes these roles.

The quality of public management matters profoundly (Meier & O'Toole, 2002), but public managers therefore have incredibly demanding and multi-faceted existences. They must 'acknowledge multiple levels of managerial accountability – to citizens, to elected officials, to public employees and to their own professional standards' (Kelly, 2005, p. 82). They are almost guaranteed, because of the variety of stakeholders they must deal with on a day-to-day basis, to be failing on some front or another. They also risk, because of the variety of roles they are required to adopt, to appear to at least some of those that work with them, to be inconsistent at least some of the time. How is it possible to be both guardian and corporate rationalizer? To be both an administrator of probity and an entrepreneur? This seems to be the challenge public managers

Table 10.2 Public manager roles

Role description	Characteristics
Administrator	Probity
	Fairness
	Service
	Enabling
Corporation manager	'Big picture' management
	Efficient
	Customer focused
Corporate rationalizer	Challenger of professional interests
Accountant	Balancer of budgets or creator of surpluses
Entrepreneur	Care pathway creator
	Adder of value
Leader	Goal setter
	Inspiration
Hero or villain	Accountability taker
Guardian	Preserver of the good of the past
	Stabilizer against unnecessary reform

are now required to meet – squaring the incompatible and extraordinarily difficult roles now demanded of them by the state.

Two main answers seem to appear as to how public services should be reformed. First, there is the greater use of markets, stressing entrepreneurial roles and making public managers increasingly accountable to individual service users rather than to collective publics. The extent to which the market can ever be allowed to run without any state hindrance, with the danger of inequalities between users resulting (which would seem to undermine key principles of public service) and concern that greater use of the private sector might result in greater measured efficiency, but also 'gaps' in provision where services cannot be supplied profitably, or where widespread, collective responses are needed (the most obvious example being when confronting natural disasters). Markets will result in the private sector making profits from public services (which readers may or may not be comfortable about), to a stressing of contractual relationships and the need for managers to work across networks of providers to avoid the fragmentation of services, and to the problem of who holds public services, as a whole, to account if they are extensively privatized and so democratic processes impinge less and less upon them.

The alternative is for the state to accept there are some services that it must play a role in providing (see Greener, 2008 for an attempt to begin to work out how this might be done), and to accept that such services must be made more democratically accountable than is presently the case, putting place a collective accountability measure to the public as a whole. Roberts (2002) suggests, in line with some of the ideas of Fox and Miller (1995), that public officials need to be accountable through 'dialogue' because the benefits of such a system outweigh the costs. In Minnesota, an attempt was held to have a wide-ranging dialogue on education that was covered by local, state and national press, reinforcing traditional accountability mechanisms by making them more transparent and visible. The publicness of the dialogue also made participants more accountable to one another, building relationships based on mutual listening and learning, and leading to adversarial politics becoming less attractive as working together had become far more attractive. However, it could also be isolating for those that call for a decision to be quickly made, and time-consuming and resource-demanding, and required public managers to learn new skills to make the process work. However, greater democracy does not come cheaply, and may not work in every situation (Irvin & Stansbury, 2004).

Where services are recognized as being public, the tension between the state attempting to run services so that they are run as fairly as possible, individual user responsiveness and collective local democracy come to the fore. Should services be standardized as much as possible, or should local variations be allowed? How do you manage the tensions between services being delivered to individual users, but collective democratic decisions having to be made about what is provided and to whom? Even with extensive dialogue processes, there are no easy answers to these questions. Public organizations, however, must find them if they are to claim their legitimacy based on collectivity and democracy. As Denhardt and Denhardt (2006) suggest 'Only when our commitment to democratic principles and ideals is clear to all will we once again be able to establish public service as the highest calling in our society' (p. 446).

Is it not possible to try and find hybrid forms that allow both markets and extensive state formations, as the Third Way discourse (see Chapter 3) attempts to achieve? This would seem to make some sense as a pragmatic response to the problems of both the market-led and democracy-led models described above. However, such a combination may have significant difficulties.

Jane Jacobs, the author of the public administration classic *The Death and Life of Great American Cities*, considered the issue of the moral foundations of commerce and politics in her book *Systems of Survival* (Jacobs, 1992). In it, in the form a platonic dialogue between a range of characters, an agreement is reached that trying to combine the moral systems of the two is likely to produce hybrids that are subjects to corruption and abuse. Jacobs' characters suggest that there is room for 'ingenuity and improvements' (p. 158) both systems, but that it is essential to be aware of the moral principles underpinning each and to make sure that they are not compromised. Jacobs' work has far-reaching implications for public managers – if she is right they must know what it is they stand for, and to only go along with reforms that make public organizations more market-oriented where they can show that their principles will not be diluted or compromised as a result.

Jacobs' work suggests that public and private management are based on different moral foundations (those of commerce and politics) and that, even if differences can be difficult to establish empirically at times, the rationale for the two different types of organization differs sufficiently for us to have to think about reforms not only in instrumental grounds, but also on moral grounds. Students often say that they might consider working in the public sector because they might be able to 'make a difference' or 'do good'. Those working in public organizations often claim that their choice of work was driven by the same beliefs (Buelens & Van den Broeck, 2007, Khojasteh, 1993). This is not to derogate those working in private organizations, but to argue that there may be different underlying moral reasons why the two kinds of organization exist, and that considerable care must be taken in both identifying and mixing the two. The quality of public services is crucial both for our individual futures and for the future of all our economies. The quality of public management within those public services is hugely important. It is crucial that we give public services the resources and status they deserve, and that the public managers within them understand their role, and the principles for which they stand. Then we can begin to get the services that we as the public, both expect and deserve.

References

6 P. (2003). Giving Consumers of British Public Services More Choice: What Can Be Learned from Recent History? *Journal of Social Policy*, 32, 239–70.

Abbott A. (1988). *The System of Professions: An Essay on the Division of Expert Labor*, Chicago IL: University of Chicago Press.

Aberbach J, Christensen T. (2005). Citizens and Consumers: An NPM Dilemma. *Public Management Review*, 7, 225–45.

Ackroyd S. (1996). Organization Contra Organizations: Professions and Organizational Change in the United Kingdom. *Organization Studies*, 17, 599–621.

Ackroyd S, Hughes J, Soothill K. (1989). Public Sector Services and Their Management. *Journal of Management Studies*, 26, 603–19.

Aitkenson G, Olseon Jr. T. (1998). Commons and Keynes: Their Assault on Laissez-Faire. *Journal of Economic Issues*, 32, 1019.

Aldcroft D. (2001). *The European Economy 1914–2000*, London: Routledge.

Aldridge A. (2005). *The Market*, Cambridge: Polity.

Alford J. (1998). A Public Management Road Less Travelled: Clients as Co-Producers of Public Services. *Australian Journal of Public Administration*, 57, 128–37.

Alford R. (1972). The Political Economy of Health Care: Dynamics without Change. *Politics and Society*, Winter 12, 127–64.

Alford R. (1975). *Health Care Politics*, Chicago IL: University of Chicago Press.

Allsop J, Jones K. (2008). Withering the Citizen, Managing the Consumer: Complaints in Healthcare Settings. *Social Policy and Society*, 7, 233–43.

Archer M. (1995). *Realist Social Theory: The Morphogenetic Approach*, Cambridge: Cambridge University Press.

Argyris C, Schon D. (1995). *Organizational Learning II. Theory, Method and Practice*, London: Prentice Hall.

Asenova D, Beck M. (2003). The UK Financial Sector and Risk Management in PFI Projects: A Survey. *Public Money and Management*, 23, 195–202.

Bacon R, Eltis W. (1978). *Britain's Economic Problem: Too Few Providers*, London: Macmillan.

Balfour D, Grubbs J. (2000). Character, Corrosion and the Civil Servant: The Human Consequences of Globalization and the New Public Management. *Administrative Theory and Praxis*, 22, 570–84.

Ball S, Bowe R, Gewirtz S. (1995). Circuits of Schooling: A Sociological Exploration of Parental Choice of School in Social Class Contexts. *The Sociological Review*, 43, 52–78.

Barber B. (2007a). *Consumed: How Markets Corrupt Children, Infantilize Adults and Swallow Citizens Whole*, London: W. W. Norton and Co.

Barber M. (2007b). *Instruction to Deliver: Tony Blair, the Public Services and the Challenge of Achieving Targets*, London: Portoco's Publishing.

Barnes M, Newman J, Knops A, Sullivan H. (2003). Constituting 'the Public' in Public Participation. *Public Administration*, 81, 379–99.

Barney J. (1996). The Resource-Based Theory of the Firm. *Organizational Science*, September–October, 7, 469.

Bauman Z. (2007). *Consuming Life*, Cambridge: Polity Press.

BBC News. (2008). £10 'licence to smoke' proposed. Accessed 15th February 2008, http://news.bbc.co.uk/1/hi/7247470.stm.

Behn R. (2003). Why Measure Performance? Different Purposes Require Different Measures. *Public Administration Review*, 63, 586–606.

Bevir M. (2010). *Democratic Governance*, New Jersey: Princeton University Press.

Blair T. (2010). *A Journey*, London: Hutchinson.

Bloomfield B, Best A. (1992). Management Consultants: Systems Development, Power and the Translation of Problems. *Sociological Review*, 40, 533–60.

Bloomfield B, Coombs R. (1992). Information Technology, Control and Power: The Centralisation and Decentralisation Debate Revisited. *Journal of Management Studies*, 29, 459–84.

Bolton S. (2001). Changing Faces: Nurses as Emotional Jugglers. *Sociology of Health and Illness*, 23, 85–100.

Bovaird T. (2007). Beyond Engagement and Participation: User and Community Coproduction of Public Services. *Public Administration Review*, 67, 846–60.

Boyne G. (1999). Editorial: Markets, Bureaucracy and Public Management. *Public Money and Management*, October–December, 19, 1–2.

Boyne G. (2002). Public and Private Management: What's the Difference. *Journal of Management Studies*, 39, 97–122.

Boyne G, Farrell C, Law J, Powell M, Walker R. (2003). *Evaluating Public Management Reforms*, Buckingham: Open University Press.

Boyne G, Gould-Williams J. (2003). Planning and Performance in Public Organizations: An Empirical Analysis. *Public Management Review*, 5, 115–32.

Bozeman B. (1988). Exploring the Limits of Public and Private Sectors: Some Boundaries on the Maginot Line. *Public Administration Review*, 48, 672–74.

Bozeman B. (2002). Public-Value Failure: When Efficient Markets May Not Do. *Public Administration Review*, 67, 145–61.

Bozeman B, Bretschneider S. (1994). The 'Publicness Puzzle' in Organizational Theory: A Test of Alternative Explanations of Differences between Public and Private Organizations. *Journal of Public Administration Research and Theory*, 4, 197–223.

Bozeman B, Kingsley G. (1998). Risk Culture in Public and Private Organizations. *Public Administration Review*, 58, 109–18.

Bradley L, Parker R. (2006). Do Australian Public Sector Employees Have the Type of Culture They Want in the Era of New Public Management? *Australian Journal of Public Administration*, 65, 89–99.

Brinton Milward H, Provan K. (2003). Managing the Hollow State: Collaboration and Contracting. *Public Management Review*, 5, 1–16.

Broadbent J, Laughlin R. (2002). Public Service Professionals and the New Public Management. In *New Public Management: Current Trends and Future Prospects*, ed. E McLaughlin, SP Osborne, E Ferlie, pp. 95–108. London: Routledge.

Brown G. (2010). *After the Crash: Overcoming the First Crisis of Globalisation*, London: Simon and Schuster.

Buelens M, Van den Broeck H. (2007). An Analysis of Differences in Work Motivation between Public and Private Sector Organizations. *Public Administration Review*, 67, 65–74.

Burt R. (1993). The Social Structure of Competition. In *Explorations in Economic Sociology*, ed. R Swedburg, pp. 65–103. New York: Russell Sage Foundation.

Burt R. (2000). The Network Entrepreneur. In *Entrepreneurship: The Social Science View*, ed. R Swedburg, Oxford: Oxford University Press.

Buxton M, Packwood T. (1991). *Hospitals in Transition: The Resource Management Initiative*, Buckingham: Open University Press.

Callaghan G, Wistow G. (2006). Governance and Public Involvement in the British National Health Service: Understanding Difficulties and Developments. *Social Science and Medicine*, 63, 2289–300.

Callon M. (1998). Introduction: The Embeddedness of Economic Markets in Economies. In *The Laws of the Markets*, ed. M Callon, pp. 1–57. Oxford: Blackwell.

Casey T, ed. (2011). *The Legacy of the Crash: How the Financial Crisis Changed America and Britain*, Basingstoke: Palgrave Macmillan.

Cassidy J. (2009). *How Markets Fail: The Logic of Economic Calamities*, London: Penguin.

Chapman R, Dunsire A, eds. (1971). *Style in Administration: Readings in British Public Administration*, London: George Allen and Unwin.

Cho K, Lee S. (2001). Another Look at Public–Private Distinction and Organizational Commitment: A Cultural Explanation. *International Journal of Organizational Analysis*, 9, 84–102.

Christensen T, Laegreid P, Wise L. (2002). Transforming Administrative Policy. *Public Administration*, 80, 153–78.

Christy R, Brown J. (1996). Marketing. In *Managing the New Public Services*, ed. D Farnham, S Horton, pp. 94–112. Basingstoke: Palgrave Macmillan.

Clarke J, Newman J. (1997). *The Managerial State*, London: Sage.

Clarke J, Newman J, Smith N, Vidler E, Westmarland L. (2007). *Creating Citizen-Consumers: Changing Publics and Changing Public Services*, London: Paul Chapman Publishing.

Clarke J, Smith N, Vidler E. (2006). The Indeterminacy of Choice: Political, Policy and Organisational Implications. *Social Policy and Society*, 5, 327–36.

Coburn D. (1992). Freidson Then and Now: An 'Internalist' Critique of Freidson's Past and Present Views of the Medical Profession. *International Journal of Health Services*, 22, 497–512.

Cole A, Jones G. (2005). Reshaping the State: Administrative Reform and New Public Management in France. *Governance*, 18, 567–88.

Conger J, Kanungo R. (1998). *Charismatic Leadership in Organizations*, New York: Sage.

Currie G. (1999). The Influence of Middle Managers in the Business Planning Process: A Case Study in the UK NHS. *British Journal of Management*, 10, 141–55.

Czarniawska B. (1997). *Narrating the Organization: Dramas of Institutional Identity*, Chicago IL: University of Chicago Press.

Darling A. (2011). *Back From the Brink: 1,000 Days at Number 11*, London: Atlantic Books.

Davies H. (2010). *The Financial Crisis: Who Is to Blame?* Cambridge: Polity.

Denhardt R, Denhardt J. (2000). The New Public Service: Serving Rather than Steering. *Public Administration Review*, 60, 549–59.

Denhardt R, Denhardt J. (2006). *Public Administration: An Action Orientation*, Belmont CA: Thomson.

Dent M. (2006). Patient Choice and Medicine in Health Care: Responsibilization, Governance and Proto-Professionalization. *Public Management Review*, 8, 449–62.

Department of Health and Social Security. (1983). *NHS Management Inquiry*, London: HMSO.

DiMaggio P. (1991). Constructing an Organizational Field as a Professional Project: U.S. Art Museums, 1920–1940. In *The New Institutionalism in Organizational Analysis*, ed. W Powell, P DiMaggio, Chicago IL: University of Chicago Press.

Du Gay P. (2000). *In Praise of Bureaucracy: Weber, Organization, Ethics*, London: Sage.

Dunleavy P, Hood C. (1994). From Old Public Administration to New Public Management. *Public Policy and Management*, July–September, 14, 9–16.

Dunsire A. (1999). Then and Now: Public Administration 1953–1999. *Political Studies*, XLVII, 360–78.

Edwards B, Fall M. (2005). *The Executive Years of the NHS: The England Account 1985–2003*, Oxford: Radcliffe Publishing Ltd.

Ehrenreich J. (1978). *The Cultural Crisis of Modern Medicine*, Boston MA: Monthly Review Press.

Elliott L, Atkinson D. (2008). *The Gods That Failed: How Blind Faith in Markets Has Cost Us Our Future*, London: Bodley Head.

Engelend E, Erturk I, Froud J, Nilson A, Williams K. (2011). *After the Great Complacence: Financial Crisis and the Politics of Reform*, Oxford: Oxford University Press.

Esping-Andersen G. (1990). *The Three Worlds of Welfare Capitalism*, New Jersey: Princeton University Press.

Exworthy M, Halford S, eds. (1998). *Professionalism and the New Managerialism in the Public Sector*, Buckingham: Open University Press.

Exworthy M, Powell M, Mohan J. (1999). The NHS: Quasi-Market, Quasi-Hierarchy and Quasi-Network? *Public Money & Management*, 19, 15.

Flynn N. (1989). The 'New Right' and Social Policy. *Policy and Politics*, 17, 97–109.

Flynn N, Strehl F. (1996). France. In *Public Sector Management in Europe*, ed. N Flynn, F Strehl, pp. 112–31. London: Prentice Hall.

Foucault M. (1977). *Discipline and Punish: The Birth of the Prison*, Harmondsworth: Penguin.

Fox C, Miller H. (1995). *Post-Modern Public Administration: Towards Discourse*, London: Sage.

Freidson E. (2001). *Professionalism: The Third Logic*, Oxford: Polity.

Galbraith J. (1958). *The Affluent Society*, London: Penguin.

Garud R, Jain S, Kumaraswamy A. (2002). Institutional Entrepreneurship in the Sponsorship of Common Technological Standards: The Case of Sun Microsystems and Java. *Academy of Management Journal*, 45, 196–214.

Giddens A. (1998). *The Third Way: The Renewal of Social Democracy*, Cambridge: Polity.

Giddens A. (2002). *What Now for New Labour?* Cambridge: Polity.

Giddens A. (2007). *Over to You, Mr. Brown*, Cambridge: Polity Press.

Gillespie R. (1997). Managers and Professionals. In *Perspectives in Health Care*, ed. N North, Y Bradshaw, pp. 84–109. Basingstoke: Palgrave Macmillan.

Gillies C. (1978). An Open Case: The Organisational Context of Social Work/Public Administration. *Journal of Management Studies*, 15, 360–61.

Goddard M, Mannion R, Smith P. (1999). Assessing the Performance of NHS Hospital Trusts: The Role of 'Hard' and 'Soft' Information. *Health Policy*, 48, 119–34.

Gould P. (2011). *The Unfinished Revolution: How New Labour Changed British Politics Forever*, London: Abacus.

Granovetter M. (1973). The Strength of Weak Ties. *American Journal of Sociology*, 78, 1360–80.

Granovetter M. (1985). Economic Action and Social Structure: The Problem of Embeddedness. *American Journal of Sociology*, 91, 481–510.

Gray A, Jenkins B. (1995). From Public Administration to Public Management: Reassessing a Revolution. *Public Administration*, Spring 73, 75–99.

Greener I. (2001). Social Learning and Macroeconomic Policy in Britain. *Journal of Public Policy*, 21, 133–52.

Greener I. (2003a). Patient Choice in the NHS: The View from Economic Sociology. *Social Theory and Health*, 1, 72–89.

Greener I. (2003b). Performance in the NHS: Insistence of Measurement and Confusion of Content. *Public Performance and Management Review*, 26, 237–50.

Greener I. (2003c). Who Choosing What? The Evolution of 'Choice' in the NHS, and Its Implications for New Labour. In *Social Policy Review 15*, ed. C Bochel, N Ellison, M Powell, pp. 49–68. Bristol: Policy Press.

Greener I. (2005a). Health Management as Strategic Behaviour: Managing Medics and Performance in the NHS. *Public Management Review*, 7, 95–110.

Greener I. (2005b). The Role of the Patient in Healthcare Reform: Customer, Consumer or Creator? In *Future Health Organisations and Systems*, ed. S Dawson, C Sausmann, pp. 227–45. Basingstoke: Palgrave Macmillan.

Greener I. (2005c). Talking to Health Managers about Change: Heroes, Villains and Simplification. *Journal of Health Organisation and Management*, May 18, 321–35.

Greener I. (2008). Markets in the Public Sector: When Do They Work, and What Do We Do When They Don't? *Policy and Politics*, 36, 93–108.

Greener I, Powell J. (2003). Health Authorities, Priority-Setting and Resource Allocation: A Study in Decision-Making in New Labour's NHS. *Social Policy & Administration*, 37, 35–48.

Grimshaw D, Vincent S, Willmott H. (2002). Going Privately: Partnership and Outsourcing in UK Public Services. *Public Administration*, 80, 475–502.

Hall P. (1993). Policy Paradigms, Social Learning and the State. *Comparative Politics*, April 25, 275–96.

Harrison S. (1982). Consensus Decision-Making in the National Health Service – A Review. *Journal of Management Studies*, 19, 377–94.

Harrison S. (1988). *Managing the National Health Service: Shifting the Frontier?* London: Chapman and Hall.

Harrison S, Hunter D, Marnoch G, Pollitt C. (1992). *Just Managing: Power and Culture in the NHS*, London: Macmillan.

Harrison S, Hunter D, Pollitt C. (1990). *The Dynamics of British Health Policy*, London: Unwin Hyman.

Harrison S, Wistow G. (1992). The Purchaser/Provider Split in English Health Care: Towards Explicit Rationing? *Policy and Politics*, 20, 123–30.

Harvey D. (2010). *The Enigma of Capital: And the Crises of Capitalism*, London: Profile Books.

Haug M, Sussman M. (1969). Professional Autonomy and the Revolt of the Client. *Social Problems*, 17, 153–61.

Heclo H. (1974). *Modern Social Politics in Britain and Sweden*, New Haven CT: Yale University Press.

Hennessy P. (1994). *Never Again: Britain 1945–1951*, London: Pantheon Books.

Hennessy P. (1997). *Muddling Through: Power, Politics and the Quality of Government in Post-War Britain*, London: Phoenix.

Hirschman A. (1970). *Exit, Voice and Loyalty: Responses to Decline in Firms, Organizations and States*, London: Harvard University Press.

Hood C. (1991). A Public Management for All Seasons? *Public Administration*, Spring 69, 3–19.

Hood C. (1998). *The Art of the State: Culture, Rhetoric and Public Management*, Oxford: Clarendon Press.

Hood C. (2006). Gaming in Target World: The Targets Approach to Managing British Public Services. *Public Administration Review*, 66, 515–21.

Hood C, Peters G. (2004). The Middle Aging of New Public Management: Into the Age of Paradox? *Journal of Public Administration Research & Theory*, 14, 267–82.

Hoque K, Davis S, Humphreys M. (2004). Freedom to Do What You Are Told: Senior Management Team Autonomy in an NHS Acute Trust. *Public Administration*, 82, 355–75.

Hutton W. (1996). *The State We're In*, London: Vintage.

Hutton W. (2010). *Them and Us: Changing Britain – Why We Need a Fair Society*, London: Little, Brown and Company.

Hwang H, Powell W. (2005). Institutions and Entrepreneurship. In *Handbook of Entrepreneurial Research*, ed. S Alvarez, R Agrawal, O Sorenson, pp. 179–210. New York: Springer.

Hyman P. (2005). *1 out of 10. From Downing Street Vision to Classroom Reality*, London: Vintage.

Illich I. (1977). *Limits to Medicine*, Harmondsworth: Penguin.

Irvin R, Stansbury J. (2004). Citizen Participation in Decision Making: Is It Worth the Effort? *Public Administration Review*, 64, 55–65.

Jackson P. (2003). The Size and Scope of the Public Sector: An International Comparison. In *Public Management and Governance*, ed. T Bovaird, E Lofler, pp. 25–39. London: Routledge.

Jacobs J. (1992). *Systems of Survival: A Dialogue on the Moral Foundations of Commerce and Politics*, Kent: Hodder and Stoughton.

Jenkins S. (2006). *Thatcher and Sons: A Revolution in Three Acts*, London: Allen Lane.

Jessop B. (1992). Fordism and Post-Fordism: A Critical Reformulation. In *Pathways to Industrialisation and Regional Development*, ed. M Storper, A Scott, London: Routledge.

Jessop B. (1993). Towards a Schumpeterian Workfare State? Preliminary Remarks on Post-Fordist Political Economy. *Studies in Political Economy*, 40, 7–39.

Jessop B. (1994). The Transition to Post-Fordism and the Schumpeterian Workfare State. In *Towards a Post-Fordist Welfare State?* ed. R Burrows, B Loader, pp. 13–37. London: Routledge.

Jessop B. (1999). The Changing Governance of Welfare: Recent Trends in Its Primary Functions, Scale and Modes of Coordination. *Social Policy and Administration*, 33, 348–59.

Jessop B. (2002). *The Future of the Capitalist State*, Cambridge: Polity Press.

Johnson G, Scholes K, eds. (2001). *Exploring Public Sector Strategy*, Harlow: Pearson.

Johnston J. (2000). The New Public Management in Australia. *Administrative Theory & Praxis*, 22, 345–68.

Kelly J. (2005). The Dilemma of the Unsatisfied Customer in a Market Model of Public Administration. *Public Administration Review*, 65, 76–84.

Khojasteh M. (1993). Motivating the Private vs. Public Sector Managers. *Public Personnel Management*, 22, 391–401.

Kickert W. (1997). Public Governance in the Netherlands: An Alternative to Anglo-American 'Managerialism'. *Public Administration*, Winter 75, 731–52.

Kickert W. (2005). Distinctiveness in the Study of Public Management in Europe: A Historical-Institutional Analysis of France, Germany and Italy. *Public Management Review*, 7, 537–63.

Kickert W, Klijn E, Koppenjan J, eds. (1997). *Managing Complex Networks: Strategies for the Public Sector*, London: Sage.

Kirkpatrick I, Ackroyd S. (2003). Transforming the Professional Archetype? The New Managerialism in UK Social Services. *Public Management Review*, 5, 511–31.

Kirkpatrick I, Martinez Lucio M. (1996). Introduction: The Contract State and the Future of Public Management. *Public Administration*, Spring 74, 1–8.

Kitchener M. (2000). The 'Bureaucratization' of Professional Roles: The Case of Clinical Directors in UK Hospitals. *Organization*, 7, 129–54.

Klein R. (1990). The State and the Profession: The Politics of the Double Bed. *British Medical Journal*, 301, 700–2.

Larson P. (1997). Public and Private Values at Odds: Can Private Sector Values Be Transplanted into Public Sector Institutions? *Public Administration and Development*, 17, 131–39.

Learmonth M. (1999). The National Health Service Manager, Engineer and Father? A Deconstruction. *Journal of Management Studies*, 36, 999–1012.

Le Grand J. (1991). *Equity and Choice: An Essay in Economics and Applied Philosophy*, London: Routledge.

Le Grand J. (1997). Knights, Knaves or Pawns? Human Behaviour and Social Policy. *Journal of Social Policy*, 26, 149–69.

Le Grand J. (2003). *Motivation, Agency and Public Policy: Of Knights, Knaves, Pawns and Queens*, Oxford: Oxford University Press.

Le Grand J. (2007). *The Other Invisible Hand*, Woodstock: Princeton University Press.

Lindblom C, Woodhouse E. (1993). *The Policy-Making Process*, Englewood-Cliffs NJ: Prentice Hall.

Llewellyn S, Tappin E. (2003). Strategy in the Public Sector: Management in the Wilderness. *Journal of Management Studies*, 40, 955–82.

Lynn L. (1999). Public Management in North America. *Public Management*, 1, 301–10.

Lynn L. (2001). The Myth of the Bureaucratic Paradigm: What Traditional Public Administration Really Stood for. *Public Administration Review*, 61, 144–60.

Mannion R, Davies H, Marshall M. (2004). *Cultures for Performance in Health Care*, Buckingham: Open University Press.

Mannion R, Goddard M, Smith P. (2001). On the Limitations and Pitfalls of Performance Measurement Systems in Health Care. In *Quality in Healthcare: Strategic Issues in Health Care Management*, ed. H Davies, M Tavakoli, M Malek, pp. 158–69. Aldershot: Ashgate.

Margretts H, 6 P, Hood C, eds. (2012). *Paradoxes of Modernization: Unintended Consequences of Public Policy Reform*, Oxford: Oxford University Press.

Marquand D. (2004). *Decline of the Public*, Cambridge: Polity.

Marston G. (2000). Metaphor, Morality and Myth: A Critical Discourse Analysis of Public Housing Policy in Queensland. *Critical Social Policy*, 20, 349–73.

McLean B, Elkind P. (2004). *The Smartest Guys in the Room: The Amazing Rise and Scandalous Fall of Enron*, London: Penguin.

McLean B, Nocera J. (2010). *All the Devils Are Here: The Hidden History of the Financial Crisis*, London: Viking.

McNulty T, Ferlie E. (2002). *Re-Engineering Health Care: The Complexities of Organizational Transformation*, Oxford: Oxford University Press.

Meier J, O'Toole L. (2002). Public Management and Organizational Performance: The Effect of Managerial Quality. *Journal of Policy Analysis and Management*, 21, 629–43.

Minister of State for Department of Health, Minister of State for Local and Regional Government, Minister of State for School Standards. (2005). *The Case for User Choice in Public Services*, Public Administration Select Committee into Choice, Voice and Public Services, London.

Minvielle E. (2006). New Public Management à la Française: The Case of Regional Hospital Agencies. *Public Administration Review*, 66, 753–63.

Moore M. (1997). *Creating Public Value: Strategic Management in Government*, Harvard: Harvard University Press.

Murray C. (1984). *Losing Ground*, New York: Basic Books.

Needham C. (2003). *Citizen-Consumers: New Labour's Marketplace Democracy*, London: Catalyst Forum.

Nettleton S, Burrows R. (2003). E-Scaped Medicine? Information, Reflexivity and Health. *Critical Social Policy*, 23, 173–93.

Newman J. (2000). Beyond the New Public Management? In *New Managerialism: New Welfare?* ed. J Clarke, S Gewirtz, E McLaughlin, pp. 45–62. London: Sage.

Newman J. (2002). The New Public Management, Modernization and Institutional Change. In *New Public Management: Current Trends and Future Prospects*, ed. K McLaughlin, S Osborne, E Ferlie, pp. 77–91. London: Routledge.

Newman J, McKee B. (2005). Beyond the New Public Management? Public Services and the Social Investment State. *Policy and Politics*, 33, 657–74.

Newman J, Raine J, Skelcher C. (2001). Transforming Local Government: Innovation and Modernization. *Public Money and Management*, April–June 21, 61–68.

Nicholson-Crotty S, Theobald N, Nicholson-Crotty J. (2006). Disparate Measures: Public Managers and Performance-Measurement Strategies. *Public Administration Review*, 66, 101–13.

Norman J. (2010). *The Big Society: The Anatomy of the New Politics*, Buckingham: University of Buckingham Press.

O'Connor J. (1973). *The Fiscal Crisis of the State*, London: Macmillan.

Oliver M. (1997). *Whatever Happened to Monetarism? Economic Planning and Social Learning in the United Kingdom Since 1979*, Aldershot: Ashgate.

Ormerod P. (2010). The Current Crisis and the Culpability of Macroeconomic Theory. *21st Century Society*, 5, 5–18.

Osborne D, Gaebler T. (1993). *Reinventing Government*, New York: Addison Wesley.

Osborne D, Plastrick P. (1997). *Banishing Bureaucracy: The Five Strategies for Reinventing Government*, New York: Addison-Wesley.

Ouchi W. (2003). *Making Schools Work*, New York: Simon and Schuster.

Ouchi W, Riordan R, Lingle L, Porter L. (2005). Making Public Schools Work: Management Reforms as the Key. *Academy of Management Journal*, 48, 929–40.

Paulson H. (2010). *On the Brink: Inside the Race to Stop the Collapse of the Global Financial System*, London: Business Plus.

Peckham S, Exworthy M, Greener I, Powell M. (2005). Decentralizing Health Services: More Local Accountability or Just More Central Control. *Public Money and Management*, 25, 221–28.

Pestoff V. (2006). Citizens and Coproduction in Public Services: Childcare in Eight European Countries. *Public Management Review*, 8, 503–19.

Peters J, Waterman R. (1982). *In Search of Excellence: Lessons from America's Best Run Companies*, London: HarperCollins.

Pierson C. (2006). *Beyond the Welfare State?* Cambridge: Polity Press.

Pollitt C. (1985). Measuring Performance: A New System for the National Health Service. *Policy and Politics*, 13, 1–15.

Pollitt C. (1986). Beyond the Managerial Model: The Case for Broadening Performance Assessment in Government and the Public Service. *Financial Accountability and Management*, Autumn 2, 155–70.

Pollitt C. (1993). *Managerialism and Public Services*, Oxford: Blackwell.

Pollitt C. (2000). Is the Emperor in His Underwear? An Analysis of the Impacts of Public Management Reform. *Public Management*, 2, 181–99.

Pollitt C. (2003). *The Essential Public Manager*, Maidenhead: Open University Press.

Pollitt C, Bouchaert G. (2000). *Public Management Reform: A Comparative Analysis*, Oxford: Oxford University Press.

Porter M. (2004). *Competitive Advantage*, New York: Free Press.

Public Finance. (2007). PFI hospitals 'costing NHS extra £480m a year'. www.publicfinance.co.uk, Accessed 3rd December 2007, http://www.cipfa.org.uk/publicfinance/news_details.cfm?News_id=30216.

Putnam R. (1993). *Making Democracy Work: Civic Conditions in Modern Italy*, Princeton NJ: Princeton University Press.

Quirk B. (1997). Accountable to Everyone: Postmodern Pressures on Public Managers. *Public Administration*, 75, 569–86.

Rainey H, Backoff R, Levine C. (1976). Comparing Public and Private Organizations. *Public Administration Review*, 36, 233–44.

Rainey H, Bozeman B. (2000). Comparing Public and Private Organizations: Empirical Research and the Power of the A Priori. *Journal of Public Administration Research and Theory*, 10, 447–69.

Rainey H, Pandey S, Bozeman B. (1995). Research Note: Public and Private Managers' Perceptions of Red Tape. *Public Administration Review*, 55, 567–74.

Rainey HG. (1989). Public Management: Recent Research on the Political Context and Managerial Roles, Structures, and Behaviors. *Journal of Management*, 15, 229.

Reichard C. (2003). Local Public Management Reforms in Germany. *Public Administration*, 81, 345–63.

Rhodes R. (1997). *Understanding Governance*, Buckingham: Open University Press.

Rintala M. (2003). *Creating the National Health Service: Bevan and the Medical Lords*, London: Frank Cass Publishers.

Roberts N. (2002). Keeping Public Officials Accountable through Dialogue: Resolving the Accountability Paradox. *Public Administration Review*, 62, 658–69.

Ross B. (1988). Public and Private Sectors: The Underlying Differences. *Management Review*, May, 28–33.

Roubini N. (2010). *Crisis Economics: A Crash Course in the Future of Finance*, London: Allen Lane.

Sabatier P. (1988). An Advocacy Coalition Framework of Policy Change and the Role of Policy-Oriented Learning Therein. *Policy Sciences*, 21, 129–69.

Sandberg J, Pinnington A. (2009). Professional Competence as Ways of Being: An Existential Ontological Perspective. *Journal of Management Studies*, 46, 1138–70.

Sanderson I. (1998). Beyond Performance Measurement? Assessing Value in Local Government. *Local Government Studies*, 24, 1–25.

Schneider S. (2005). Administrative Breakdowns in the Governmental Response to Hurricane Katrina. *Public Administration Review*, 65, 515–16.

Schofield J. (2001). The Old Ways Are the Best? The Durability and Usefulness of Bureaucracy in Public Sector Management. *Organization*, 8, 77–96.

Schwartz B. (2004). *The Paradox of Choice: Why Less Is More*, New York: Harper Collins.

Sheaff R. (1990). *Marketing for Health Services: A Framework for Communications, Evaluation and Total Quality Management*, Buckingham: Open University Press.

Shiller R. (2008). *The Subprime Solution: How Today's Financial Crisis Happened, and What to Do about It*, Woodstock: Princeton University Press.

Smith J, Walsh K. (2001). The 'Redisorganisation' of the NHS. *British Medical Journal*, 1 December, 323, 1262–63.

Smith Ring P, Perry J. (1985). Strategic Management in Public and Private Organizations: Implications of Distinctive Contexts and Constraints. *Academy of Management Review*, 10, 276–86.

Smith W, Lewis M. (2011). Toward a Theory of Paradox: A Dynamic Equilibrium Model of Organizing. *Academy of Management Review*, 36, 381–403.

Spicer M. (2001). *Public Administration and the State: A Postmodern Perspective*, Tuscaloosa, AL: University of Alabama Press.

Spicer M. (2004). Public Administration, the History of Ideas, and the Reinventing Government Movement. *Public Administration Review*, 64, 353–61.

Stewart J, Walsh K. (1992). Change in the Management of Public Services. *Public Administration*, 70, 499–518.

Stiglitz J. (2010). *Freefall: Free Markets and the Sinking of the Global Economy*, London: Penguin.

Stillman R. (1997). American vs. European Public Administration: Does Public Administration Make the Modern State, or Does the State Make Public Administration. *Public Administration Review*, 57, 332–38.

Stoker G. (2006). *Why Politics Matters: Making Democracy Work*, London: Palgrave.

Stone D. (2012). *Policy Paradox: The Art of Political Decision Making*, London: Norton.

Sukel W. (1978). Contrasting the Private and Public Sectors. *Industrial Management*, March–April, 18–19.

Talbot C. (2000). Performing 'Performance' – a Comedy in Five Acts. *Public Money and Management*, 20, 63–68.

Tallis R. (2005). *Hippocratic Oaths: Medicine and Its Discontents*, London: Atlantic Books.

Thaler R, Sunstein C. (2008). *Nudge: Improving Decisions about Health, Wealth and Happiness*, London: Yale University Press.

Thomas R. (1978). *The British Philosophy of Administration: A Comparison of British and American Ideas 1900-1939*, London: Longman.

Torfing J. (1999a). Towards a Schumpeterian Workfare Postnational Regime: Path-Shaping and Path-Dependency in Danish Welfare State Reform. *Economy and Society*, 28, 369–402.

Torfing J. (1999b). Workfare with Welfare: Recent Reforms of the Danish Welfare State. *Journal of European Social Policy*, 9, 5–28.

Torfing J. (2001). Path-Dependent Danish Welfare Reforms: The Contribution of the New Institutionalisms to Understanding Evolutionary Change. *Scandinavian Political Studies*, 24, 277–310.

Turner B. (1987). *Medical Power and Social Knowledge*, London: Sage.

Vigoda E. (2002). From Responsiveness to Collaboration: Governance, Citizens, and the Next Generation of Public Administration. *Public Administration Review*, 62, 527–40.

Walsh K. (1996). *Public Services and Market Mechanisms: Competition, Contracting and the New Public Management*, London: Palgrave Macmillan.

Wildavsky A. (1997). *The New Politics of the Budgetary Process*, New York: Longman.

Wilding P. (1982). *Professional Power and Social Welfare*, London: Routledge and Kegan Paul.

Wilsford D. (1995). States Facing Interests: Struggles Over Health Care Policy in Advanced Industrial Democracies. *Journal of Health Politics, Policy and Law*, 20, 571–613.

Wilson J, Thompson A. (2006). *The Making of Modern Management: British Management in Historical Perspective*, Oxford: Oxford University Press.

Wright Mills C. (1956). *The Power Elite*, Oxford: Oxford Press.

Index

accountability, 50, 54, 55, 56, 61, 62, 65, 68, 69, 71–3, 76, 111, 114, 117, 118–22, 124, 130, 143–5, 150, 170, 171, 177, 185, 186, 207, 210, 216–18, 220, 223, 224

administration, *see* public administration

autonomy, 34, 56, 70, 101, 103, 106, 109–11, 123, 133, 202, 219–20

Boyne, G., 59, 80, 122, 189, 197, 209

centralisation, 40, 49, 54, 55, 103, 171, 184, 186, 208, 218–20

charging (for services), 52, 59, 60, 81, 82, 83, 87, 88, 92, 104, 139, 154, 158, 159, 160

Christensen, T., 51, 67, 177

citizens (services users as), 5, 7, 34, 36, 37, 38, 41, 42, 57, 60, 61, 67, 68, 69, 82, 121, 142, 144, 145, 148, 149, 152, 153, 169, 177, 182, 206, 208, 213, 216–18, 222

Clarke, J., 33, 77, 143, 153, 182–3

competition in public services, 2, 6, 21, 22, 35, 37, 38, 68, 82, 143, 156, 157, 158, 160, 162–5, 168, 172, 174, 178, 180, 182

co-production, 130, 145–7, 150, 151–3, 189, 217

collectivized individualism, 130, 148–9, 150, 151

confidentiality, 91, 107, 109, 111–12, 113, 118, 124, 174

consumerism, 2, 6, 36, 41, 44, 57, 59, 60, 68, 72, 123, 126, 128, 131, 132, 143, 148, 149, 153, 155, 174, 177, 188, 192, 206, 207, 208, 216–18, 220

contracts for services, 43, 44, 59–60, 63, 68, 78, 88, 91, 164, 166–8, 170–1, 172–3, 174, 175, 193, 221, 223

control (systems of control), 36, 40, 54, 56, 58, 64, 89, 103, 106, 109, 111, 112, 115, 118, 128, 178, 185–6, 187, 202, 208, 213–15

contradictions in public management, 3–6, 45, 46, 56, 64, 65, 69, 76, 153, 206–25

crowding out, 30, 32

customer focus/service, 2, 3, 4, 5, 6, 7, 68, 69, 72, 73, 76, 78, 123, 130–2, 132–43, 149, 151, 177, 198, 209, 209, 210–13, 214, 220, 223

decentralisation, 40, 48, 50, 103, 104, 184–6, 208, 218–20, 222

democratic accountability, 9, 53, 54–6, 57–8, 61–2, 63, 65, 67, 68, 69, 74–6, 77. 82, 99, 121–2, 124, 126, 142, 143, 148, 167, 169, 174, 185–6, 188, 207, 218, 220, 221, 222, 223, 224

discretion (at work), 40, 107, 113, 124, 202, 204, 219

doctors, 4, 5, 44, 74, 85, 94, 105, 108, 109, 110, 111, 112, 113, 114, 116, 119, 121, 126, 127–9, 131, 133, 136, 138, 141, 146, 154, 175, 176, 179, 181, 188, 192, 193, 211, 222

Dunsire, A., 53–6, 79

efficiency, 2, 3, 4, 5, 13, 14, 22, 25, 29, 36, 37, 38, 39, 42, 44, 49, 50, 56, 61, 67, 69, 73–4, 76, 82, 83, 87, 88, 123, 127, 133, 134, 135, 137, 142, 149, 151, 155, 160, 162, 164, 166, 168, 174, 207, 209, 210, 211, 212, 214, 215, 220, 223

election of public managers, 69, 74–6, 121

entrepreneurialism, 18, 33, 35, 41, 43, 68, 78, 208, 209, 213–15, 221–2, 223